W9-ACF-948

MARY MARTIN,
BROADWAY LEGEND

Mary Martin during her early Broadway period, ca. 1946. (Courtesy of Mary McCord/ Edyth Renshaw Collection on the Performing Arts, Hamon Arts Library, Southern Methodist University).

MARY MARTIN,
BROADWAY LEGEND

Ronald L. Davis

UNIVERSITY OF OKLAHOMA PRESS : NORMAN

Also by Ronald L. Davis

A History of Opera in the American West (Englewood Cliffs, N.J., 1965)
Opera in Chicago (New York, 1966)
The Social and Cultural Life of the 1920s (New York, 1972)
A History of Music in American Life: The Gilded Years, 1865–1920
 (Huntington, N.Y., 1982)
(with Paul Boller) *Hollywood Anecdotes* (New York, 1987)
Hollywood Beauty: Linda Darnell and the American Dream (Norman, 1991)
The Glamour Factory: Inside Hollywood's Big Studio System (Dallas, 1993)
John Ford: Hollywood's Old Master (Norman, 1995)
Celluloid Mirrors: Hollywood and American Society Since 1945 (Fort Worth,
 1997)
Duke: The Life and Image of John Wayne (Norman, 1998)
Van Johnson: MGM's Golden Boy (Jackson, Miss., 2001)
William S. Hart: Projecting the American West (Norman, 2003)
Zachary Scott: Hollywood's Sophisticated Cad (Jackson, Miss., 2006)

Library of Congress Cataloging-in-Publication Data

Davis, Ronald L.
 Mary Martin, Broadway legend / Ronald L. Davis. — 1st ed.
 p. cm.
 Includes bibliographical references (p.)
 ISBN 978-0-8061-3905-0 (hardcover : alk. paper)
 1. Martin, Mary, 1913–1990. 2. Singers—United States—Biography. I. Title
ML420.M332D38 2008
782.1'4092—dc22
[B]
 2007028943

1 2 3 4 5 6 7 8 9 10

In loving memory of

Bessie Mae Sue Ella and Jac Austin,

who brought gentility and gracious living
into the modern world

Contents

Illustrations

Preface

Mary Martin became one of the most beloved musical comedy stars in Broadway history, beginning with her overnight success singing a Cole Porter song, "My Heart Belongs to Daddy," in *Leave It to Me*. A Paramount contract followed, but after a modest movie career the star returned to Broadway in *One Touch of Venus*, among the most popular shows in New York during World War II. A national tour in Irving Berlin's *Annie Get Your Gun* broadened Martin's reputation, and in 1949 she won her greatest critical acclaim in Rodgers and Hammerstein's blockbuster hit *South Pacific*, playing opposite Metropolitan Opera basso Ezio Pinza. *Peter Pan*, *The Sound of Music*, and *I Do! I Do!* on the stage won additional plaudits for the star from Texas, and a series of television specials during the 1950s, especially a recreation of *Peter Pan*, contributed to her rise as a Broadway legend.

Mary Martin's place in the history of American musical theater is singular. During the 1940s and 1950s, she and Ethel Merman dominated the Broadway musical stage. It was an era when female stars reigned supreme in musicals, and none blazed brighter than Martin and Merman. In many ways the two were opposites. Ethel Merman's approach was bold and brassy, and her voice belted bravado. Mary Martin exuded an impish down-homeness that masked a feisty

interior, while she had two singing voices, a high soprano and a mellow alto. Both stars had shows written for them, but Mary seemed too sincere and friendly to be viewed as a grand diva. Still, after their joint television appearance on Ford's fiftieth anniversary show in 1953, Martin and Merman became household names, although inescapably linked to Broadway.

Early in my last year of elementary school, my maternal grandmother took me to see a matinee performance of *Annie Get Your Gun* during the national tour that Mary Martin launched in Dallas in the fall of 1947. That Sunday afternoon, sitting high in the balcony of Fair Park Auditorium, I fell in love with musical comedy. I bought the original cast album of the show and played the 78 rpm records until they were white, always imagining Mary Martin warbling Annie's songs rather than Ethel Merman, the Broadway star who had created the role. Before the musical opened its tour during the State Fair of Texas, it had been well publicized that Martin was from nearby Weatherford, and I yearned to see the enchanting singing actress again when she made her tremendous hit in *South Pacific* on Broadway two years later. But Manhattan was a long way from Texas for the adolescent son of working-class parents during the postwar era, and traveling there to sample the riches of New York theater wasn't in our family budget. I had to content myself with a ticket to the touring company of the Rodgers and Hammerstein show and with the original cast recording, both of which I financed from my allowance.

I saw Janet Blair in *South Pacific* when the national company played in Dallas, but again I sat far enough back in Fair Park Auditorium that it was easy for me to imagine that I was seeing Mary Martin as Nellie Forbush. When Martin toured with her one-woman show in 1959, I saw it twice—once during a trip home to Dallas and again while sitting on bleachers in Gregory Gymnasium at the University of Texas in Austin, where I was in graduate school.

Five years later, I was teaching at Michigan State University when Mary Martin tried out the ill-fated *Jennie* in Detroit before that production opened its brief run in New York. I seem to have been one of the few people who actually liked the show.

In 1966, I finally saw the singing star from Weatherford perform in New York shortly after *I Do! I Do!*, the final musical of her career, opened on Broadway. I loved that show, too, and I particularly remember Martin's stepping down onto a small platform at the lip of the stage and singing "What Is a Woman?" in her rich middle-aged voice. By then I was back living in Dallas and teaching American history at Southern Methodist University.

One day after class a short time later, a student who had heard me talk about Mary Martin approached me and said, "Dr. Davis, you need to meet my aunt." The coed's aunt turned out to be Bessie Mae Sue Ella Yeager Austin, Mary Martin's best friend during her Texas childhood and a lifetime intimate. I had recently started the SMU Oral History Program on the Performing Arts and quickly arranged to interview Bessie Mae for our project. She proved such a delight that Bessie and her husband, Jac Austin, a Dallas realtor, became my good friends. I've often said about Bessie Mae Sue Ella that if she met Jack the Ripper, she'd say to him, "Well, darlin', you've just got to come to dinner one night next week." And not only would Jack have accepted the generous southern lady's invitation, he'd have behaved himself. That was the kind of magic Bessie Mae exuded.

Through the years, the Austins recounted stories for me about their times with Mary Martin. Eventually, they took me to meet the Broadway star in Fort Worth during one of her gigs as a spokeswoman for Fieldcrest, for whom she designed a line of sheets and pillowcases. We attended her talk at Casa Mañana, visited with Mary in her dressing room, and I experienced the thrill of having my favorite musical comedy star chuck my cheek and tell me how handsome I was! Mary truly had a way of making everyone she met feel special.

When Martin unveiled a statue of herself as Peter Pan in Weatherford on July 4, 1976, the Austins invited me to drive over to Parker County with them for the occasion. I met Mary again, tried to convince her that she should tape a lengthy oral history for the SMU project, and experienced the star's skill at saying neither

yes nor no. She turned me over to her publicist, Ben Washer, who was equally gracious but no less vague about when I might interview Miss Martin.

In 1984, while on a book tour with the paperback edition of her memoirs, the star spent some time in Dallas with the Austins. Bessie Mae arranged for me to have an hour-and-a-half oral history session alone with the actress in the guest quarters at the Austins' high-rise condominium. Mary and I had gotten up to 1946 in the narrative when she had to leave for a luncheon where she was being honored. Over salad, Mary apparently paid me a compliment by telling Bessie Mae that I had made her think during our interview!

Another four years passed before I could corner the busy star again. Early one morning in 1988, Bessie Mae called and said, "Ron, you've simply got to go to San Miguel de Allende with Jac and me this summer. Mary's going to be in Mexico for two months, and she's going to be bored. That'll be the perfect time for you to finish your oral history with her." It was truly an offer I couldn't refuse.

Ten days with Mary Martin in Mexico was like living out a fantasy. The intense period of work was matched by pleasure beyond compare. By then I had interviewed in the neighborhood of four hundred people for the SMU project, most of them celebrities. But I discovered in Mexico that it was one thing to have questions prepared to ask a star and another to "hang out" with them. Although Mary was exuberantly friendly and fun, I had trouble relaxing with her in a purely social situation. I didn't want to come across as an adoring fan or seem overly familiar. Professors have seldom been accused of lacking something to say, but I suddenly found myself hanging back, letting Mary and the Austins carry the conversation. I felt downright awkward and out of place.

The ice was broken shortly before noon on my first day in San Miguel when Jac and Bessie Mae were trying to decide what they should have the señora at their leased house prepare for lunch. Mary was chattering happily with Susan Grushkin, her secretary-companion, and me while the Austins were having their domestic deliberation. Finally, the gentlemanly Jac, who adored Mary, raised his voice slightly and bellowed, "Mary, would you shut up a minute?

I'm trying to talk to my wife!" I was stunned, but quickly realized that I was with friends who had known each other for so long, and were so natural with one another, that superficial manners didn't apply. Somehow that informality freed me to enter in and be myself.

Before I left Dallas, the Austins' youngest daughter, Mary Anna, a casting director and partial namesake of Mary Martin, called and said, "Ron, while you're in San Miguel, you should interview Robert Buckner. He was a major writer at Warner Bros." I did interview Buckner and thought so highly of the session that Bessie Mae and Jac asked if they could hear part of it. They ended up listening to the entire two hours and raved so about the interview the next day to Mary that I grew self-conscious. After all, by then I'd spent far longer periods interviewing Mary, and her friends had shown no interest whatever in hearing those sessions. Mary wasn't disturbed by their neglect, but I was! Eventually, I interrupted the Austins' praise of the Buckner interview to ask, "What about Mary's splendid interview? There's not only her fabulous career recounted but also insight into all the incredible people she's worked with—Sophocles, Aeschylus, Euripides." Mary let out a Mary Martin giggle at that and exclaimed, "I'm not *that* old!" but she clearly enjoyed my attempt at humor. A few minutes later she walked over to where I was standing and put her arm around my waist. From then on, I had no trouble relating to her in an easy manner.

A few days after that, Jac hired a car and driver to take us to Guanajuato. We saw the sights there, went through the market, ate lunch outdoors at a sidewalk cafe, and proceeded to stroll through the town. As we did, we paired off in twos—Jac and Bessie Mae in front, Mary and Julian (our driver, who happened to be San Miguel's popular young bullfighter) in the middle, and Susan and me bringing up the rear. As we started down a hill, Susan and I noticed a pink house across the street with *de las señoritas* on a sign outside. She and I gave each other a quizzical look, with both of us wondering aloud if that was the kind of house we thought it was. Julian overheard and gave us a grinning nod. So we talked Mary into going over and standing under the brothel sign while Susan and I took pictures of her. Mary was laughing so hard that we had to caution

her to stand still while we snapped our photos. After she'd rejoined us, I said, "Now, Mary, those pictures are going into the SMU archives! And they'll have as the caption: "But my heart belongs to daddy." Mary laughed at the reference to her signature song.

When the star died two years later, Susan invited me to the Mary Martin memorial at the Majestic Theater in New York. I felt honored to be there, and the occasion, with a reception at Sardi's afterward, was truly a joyful and touching way of saying goodbye to a Broadway legend.

MARY MARTIN,
BROADWAY LEGEND

Texas Tomboy

Mary often claimed that at her birth a curtain lifted in her mother's bedroom to signal the event to inquisitive folks in Weatherford, Texas. "It must have been a good omen," she said. "Curtains have been going up for me ever since." That initial shade went up for Mary Virginia Martin on Monday, December 1, 1913, horse-trading day in Weatherford, in the family's white, two-story frame home on West Lee Avenue. Mary's father, Preston Martin, one of the town's leading lawyers, later joshed that he traded off a horse and got Mary, the younger of his two daughters, in return.

Weatherford in 1913 was a town with a population of about 5,000, the county seat of Parker County, some thirty miles west of Fort Worth. Incorporated in 1858, Weatherford in its first decade was the principal frontier settlement in northern Texas, a refuge for outlying residents who sought protection from the periodic Indian attacks that lasted until the early 1870s. Located on the stagecoach route between Fort Worth and Fort Belknap and on the later Texas and Pacific Railroad line, Weatherford became a shipping point and emporium for Parker County farmers and ranchers. In 1913 the community still had the flavor of a western agricultural town. Horses far outnumbered cars, and electric lights were new, a comfort most homes in the outlying areas did without. Although

Weatherford merchants in the 1920s sold oil field equipment and furniture, the pride of the county was its watermelons, which citizens boasted were the biggest and best. Long after Mary had become the toast of Broadway, a sign on the outskirts of town read: "Weatherford, Texas, home of watermelons and Mary Martin." Mary's retort was, "I never got top billing in my hometown."

Folks in Weatherford referred to Preston Martin as Judge Martin, although his nephew, Don Martin, a local businessman and cattleman, denied that his uncle was ever a judge. "He was just called that because he was one of the town's prominent attorneys," the younger Martin said. "Everyone in town knew him as a great and wonderful friend." Preston was president of the Weatherford school board for twenty years, the man who handed out diplomas on graduation day, and was celebrated in the county for his orations at the funerals of friends. "There was never a dry eye during one of Judge Martin's elegiac orations," said Carlos Hartnett, a Weatherford native. Mary, who grew up idolizing her father, considered him the wisest man in town. Born in Mississippi in 1872 of Scotch descent, Judge Martin indulged his energetic daughter and called her "Poog," declaring Mary "a heller." Yet he left most of the discipline of his children to his wife, Juanita, who was the family ramrod. Preston— a tall, good-looking, silver-haired man—was of a more gentle and caring disposition. "I have seldom known anyone who had the depth of feeling for other human beings that my father had," an adult Mary said. From him, she got her joyous nature and her ready capacity for making friends.

Juanita Presley Martin was born in Brenham, Texas, in 1878, of Scotch-Irish ancestry. Her family moved to Fort Worth, where she developed into a cultured young woman with little liking for rural living. She came to Weatherford to teach music at the local community college. A fine violinist, Juanita met Preston, then a law student, while they were both out bicycling. "Aren't you the little fiddle teacher?" he asked her. Shy Juanita, upon sufficient query, admitted that she was indeed head of the string instrument department at Weatherford College. Her mother and father had been killed in an accident, so her sisters had raised her. One of the sisters was married

to a violin teacher from Germany, and Juanita had taken lessons from him and soon practiced on the instrument eight hours a day. Organized and ladylike, she was not the easy, outgoing person that Preston was, but the two fell in love and were married in 1899.

The next year Geraldine was born. Thirteen years later, when Jerry was a budding adolescent, a baby sister was announced, somewhat to the surprise of even her parents, and soon took center stage in the Martin household. A happy baby who grew into a pert, vivacious child, Mary seemed to usurp the attention of everyone, including the family's black maid, Billie Jones, who also served as the baby's nurse. Mary claimed Billie "practically brought me up." Earlier, the Martins had had a son, a few years younger than Jerry, but he died in childhood, and doctors had said that it was not safe for Juanita to have another baby. Mary arrived as an unexpected gift.

Once she married, Juanita had given up her teaching career and devoted herself to homemaking and civic affairs. One day, before Mary was quite five years old, Juanita pulled out her violin and started playing. Mary, remembered thinking, "My, that's the most beautiful thing I've ever heard!" Soon the youngster began begging to take violin lessons herself. "I did for a while," Mary recalled, "from a teacher at Weatherford College." But the high-strung child was too impatient to learn to read music and preferred playing by ear. "It came too quickly for me," Mary said. "If I heard a tune once, I could play it."

From her father Mary learned a skill with words and at an early age developed a love for reading. From her mother she acquired an eye for design, as well as her penchant for music and acting. Early in life Mary showed a habit of pretending, and Mrs. Martin decided that she should study expression. When her violin lessons proved more frolic than serious, Juanita suggested that Mary switch to singing and dance lessons. Doting parent that she was, Juanita began to fantasize that her rambunctious daughter might ripen into an opera singer, and she saw to it that Mary was exposed to the classics as well as the current popular songs.

Preston liked music, too, but his preferences leaned more toward old favorites like "Wait Till the Sun Shines, Nellie" and "When

the Red, Red Robin Comes Bob, Bob Bobbin' Along." He used to caution Mary, "It's all right to sing seriously but don't take up serious singing!" The girl learned all of her dad's choices in music and, delighted to be the center of his attention, warbled them for his pleasure. "I just sang from morning till night when I was a child," she said. "Mother and my sister Jerry claimed that I sang in my crib before I ever learned to talk."

At age five, Mary sang "When the Apples Grow on the Lilac Tree" at a local Fireman's Ball and fell in love with an audience. The song, about a little girl who tells a boy her age that she will give him a kiss when apples grow on the lilac tree, brought down the house, and Mary's destiny was sealed. "I didn't fall in love with one face in that audience," she said, "I fell in love with all of them. It's been that way ever since." At age six, she gave her first dance recital, in which the leading number was "The Birth of a Butterfly from Its Cocoon." The cocoon was a burlap sack, and Juanita made the butterfly's dress from many shades of net adorned with hand-sewn beads.

Despite her addiction to music and performing, Mary was an active, joyous child who spent much of her time outdoors. "Even as a baby I quickly learned how to crawl out of my crib," she said. "They'd put up barriers, and I learned how to go over them." Within a few years she was climbing trees, scampering up hills, and riding her Shetland pony bareback. "I was more boy than girl then," Mary said. "My mother would make all these beautiful, hand-made dresses for me, but she finally gave up and put me in rompers." Once the Martins' "heller" tried to fly from the roof of the garage, holding an open parasol, which turned inside out on the way down. Mary landed hard and broke her collarbone. Skinny tom-boy though her impish daughter was, Juanita insisted that the girl learn proper manners and the social graces and was strict about their enforcement.

Like most county seats in Texas, Weatherford centered on the courthouse square. In the old days, delighted with the town's reputation for being the watermelon capital of the world, civic leaders had erected a painted tin replica of a melon about fourteen feet

long on the courthouse lawn. "I thought the square was my own personal property," Mary wrote in her autobiography, "because I loved it so and I knew everybody in every store all the way around." Her father's office was on the second floor of the southeast corner of the square, looking right out on the dazzling white courthouse, which resembled a giant wedding cake. Mary remembered horses and wagons tied up on the streets of the square on Fridays and Saturdays. During the season, wagons full of watermelons were driven into town at night so that the loads could be shipped out by rail the next day. "Early in the morning there'd be two lines of wagons side by side for a mile," Don Martin remembered. At the same time, "many Weatherford folks were in the cattle business. They drove cattle right down the main streets." Mary enjoyed pleasant times drinking sodas in Corcanges' drugstore on the square and once wandered into the courtroom where her father was arguing a case against his best friend, another prominent Parker County attorney. "It scared me to death," Mary said. "My father and his closest friend were yelling at each other. I thought, 'How can my daddy do such a thing in front of all these people?' And when the friend yelled back at Daddy, that made me mad. I never went into the place again."

On the lawn in front of the courthouse was a bandstand where the town band played on Saturday nights. As a child, Mary sang there with a trio of young girls dressed in bellhop uniforms. They sang favorites like "Moonlight and Roses" while their parents beamed approval. Even before she started to school, Mary said, she would "dance and sing at the drop of a hat." She performed at church socials, for ladies' clubs, and on Mother's Day programs at the Methodist Church. "Her mother pushed her," Don Martin maintained. "As a little kid Mary performed all the time, but her mother was behind that."

Adored and pampered child though she was, Mary grew up too generous, people-oriented, and likable to be termed a spoiled brat. "She was a gal that loved everybody," Mary's cousin Don said. "She was full of life and never saw a stranger." The youngster played with Ralph Kindel, the boy next door, and Virginia May Milmo,

who lived across the street, and considered Ford White, whom she sang with at the Fireman's Ball, her first beau. Her biggest fault seemed to be in showing off. She learned to do cartwheels, hung by her heels from a trapeze, swam in a lake at the Country Club, and coveted a pair of boxing gloves she'd seen in Mr. Richards' sporting-goods store. "Mother tried to make me into the most feminine thing you ever saw," Mary said. "But all the time she was trying so hard to make me feminine, I wanted to be a boy." Mary ruined most of the lacy dresses Juanita made for her, and the active girl always seemed to have ugly bruises or a scraped knee from falls.

During much of Mary's childhood, Jerry, whom she called Sister, was either away at school in New York or married and living in Dallas. To help fill that void, her parents arranged for their little tomboy to spend weekends with Bessie Mae Sue Ella Yeager, the demure daughter of close friends of theirs in nearby Mineral Wells. "I don't think either of us remember when we first became friends," an adult Bessie Mae Sue Ella said. "When Juanita Martin was teaching violin at Weatherford College, she lived with my great uncle and his wife. So there's always been a family connection." At eight or nine years of age, the two girls began spending Saturdays together, usually sleeping out on the Martins' screened-in porch. "Mary always projected such energy," Bessie Mae recalled. "I wanted to do everything Mary did, and she had me doing things I didn't know I *could* do—and some I didn't want to do! I rode horseback and later, when we were older, played tennis, but I didn't want to get up as early as Mary did."

Bessie Mae loved Sunday dinners at the Martins' home. "Billie, their maid, was the greatest cook in the world," she remembered, "and Jerry and her husband, Robert, would come over every weekend. Mrs. Martin had put together the most beautiful tablecloth out of lace, and we ate on that every Sunday." After dinner Preston and Juanita would take a nap, while Mary had Bessie Mae out doing antics in the yard, barn, or orchard. By then the Martins had moved to 314 West Oak Street, a few blocks from the town square. An imposing two-story stucco house on a big lot, with huge living and dining rooms and wings on both sides, the Victorian mansion

included a sunroom, a den in back, and four bedrooms upstairs. "It was very much a home and most comfortable," Bessie Mae said, "and Mrs. Martin was a wonderful homemaker and there was always music." In the evenings and sometimes on Sunday afternoons, the Martins gathered around the piano and sang. "Of all the families I've known," Mary said as an adult, "the ones that sang at home were always the happiest."

Sometimes Juanita would drive Mary over to Mineral Wells to spend the weekend with the Yeagers. Bessie Mae's father, a physician, called Mary "Boy" because of her athletic nature. Whereas Weatherford was an old-fashioned country town, Mineral Wells was a sophisticated little resort community with big hotels. People came from all over to drink the waters there. "In small towns children had such freedom in those days," Bessie Mae said, "although there was more freedom in Weatherford than there was in Mineral Wells because we had so many visitors coming into town." The two girls would ride donkeys up East Mountain, sang duets together, and spent Saturday afternoons at the movies. "Bessie Mae Sue Ella has always been so much fun," Mary reflected as a Broadway star. "She has the cutest little squeaky voice and would come out with the funniest things." The two girls really came to be more like sisters than friends. Long after Mary had become famous, someone said to Bessie Mae, "You and Mary kind of talk alike," referring to their Texas accent. Bessie Mae replied, "We used to, but she got over it!"

Mary was crazy about Bessie Mae Sue Ella's name and later used it in most of her shows. As schoolgirls, the two went to camp together in Siloam Springs, Arkansas, up in the Ozarks. Juanita drove them to Arkansas and stayed nearby. "She always hovered," Bessie Mae said, "but she was there to dream up happy things for us to do. Juanita Martin was very imaginative about everything and very ambitious for Mary." Later, Mary went to camp near Kerrville, Texas, where she learned to play the ukulele.

Bessie Mae Sue Ella discovered Mary's genius for performing when her parents took her to Weatherford to see her friend in a program, in which the future star interpreted Robert Browning's "The Laboratory" in dance. "It was one of the most exquisite, fanciful

things I have ever seen," Bessie Mae recalled. "Mary had a magnificent teacher, Miss Flo Hutchins, who introduced her to that type of literature. She turned those rhymes into a beautiful ballet"

At age twelve, Mary began taking voice lessons from Helen Fouts Cahoon in Fort Worth. A friend of the Martins, Cahoon taught music at Texas Christian University, and she helped Mary develop a distinctive style of singing. At that point in her life, Mary dreamed of becoming a coloratura soprano. How much of the girl's drive was Juanita's doing is a matter of conjecture. Mary denied that Juanita was a stage mother, but admitted that she acquired Juanita's "strong constitution." "Mother would get very upset because I'd put everything off until the last minute," an adult Mary said. "When I was to do a recital, she'd just have a nervous breakdown. She'd say, 'But you don't know the songs!' I'd say, 'I'll know them, don't worry about it.' Mother would insist, 'If you're going to do this, you have to memorize the material. Don't wait, don't put it off.' But I'd wait until the last minute. I could learn things very quickly in those days." Bessie Mae Sue Ella, like Don Martin, maintained that Juanita Martin was a pusher and navigated much of Mary's reputation as the most talented girl in Weatherford.

Before she became Mary's teacher, Helen Fouts Cahoon had given a concert that the Martins attended. Afterward, Mary was strangely silent. Mrs. Cahoon studied the reddish-haired girl, whom she knew was given to playacting, and asked, "What do you want to be when you grow up?" Without hesitation, Mary replied, "I want to grow up and sing—in opera." Cahoon agreed to take the novice on as a pupil and found her first lesson a revelation. "Mary had an absolutely pure ear," the teacher said, "and I soon realized she had stick-to-itiveness. She wouldn't give up."

As a high school student, Mary gave a two-hour recital with her friend Bessie Mae Sue Ella, who played the violin, and doted on the attention it brought. Mary felt perfectly at home before an audience. "Give me four people and I'm on," the future star often said. "Give me four hundred and I'm a hundred times more on." She began performing wherever she could—for the Lion's Club, at the Elks Club, for the Rotarians, and in church choirs. Once

she popped out of an oversized rose at a garden party, threw rose petals, and announced a couple's engagement. Yet, as ambitious as Mary was, she fantasized living in a rose-covered cottage with a picket fence and having an idyllic small-town marriage.

Although the Martins were Methodists, Juanita had very progressive ideas about religion and encouraged Mary to consider other denominations when picking her own church. "If you wish to join a congregation, you have to study it," Juanita Martin told her daughter. After trying the Baptists, the Presbyterians, and practically every other church in town, Mary decided to become an Episcopalian. For a time she sang in the choir at Weatherford's little Episcopal church, around the corner from her home. "The only reason I quit was that the priest's wife sang louder than I did," Mary said years later. "She was so loud and so bad, it was just awful. I finally just went to Sunday school and stopped going to church."

In addition to studying voice with Helen Fouts Cahoon, Mary also took dancing lessons in Fort Worth for a brief time from Elizabeth King, who had taught future Hollywood actress Ginger Rogers. Yet Mary claimed that most of what she knew about show business in those days she learned from the movies. Week after week she went to the Palace Theater, Weatherford's only movie house, and sat enthralled by the singers and dancers she saw on the screen. The Palace was where, as a small child, Mary first saw *Peter Pan*, the silent film that starred Betty Bronson, and immediately fell in love with the character. Later she watched Al Jolson, Ruby Keeler, Dick Powell, Eleanor Powell, and the other musical stars of the early talkies. "I was the Palace's best customer," Mary said. "The movies were the only way I knew there was a place outside of Weatherford to perform. They were my babysitter. Mother would let me go to the movies, and I'd see them four or five times, because the people that owned the theater were distant cousins. I'd watch these fabulous stars perform and then go home and do what they did. Unfortunately, learning the routines from the screen, I never knew left from right—and still don't."

But even as a small child, Mary had an awareness of what money could buy. After watching a movie she used to go into the Palace's

box office and play with the coins in the till. "She liked to scoop up the nickels and let them trickle through her fingers," remembered C. W. Sadler, the theater's co-owner. "The cashiers always welcomed her."

Through her parents' guidance, Mary learned acceptance of other viewpoints and lessons in self-perception. When she was in the seventh grade she had an enemy, a girl in her class whose principal mission seemed to be to point out Mary's shortcomings. Day after day the girl's volley of grievances grew: Mary was too skinny, she was a tomboy, she talked too loud, she was stuck up, she wasn't a good student in school. Finally in tears of rage Mary ran to her father for comfort. Judge Martin listened patiently to her outburst and then asked, "Are the things the girl says true?" Mary looked at him with solemn eyes. "Haven't you ever wondered what you're really like?" Preston Martin asked his daughter. "Now you have that girl's opinion. Go make a list of everything she said, mark the points that are true, and ignore the rest." Mary did as her father directed and discovered to her surprise that about half of the girl's criticism was accurate. "Some of the things I couldn't change (like being skinny)," she said, "but a fair number I could—and suddenly wanted to change. For the first time in my life I got a fairly objective view of myself." She took the list she'd made to her father, but he refused to look at it. "That's just for you," he said. "You know better than anybody else the truth about yourself."

During their high school years Mary and Bessie Mae Sue Ella shared many of their social activities, although Bessie Mae was a year older than Mary. There were tea dances and house parties for boys and girls in Weatherford, Mineral Wells, and Fort Worth, a girl's club called the Barnaby Club, and a high school sorority in Dallas called Beta Sig. "Mary and I were the out-of-town members of Beta Sig," Bessie Mae Sue Ella remembered. "My older sister lived in Dallas, so we'd go over and stay with her." The two friends bought most of the new records of popular songs and eagerly awaited Fridays, when new releases became available. "We couldn't wait to get the latest recordings by Rudy Vallee and Gene Austin and our

other favorite artists we'd heard on the radio and bring them home and listen to them," Bessie Mae said.

In her junior year at Weatherford High School, Mary was voted the class vice-president and the most popular girl. *The Melon-Vine*, the student annual, described her as "a beautiful personality and a friend to all." Wearing bobbed hair, Mary was prominent in most of the school's social activities. She became a member of the Irene Crawford Literary Society and the Theta-Theta Society, which hosted a party each fall to welcome the football team, the Kangaroos, had picnics, and sponsored a Thanksgiving banquet and a New Year's Eve bash. Mary served as hostess of a bridge party the group gave in 1929, and when thirty-five classmates held a Halloween party in the barn at Myra Akard's house, Mary and Myra led the guests in dancing the Virginia Reel. The young people at the event also had their fortunes told, played games, danced to a portable record player, feasted on popcorn balls, hot chocolate, and marshmallows, and enjoyed a grand time despite a drowning rain outside.

In May, the junior class entertained the seniors with a celebration at the Martins' home, where there was plenty of room for dancing and parlor games. The evening culminated with a promenade around the town square, during which the revelers wore paper hats, blew horns, and threw streamers and confetti. A joke exchange supposedly had Myra Akard asking Mary, "Why do you call your sweetie Paul Revere?" Never at a loss for words, Mary answered, "It's just the way he makes his midnight call to arms."

That same year Mary gave a two-hour recital with Bessie Mae Sue Ella, who played the violin and sang. A short time later, in March 1929, Mary reciprocated when Bessie Mae gave her own recital in the high school auditorium in Mineral Wells. The program for the event read: "Bessie Mae Yeager in Expression, Voice, Violin Recital, Assisted by Mary Martin, Soprano." The auditorium, first floor and balcony, was filled to capacity for the performance, and the review in the local paper was a rave. "The stage setting was truly an art triumph," a clipping from March 21, 1929, reads. "A Japanese garden scene was depicted in view of the fact that the concluding feature

of the program portrayed the last act of *Madam Butterfly*. Miss Martin's sweet voice was very lovely in song. She gave several selections in Italian and her numbers were received with enthusiasm by the audience."

In her senior year of high school, Mary went to Dallas as "Princess" from Weatherford to appear in a State Fair of Texas beauty show. She was waiting on a float just outside the tunnel leading into the Cotton Bowl when a drunken rodeo cowboy came along on his horse from the nearby grandstand where he'd been performing. He threw a rope around Mary's shoulders and proclaimed in a loud voice that she was the prettiest girl at the fair and that he intended to take her home with him. Mary was good-natured about the intrusion at first, but when time came for the float to go into the Cotton Bowl, she began pleading with the cowboy to unfasten her. A Texas Ranger walked up about that time and ordered the cowboy to free her. After the beauty show, Mary and a friend went to see the musical the State Fair was offering that year, which was *Bittersweet* starring Allan Jones, who would be Mary's costar in her first movie a decade later.

Her friend on the trip to Dallas had argued that Mary was making a mistake by piling her hair on top of her head. "I don't care how it looks," Mary retorted. "I'd rather look different than beautiful." Mary knew that she was not a beautiful girl by traditional standards, but she did her best to appear as striking as possible. At age fourteen she started putting chamomile tea on her hair to brighten the look. "I don't remember having seen the real color of my hair since then," Mary remarked years later. Preston Martin, whom friends also called "Pet," had instilled in his daughter a great deal of personal assurance during her adolescence. He told her, "Mary, there is one way never to be talked about and never criticized—by saying nothing and doing nothing. Of course, as a result, you'd *be* nothing." Blandness was never Mary's style, and she sensed early that she was going to be famous. While still in high school she spent hours experimenting with different ways of writing her name, so that when she became a movie star she could make a statement when signing autographs.

Mary was supposed to play the lead in the senior play at Weatherford High, which was a musical. A few days before the performance, a group of her friends had a picnic at a nearby lake and invited Mary to come along. It was a chilly day, and Juanita urged her daughter to stay home and avoid the possibility of catching a cold. Mary raised such a fuss about being left behind that her mother finally relented after Mary promised not to go swimming. When the others went into the water, Mary couldn't stand not being part of the action, so she put on her bathing suit and went out in a rowboat. Later, when she headed for shore, some of the boys began rocking the boat, and just as Mary was about to beach the craft, it tipped over. "Trying at all costs to avoid contact with the water," Mary said, "I took a leap for shore. I made it, but I landed squarely on a broken bottle and slashed my heel to the bone." The gash ruled out her appearing in the senior play. "My understudy made a big hit while I languished in the hospital," Mary recalled.

Because Bessie Mae Sue Ella the year before had gone to Ward-Belmont, a finishing school in Nashville, Tennessee, Mary was sent there in the fall of 1930 after her graduation from high school. She was sixteen years old, and it was the first time she'd ever been away from her parents. "Mary was miserable," Bessie Mae recalled, "just completely miserable. She was homesick and, intelligent person though she has always been, academic work was never for Mary." The future star studied voice at Ward-Belmont with Dr. Stetson Humphrey, but aside from singing and the social life, Mary found the school dull. She hated math, English literature, and medieval history, and admitted lifting sentences from a book for an assigned paper on Benjamin Franklin.

One of the few bright spots in her brief "higher education" was a chance to see silent screen stars Vilma Banky and Rod La Rocque during a personal appearance tour through the upper South. They were the first live actors Mary had ever seen. "It opened another world to me," she said. But otherwise, apart from a few friendships there, Ward-Belmont seemed pretty much a bore. Mary hated all the rules about makeup, dating, and chaperones, and her homesickness got worse when Bessie Mae Sue Ella had to return to

Texas because of a foot infection. "Mary wanted to go, too." Bessie Mae said. "Ward-Belmont was definitely not for her." Forced to stay, Mary roomed with Shirley Lege of Dallas and sank deeper into despair. She missed her family, particularly her mother, who had always been there to help make decisions for her. "I never realized how close I was to her," Mary said later.

After two and a half months of misery, the homesick girl talked her mother into coming to Nashville for a visit and suggested that she ask Ben Hagman, a boy from Fort Worth she had known for two years, to drive her. Twenty-one-years-old, Ben had been a football player in high school and was an accountant, currently studying law with the goal of going into partnership with Preston Martin. One of three brothers, Ben possessed his own flair, and Mary had dated him during her senior year at Weatherford High. Ben was a forceful, straightforward fellow and, like Mary, never seemed to meet a stranger. The summer after she graduated from high school, their romance had grown heated enough that Juanita and Preston were relieved when time came for Mary to leave for Ward-Belmont.

When Juanita Martin arrived in Nashville with Ben, she found Mary in an alarming state of nerves. The unhappy student had been assigned to write a term theme on "Flower Decoration in the Genteel Home," and she had no notion of how to begin. Juanita listened to her daughter's lexicon of complaints about school and for some inexplicable reason let Mary and Ben talk her into allowing them to get married. They drove across the state line to Hopkinsville, Kentucky, where on November 3, 1930, the underage bride and a boy she knew only superficially were wed in the Episcopal Church there. "How hillbilly can you get?" Mary would later say. The bride thought they needed music at the ceremony, so she walked down the aisle singing "Oh Promise Me."

After the nuptials, the three-member wedding party drove straight to the gates of Ward-Belmont. Mary kissed her mother and Ben goodbye and went back to her room in the freshman girls' dormitory. "I just never thought what marriage would be," she said. "I was not equipped, and I only loved Ben like a brother." Mary decided to tell only a few of her close friends at school that she had gotten

married, but the word spread fast. Within a few hours she was
called to the dean's office. Upon discovering that the rumors he'd
heard were true, the dean, a proper southern gentleman, asked if
the marriage had been consummated. Mary claimed she didn't
know what that meant. The dean fumbled for words but finally
said, "Have you lived with him?" A startled Mary replied, "Oh, no, of
course not." Relieved, the dean said, "Fine, we can have the marriage
annulled, and you can stay in school." "Oh, no!" Mary retorted.
Her whole reason for getting married was to get out of Ward-
Belmont. "I had to do some fast talking and managed to get myself
home," she recalled. "I got married so I wouldn't have to write
that term paper."

As an adult, Mary maintained that she never understood why
her mother had permitted her to marry so young. "I guess she just
wasn't used to saying 'no' to me," she supposed. "And maybe Mother
liked the idea of having Ben as the son she never had. Later, I
blamed her for that early marriage. Now I realize that my mother
just didn't know what to do with me."

The adolescent bride returned to Texas on a train. At Fort
Worth her eager groom boarded the coach and slipped a wedding
ring on Mary's finger. They spent their honeymoon at the Martins'
house in Weatherford, and their first night together in Mary's old
bedroom. "Our marriage was not consummated for a week or so,"
Mary said, "but almost from the moment it was, I was pregnant."
Preston and Juanita Martin bought the newlyweds a small house
in Fort Worth, a car, and some furniture, and Mary started trying
to be a housewife, which she knew nothing about. "Mrs. Martin
would drive over several times a week," Bessie Mae Sue Ella recalled,
"and take Mary's lingerie and laundry home with her and have Billie
wash and iron everything. Then she'd bring it back to Mary."

Bessie Mae was shocked when she heard that her friend had
married, but she wasn't surprised at all when she saw how unhappy
Mary was with her attempts at homemaking. Ben and Mary were
totally different personalities, except for their love of people. He
was from reserved Swedish stock, serious about launching a legal
career, whereas Mary was the talkative teenager. His family had

owned lumber mills in Wisconsin before migrating to Texas, and Ben loved nothing more than to spend his leisure time hunting, fishing, and having a few drinks with his buddies, activities that excluded Mary. She wasn't used to being left out, nor was she used to living a Spartan existence. The Great Depression had hit Texas by 1930, and while the state's economy was better than in the Dust Bowl to the north, Ben was still a struggling accountant, studying law on the side, and times were hard. Mary felt isolated from her family and from much of her husband's world. Starved for companionship, she invited Bessie Mae Sue Ella to Fort Worth for a visit. "Mary had a watermelon party for me in her yard," Bessie Mae remembered, "and she invited all of the friends we'd known in Fort Worth. We had a really wonderful time, but I think Mary was beginning to realize that she was a married woman, pregnant, and that she was removed from this group of people that she'd danced with from the time she was in junior high school. Her life had changed and she was fighting the adjustment."

On September 21, 1931, just ten months after Mary and Ben married, their son, Larry Martin Hagman—future star of the television series *I Dream of Jeannie* and the infamous J. R. Ewing on the prime-time soap opera *Dallas*—was born in Fort Worth. The infant's seventeen-year-old mother was no more prepared to become a parent than she was to be a housewife. Mary called her son "Lukey" and viewed him almost like a baby brother. "She was a kid herself—too young to be a wife, too young to be a mother, and too full of ambition to settle down," Larry wrote years later. Inept at the duties that faced her and despondent over the stifling life she saw ahead of her, Mary wrestled with confused emotions and a sense of being trapped. The normally sunny, sparkling girl began to look listless and peaked. When her disposition appeared to grow worse, Juanita Martin took her daughter to Mineral Wells and had Dr. Yeager, Bessie Mae's father, examine her. After a thorough examination the kindly doctor said, "There's nothing wrong with her physically. It's just that too much has happened to her in too short a period. Let Mary stay here with us for two weeks. I will see her daily and take care of her physical well being." Then Dr. Yeager's voice grew

stern. "But, Juanita, I don't want you to call her, and I don't want Ben to come to see her. Mary needs to refresh herself."

Mary stayed with the Yeagers for the prescribed rest, and a woman who worked for the family gave her a hot bath every morning and a massage. Previously, the woman had been a masseuse at one of the bathhouses in Mineral Wells. "She said Mary was as tight as a little race horse," Bessie Mae recalled. "I think marriage and motherhood coming so fast had just been too much for her. Mary envisioned more for herself."

A short time later Larry was baptized in Weatherford, and Bessie Mae Sue Ella was named the boy's godmother. Juanita Martin gave a party to commemorate the occasion, and it was clear to Bessie Mae then that Larry had already become more Juanita's child than Mary's. "Mary just bore him," Bessie Mae said, "Juanita dominated him." Many years later Mary reflected, "Mother always wanted a boy, and with Larry's birth she had one. She had me, and I was more like a boy than a girl, but when Larry came along, she had a real son. She really raised him until he was twelve years old."

When Ben joined Preston Martin's law firm after passing the bar exam in Austin, the young couple moved to Weatherford and back into the house with Mary's parents, an uneasy arrangement for young married people under the best of circumstances. Larry was a sweet-natured boy, and while Mary wasn't ready to assume responsibility for his rearing, she resented her mother's taking charge. Mary took her son for a walk once, during which he was stung by a bee. When the boy was a little older, he fell off a Shetland pony and broke a bone. When Juanita found out about these mishaps, she blamed Mary, asking, "What did you do to *my* Larry?" Mary knew that as long as she lived in her parents' house, things would never be any different. "I wasn't happy with that," she said, "but I didn't know what to do."

In addition to everything else, with Billie and her mother taking care of Larry and running the household, Mary didn't have enough to occupy her time. After two years of sitting idle in a state of emotional turmoil, she was receptive when her sister Jerry suggested that she open a dance studio. Jerry taught her some basic steps she had

learned as a physical education major at Columbia University, and
within a month Mary had enrolled thirty pupils, ranging from a
two-year-old girl to a man from Oklahoma at least sixty. In 1932
eighteen-year-old Mary opened the Mary Hagman School of Terpsi-
chore in what had been her Uncle Luke's grain storage loft. She swept
out the remains of the wheat and corn, had a piano toted up the steep,
wobbly staircase, added a barre for ballet training, and announced
that she was in business. To counteract the strong religious prejudice
against dancing in the Bible Belt, Mary emphasized the health bene-
fits of dancing as exercise. She was also aware that tap dancing had
become a fad in the neighboring cities. Mothers eager to have their
daughters in the social whirl soon proved Mary's best customers.

The first step she taught her students was the waltz clog, but
Mary quickly realized that she didn't know much more. Most of what
she knew lacked precision since it came from watching Hollywood
stars cavorting on the screen. Aware of the need for continuous
fresh material, she boarded a bus each week and took dance lessons
at night in Fort Worth to stay one step ahead of her pupils. "It was
a scramble," Mary said, "but it was fun." Gradually, she expanded
her teaching to include tap, ballet, acrobatic, and ballroom dancing.
Eventually, she learned from her instructor in Fort Worth the
Shim Sham, the Shuffle Off to Buffalo, and a triple time-step with
break. Mary became so fond of her students that she spent most
of her earnings making them costumes.

Meanwhile, she and Ben drifted farther apart. He spent most
of his evenings preparing for his new career, while Mary developed
renewed zest from her success as a dance teacher. As her old drive
and fortitude returned, she began talking about a divorce. Mary
showed signs of growing up, and it was clear to everyone in the
Martin household that her marriage to Ben had been a mistake.
Still, there had never been a divorce in the family, and Preston urged
Mary to wait a year before making a final decision. She agreed,
although Ben moved out of the Martin home. The two remained
amicable and wouldn't legally divorce until 1935, but their marriage
had been on tenuous ground from the start. Juanita Martin confessed
to Bessie Mae Sue Ella that she doubted that sex would ever be

important to Mary. It was perhaps the most perceptive statement one could make about Mary's sexuality

At the end of her first year as a dance instructor, Mary decided that she had to learn a great deal more if she was to shepherd her pupils through another year of classes. She looked into schools that taught dance teachers and determined that the famous Fanchon and Marco School of the Theatre in Hollywood would meet her needs best. Her father agreed to pay for the trip to California and advanced her money for tuition. Nineteen-year-old Mary, back to her happy self, drove to California in the summer of 1933 with Bessie Mae Sue Ella's cousin, Ben Yeager, who was in medical school, and two of their older friends. "They had a marvelous time," Bessie Mae said, "and laughed all the way, except that Mary got restless and kept wanting to know when they were going to get there."

Fanchon and Marco were a brother and sister team that became successful in sending out road shows all over the country. For their school on Sunset Boulevard in Los Angeles they hired experienced teachers, one of whom was Nico Charisse, who taught modern and Spanish dancing and married Cyd Charisse before she became a film star. Mary thrived on the exposure she got at the school and made the most of her father's investment. "I didn't waste one waking moment," she said. "I studied eight hours a day and then practiced for hours anywhere I could find an empty room in the school." From Nico Charisse she learned to tango and took classes in tap, acrobatic dancing, ballroom, and ballet. "Most of the teachers that studied at Fanchon and Marco were way ahead of me because they came there every summer," Mary said. "We did precision dancing, and that thrilled me—a big chorus of us all kicking. I was young and thin, and they put me in the front row. I would work my way to the back because I had to watch somebody to be able to do the steps. I didn't know anything. The friends I met in classes would go off to the beach on the weekends, and I would still be at the school practicing." But for the first time since her marriage Mary felt free and alive.

She returned to Texas, captivated by the excitement of show business, to find a surprise waiting. While she was away, her father

and mother had built a studio for her. The one-story brick cottage was across the street and down a half-block from the Martins' home. It had a stone floor, a wood-paneled reception room, a fireplace, and French doors that opened into the studio itself. Juanita had designed the building, which had windows on three sides, a wall of mirrors, a ballet barre, and a dressing room with bath and showers for the students. Mary's classes immediately grew to be enormous. "Everybody in Weatherford wanted to find out what I'd learned in Hollywood," she said. The trip markedly enhanced her reputation as the most talented girl in town, and she was referred to locally as the "Weatherford Whiz." She added voice lessons to her curriculum and did so well with her school that she opened a second one in Mineral Wells, twenty miles away.

Mary drove over to the resort town twice a week, and the head of the Crazy Water Crystals Company made a deal with her. He would allow Mary to use the rooftop ballroom of the Crazy Water Hotel in Mineral Wells for her dancing classes; in return, she would sing in the lobby with the hotel orchestra on Wednesdays and Saturdays. "This was my first singing job," Mary said, "though no money changed hands." From that time until she left Texas, she sang twice a week at noon with Jack Amlong and his band in the lobby of the Crazy Water Hotel. "So many people that gathered there were ill," Mary recalled. "They'd come in their wheelchairs to hear us. I had to sing hillbilly songs, which I just loathed. I wanted to sing things like 'Stormy Weather,' which I did, but I also had to do songs like 'Hand Me Down My Walkin' Cane.'" From Jack Amlong she learned to sing into a microphone, and Amlong's pianist taught her how to phrase blues numbers. But she also whistled and learned to yodel at the Crazy Water Hotel and on occasions even sang hillbilly songs with the Light Crust Doughboys when they came through the area on tour. Since the shows in the hotel's lobby were broadcast, advertising Crazy Crystals, Mary developed a regional following and became known as "Mary Hagman, the Crazy Girl."

Dallas arts patron Ruth Altschuler remembered meeting Mary while she was singing in Mineral Wells. "She wasn't a beautiful girl," Altschuler said, "but she just exuded personality." The *Dallas Morning*

News amusement critic, John Rosenfield, became acquainted with Mary through the broadcasts from the Crazy Water Hotel and became a lifelong friend. "She was a girl of less beauty than style," Rosenfield wrote in a column in 1959, "less voice than instinct, but a girl with an unusual combination of youth, femininity, imagination, and lyric poetry."

Again out of routines to teach her pupils, Mary returned to California during the summer of 1934 to study at the Fanchon and Marco School. This time Juanita and Larry drove to Los Angeles with her. They rented a house in the Hollywood hills, and Mary went back to taking lessons all day and practicing at night. One afternoon she wandered into the wrong classroom. Various girl students were getting up and singing the same song, "How Red the Rose, How Blue the Sky." Mary sat down to listen. Eventually someone said to her, "You're next." By that time she'd learned the words to the song, so Mary got up and sang it. She went to her next class, and when it was over she was told, "Miss Fanchon wants to see you in her office." Mary had never met Miss Fanchon and was terrified, certain she had done something wrong and was about to be kicked out of school. When she walked into the office, she recognized a woman she'd seen while she was singing "How Red the Rose." Fanchon told Mary she'd won the audition she'd just participated in. Unaware that she'd ambled into an audition, Mary listened in shock as Fanchon told her, "You leave at 7:30 in the morning for San Francisco with a Fanchonette stage unit. You will sing that song while they dance."

The next morning Mary and twenty-four Fanchonettes boarded a train for San Francisco, and for a week Mary sang "How Red the Rose" in the wings of the Fox Theater six times a day while the other girls performed a precision dance routine wearing rose-colored costumes. "I found it delightfully habit-forming," Mary said. "So much so that when I went back to Weatherford, teaching dancing wasn't exciting anymore." Before the summer was over, Fanchon offered Mary a regular job at $75 a week, but Preston Martin was not in good health by then, and the ambitious girl felt that she had no choice but to return to Texas.

That fall Mary enrolled three hundred students in her classes and opened a third school in Cisco, Texas, in one of Conrad Hilton's first hotels. She hired a dance assistant, a woman who kept books for her, and an accompanist. In addition to her teaching, Mary also was busy preparing for her pupils' dance recitals in both Weatherford and Mineral Wells and singing in the lobby of the Crazy Water Hotel. But she had tasted the glamour of professional show biz and hungered for more. She began doing more singing in Fort Worth and the surrounding towns and learned to hold the attention of an audience as she grew in her craft. When a crank who thought dancing was sinful set fire to her studio, some of the joy of teaching also went up in smoke. Mary couldn't stop crying as she viewed the damage. "I didn't know it," she wrote in her memoirs, "but I was on the ragged edge of a small breakdown." Although the studio was rebuilt, Mary by then had aspirations far grander than being the best dance instructor in Parker County. Hollywood had cast its spell, and she was growing tired of singing for local benefits and Country Club dances.

After the bustle of Los Angeles, life in small-town Texas seemed so mundane. Once while waiting for her cue to entertain at a dance, Mary stood outside talking with Bessie Mae Sue Ella. "It was at Easter time," Mary recalled, "and I had on a hat and a very fluffy dress. Somebody threw dishwater out a window, and it went all over me. Bessie Mae just went into hysterics, but I had to rush in and put on something else before I could sing." She yearned for a chance to break into movies and refused to accept the pitfalls her parents and friends pointed out when she talked of returning to the West Coast to try her luck.

Meanwhile, Larry was left in the care of his grandmother, whom he called Nanny, and Billie Jones, the Martins' loving maid. Billie, a rotund woman, took the boy with her to Weatherford's black church, which Larry said he liked better than the one his grandparents attended, and also to the movies at the theater down on the town square. "I remember the manager would let me and other white kids go upstairs with our nannies," Hagman wrote after his success as J. R. Ewing in *Dallas*, "but the nannies couldn't go downstairs

with us." The boy called Preston "Papu," and Larry remembered that his granddad bored him to death as a child with his endless lectures. "Judge Martin definitely had a gift for gab," said Mary's childhood friend, Virginia May Milmo. "He used to come over and have a cocktail with my Papa. Mrs. Martin was always going someplace, so she never visited very much, but everybody in town knew Mr. Martin."

To enhance the allure of her performing, Mary had selected a dozen of her best teenage students as a backup group and tagged them the Martinettes. Patterned after the Fanchonettes, who did production numbers at the Paramount Theater in Los Angeles, the Martinettes danced in shows around the small towns west of Fort Worth. When Broadway producer Billy Rose came to Texas in 1935, scouting for local talent for the chorus of the centennial extravaganza he planned to stage at Casa Mañana in Fort Worth, Mary loaded the Martinettes into two cars, and off they went to audition. When they arrived at the Texas Hotel in Fort Worth, where try-outs were being held, they found the place a madhouse. Mary pushed her way up to Rose, who told her she'd have to wait her turn. Mary and the girls got into costume, but waited until midnight before Rose was ready to see what the Martinettes could do. Mary, decked out in a full dress suit with top hat and tails reminiscent of Fred Astaire, danced and sang in front while the girls danced behind her. According to Mary, "Billy Rose kept getting lower and lower in his chair. He thought the girls were good, but me dancing in front as Fred Astaire was what was giving him a nervous breakdown."

When they finished their routine, the worldly producer asked Mary if she could sing any other songs. "Oh, yes," she said, "there's one I'd like to sing," and for some bizarre reason she broke into "Gloomy Sunday," making the number as dramatic as possible. "It was a song that had people committing suicide," Mary said later, "but that's what I chose to sing!" When she was done, Rose asked why she had picked that particular song. "Because I like it," she said, "it's so touching." The exasperated producer told her, "Well, don't ever sing it on another audition."

Rose ended up hiring three of the Martinettes, but rejected Mary. He told her that she was too good for the chorus and not

good enough for a specialty number. He advised her to go back to Weatherford, have more babies, and forget show business. "He thought I had no talent at all," Mary said, but the rejection made her more determined than ever. "I was so mad at him I wanted to shoot him," Mary said. Later Rose called her for an interview and explained the limitations of the theatrical profession to her. He urged her to stick to her dancing school. "I sat there furious," Mary said, "almost choking." Juanita had driven to Fort Worth with her daughter for the interview, and when Mary came out of her talk with Rose, she said, "Mother, I'm going back to California and I'm going to have a career." Her voice was like steel.

Preston agreed to finance Mary's efforts to break into movies and said he'd arrange for her divorce while she was gone. "I think Ben was very loathe to be divorced from Mary," Bessie Mae Sue Ella said, "but he understood that the marriage wasn't working. I do think he wanted custody of Larry, but that was not feasible. Mrs. Martin would never have given Larry up."

Juanita insisted that Mary have a companion with her when she returned to California and arranged for their friend Mildred Woods to accompany her headstrong daughter. "Folks in Weatherford didn't get very far from home in those days," said Don Martin, so when his cousin, a married woman with a four-year-old child, left for the perils of Hollywood, she was both the town's pride and the town scandal. "I couldn't take Larry away from mother," Mary insisted. "Leaving him in Texas was very tough on him, and on all of us. He felt abandoned and harbored resentment toward me for many years. But I had no choice; my need for a career was too strong. . . . I'll never stop being grateful to Billy Rose. His advice that I should stay out of show business crystalized my desire to go in."

Audition Mary

Mary flew to Hollywood in 1935 with $500 in her purse, an unmistakable Texas twang, and a pleasing soprano voice capable of singing popular songs, blues, and light opera. Before she left Weatherford she had promised her father that, as soon as the $500 was gone, she would come home. "Let conscience be your guide," Preston Martin told his adventuresome daughter as she prepared to leave her child, her business, and her security behind. But Mary's conscience told her that she was doing the right thing, the only thing she knew that would make her happy and bring her the fulfillment she longed for. When Billy Rose rejected her for his Casa Mañana show, something clicked in Mary's head, and she determined to shape her own destiny. Since motion pictures were the only facet of big-time show business she had ever seen in Weatherford, Hollywood was the logical target for her. Fan magazines were full of stories about hopefuls who had been discovered for movies while selling lingerie or sipping sodas at drugstore counters. Mary knew that she had an advantage over the vacuous glamour girls and beauty queens that poured into Tinseltown by the zillions, something most of them didn't have—she had talent.

Juanita Martin would have no part of Mary's plan to return to California until her willful daughter agreed to take Mildred Woods,

a schoolteacher's daughter and trusted family friend from Peaster, Texas, with her as companion, chaperon, and part-time secretary. Mildred had helped Mary manage her dance studio and possessed the organizational skills that Mary lacked. She was a short, chunky woman, two years older than Mary, full of provincial attitudes and covered with freckles. "From the beginning," Mary said, "we felt like sisters." From Juanita's standpoint, Mildred made the ideal companion for her daughter, and she made them both promise that neither would go out at night without the other.

At first the girls stayed at one of the nicer apartment houses in Los Angeles, but their money began to run out fast. They moved to a one-room kitchenette with a Murphy bed near the Fanchon and Marco School, and Mary began a frantic two-year effort to win the attention of movie studios. She and Mildred shared some articles of clothing, and Millie helped Mary get fixed up with the appropriate outfit and makeup before she went on interviews. Getting an agent to handle an unknown singer with a hick accent proved the first hurdle, and Mary claimed that she talked herself into a "whispering bass" trying to find one.

Next came a marathon series of auditions. Mary tried out for everything, sometimes as a blues singer, other times as an operatic soprano or crooner, occasionally as a dancer, but nothing seemed to be what producers were looking for. "Sometimes I truly did ten auditions a day," Mary said. She tried all the vocal styles she knew, from earthy song plugging to high coloratura. She sang like Frances Langford, and when that didn't work she shifted to a Kate Smith imitation. "I even did a good Bing Crosby," Mary said. Actually, she had what she later called "a sort of illegitimate legitimate soprano" in her Hollywood days. But an early teacher in California told her, "Sopranos are a dime a dozen. Throw away that voice and use your lower register."

There were some bleak periods during those two years of auditioning. Preston Martin kept sending Mary money, but still she and Mildred had to move into cheaper and cheaper quarters on streets far from glamorous. They lived on Franklin Street, on Fountain, and at a place near Hollywood and Vine. Mildred remained a

constant source of encouragement. "You wait," she'd say when Mary grew discouraged. "You'll show 'em!" Mary took strength from what her mother had taught her: if you want to do something, all you have to do is try hard enough. Accomplishment is simply a question of work.

But when Mary at last gained entrance into the studios, the answer was always the same. Her nose was too big, her neck was too long, her chin was too small, her forehead was too high, her chest was too flat, and she didn't photograph well. Time and again, Mary was told that she'd never make it in movies. Talent department representatives told her she couldn't act, and studio vocal coaches said her voice was undisciplined. Eventually, she auditioned for every studio in town, not once but repeatedly, until she became known around town as "Audition Mary." She was told that to make the grade as a soprano she'd have to learn to read music and change her name to something like Mary Martini, or at least change her first name to a spelling with greater marquee value such as Merrie or Merry, suggestions the Weatherford girl found ludicrous. "Hollywood studios kept trying to make me into a glamour girl," she said. "So did booking agents and nightclubs where I auditioned." Everybody seemed to see something different in her. She was made up to look like Claudette Colbert, as Rosalind Russell, as Jean Arthur, as first one movie queen and then another. Her hair always seemed to be the wrong color, so it was dyed and redyed to enhance whatever image Hollywood masterminds were trying to concoct.

What Mary had going for her was personality, ambition, a pleasant voice, vitality, good legs, nice eyes, and a fundamental stubbornness. Finally, Paramount agreed to make a silent test of her. So did Metro-Goldwyn-Mayer, Universal, and Twentieth Century-Fox. For a while the Metro test looked promising. She was called back to the studio at intervals for two weeks. Then came the verdict, which essentially was, "Go home, little girl. Don't break your heart over Hollywood." But Mary wasn't used to failure, and she simply vowed to try harder. "There are two types in Hollywood," she said: "the girls who take what is given to them and get along fine and others who fight for every inch." Mary decided she fell into the latter category.

About the only person who seemed to feel Mary had any special quality was Lillian Burns, later the powerful drama coach at MGM. In 1935, Burns was working in the talent department at Republic, one of the lesser studios that specialized in making budget Westerns. "I worked in a room next to where the horses were," the coach said. Burns heard Mary read when she auditioned for Republic and saw that she had a unique charm. The coach gave her a scene that Claudette Colbert and Fred MacMurray had done in a movie at Paramount, one where she sat on a bench and ate popcorn while she and an actor talked. "Mary was wonderful," Burns said. "I knew then that this girl had a future." But the man who read lines with Mary, an ex-vaudevillian, remarked that she was no beauty. "He was dead as far as I was concerned," the discerning drama coach remembered. "I never forgave him for saying that about a darling girl so obviously talented." But Republic turned thumbs down on Mary, just as Metro and Fox and the rest did.

The discouraged girl did dub a song for actress Margaret Sullavan in a movie at MGM. She sang "Pack Up Your Troubles in Your Old Kit Bag" and earned two hundred dollars for a few minutes' work. Another time she dubbed for stripper Gypsy Rose Lee in a nightclub blues number at Fox, singing way down in her gullet. Studio executive Buddy DeSylva got Mary a job as a dancing teacher at Universal for another two hundred dollars, and she ended up with a fleeting moment in *The Rage of Paris*. She had tried to teach French actress Danielle Darrieux how to sing and dance a number for the movie, but Darrieux said she couldn't possibly do the hotcha the way Mary demonstrated and ran off the set, leaving Mary to take over.

Early in her Hollywood foray, Mary auditioned for Oscar Hammerstein II at the house that the renowned Broadway lyricist was renting in Beverly Hills. Like most everyone else, Hammerstein saw that Mary wasn't ready for stardom and didn't fit Hollywood's traditional concept of beauty, but he did work with her for a few days, gave her some pointers on how to phrase a lyric, and arranged for her to sing for composer Jerome Kern. After Hammerstein and Mary became friends, during the preparation of *South Pacific* for

the stage in 1949, the lyricist acquired a snapshot of the show's dazzling star taken as a teenager, which he kept on his desk. Over the photo he wrote, "There is hope for everyone."

Jerome Kern was collaborating with Hammerstein and holding auditions for the St. Louis Municipal Opera when Mary met him. The composer asked her to describe her approach to singing. Mary explained how she'd tried one thing and then another. The sagacious songwriter told her that imitating other singers was a mistake. "You must learn to sing your own way," he said. Mary recognized that Kern's advice was the truth she needed to hear. "If I was ever to be a success," she said, "it would have to be as myself."

Through the efforts of Fanchon and Marco, Mary made her first appearance on a national radio network while she was auditioning in Hollywood. The program was called *Gateway to Hollywood*, on which winners from various sections of the country competed for a short-term movie contract. None was forthcoming for Mary, but the show did result in other radio work for her, including appearances on the *Good News* programs and other broadcasts hosted by Rudy Vallee, Eddie Cantor, and Buddy Rogers. Mary thought those exposures surely would lead to bigger things, but nothing happened. As the months wore on and one discouragement followed another, the Weatherford fireball grew downhearted. Mildred, on the other hand, never lost hope. "She had lots more faith in me than I had in myself," Mary said.

One day Mary was walking down Hollywood Boulevard when she ran into her old voice teacher, Dr. Stetson Humphrey, from Ward-Belmont. Humphrey asked her what she was doing in Los Angeles, and heard how she'd been auditioning all over town with no luck and how dejected she was. "Mary," Humphrey said in a somber voice, "would you be willing to do nothing but study for six months?" She rushed home to consider the matter and to consult with Mildred, who counted up their remaining funds. Torn with indecision, Mary put in a long-distance telephone call to her father. "By all means stay and do it," Preston Martin said. "I can see you through another six months." Mary began working in earnest with her Ward-Belmont teacher—daily hours of scales, sight reading,

studying the operatic literature and lieder. She and Mildred moved to a cheap little bungalow court and did their own cleaning, washing, cooking, and mending. It was a dismal existence, but by the end of six months Mary knew that her singing had improved. Humphrey had helped her get back her true voice after she had spent months trying to lower it.

There wasn't enough money for much of a social life during those two years of auditions. Mary remembered one occasion when she got herself to the Hollywood Bowl, climbed a tree, and watched a concert from its branches. When her friend and neighbor from Weatherford, Virginia May Milmo, came to Los Angeles to study tap dancing at the Fanchon and Marco school, the two girls renewed their acquaintance and shared copies of the hometown newspaper the Martins sent. "I never knew how Mary had the nerve to stay in California as long as she did after being married and having a child," Milmo said. "She just had perseverance and wanted a career so badly. And she had talent."

With finances running low and the six months allotted for concentrated study nearing an end, Mary began looking for work. After much effort she landed a job in one of Los Angeles' lesser nightclubs. "Unfortunately, I couldn't top the dishes," Mary later said. "The customers took me as a matter of course." Another time she was singing "Shoeshine Boy" at a small club called The Casanova when Bing Crosby walked in. The famous crooner was so impressed with Mary's rendition that he had her singing the song over and over until three o'clock in the morning. Before he left, Crosby promised to help her get a job in movies. But weeks passed and Mary never heard from him.

Instead, she got a phone call offering her forty dollars a week to sing at the Cinegrille, a bar in Hollywood's Roosevelt Hotel. It would be the longest engagement she'd had, and the management there expected her to sing songs like "Indian Love Call" for ladies in the hotel's lounge at tea time and bar songs at night. Mildred went along as chaperone every evening while Mary sang numbers like "The Very Thought of You," "It's De-Lovely," and "Exactly Like You" with a small combo amid a mass of smoke and commotion.

The people in charge of the hotel were elderly and assumed a protective attitude toward Mary, making sure nobody bothered her or dared to offer her a cocktail. Working at the Cinegrill was great training, and Mary later claimed that she mastered her craft "sitting on top of a piano singing in a bar." Still, when word reached Weatherford that Mary was working in an establishment where liquor was sold, Juanita Martin became so alarmed that she packed Larry into her car and drove to California to see what was going on. "Mother met the people that ran the hotel and figured out that nothing would happen to me," Mary said. "She made sure Mildred was always there to see that everything was all right. I never went anywhere without Mildred." But Juanita stayed in California with Larry just to make sure.

When another bar, Gordon's, offered her four hundred dollars a week to sing from eight o'clock until midnight, Mary thought she was rich. She put Larry in a private school and moved into an apartment in the Highland Towers with her mother and Mildred. Afraid that Larry would grow up a sissy, since he was surrounded by women, she enrolled him in a military school, which he hated. Fortunately for him, the internment didn't last long.

Late in the summer of 1937, Audition Mary got her most decisive break to date when she wangled a bid to sing on a Sunday night talent show at the famous Trocadero Club on the Sunset Strip. Agents, talent scouts, and Hollywood producers and celebrities frequented the nightclub, and Mary decided to give her appearance there everything she had, yet be completely herself. She made no attempt at glamorization; instead, she effected a different look, simple and collegiate, by wearing a short accordion-pleated black taffeta skirt, a white blouse with a red velvet sash, a white bolero jacket, a black velvet beanie with a ribbon in her hair, and saddle shoes. She waited off to the side of the jam-packed club wondering if her turn to perform would ever come. When she heard her name called, Mary stepped into the spotlight and sang "The Weekend of a Private Secretary," a slightly risqué song about the escapades of a secretary during a whirlwind trip to Havana. Mary donned horn-rimmed glasses for the number and sang out full-voice with her

natural lilt. Then she made an abrupt switch to Arditi's aria "Il Bacio," which showed off her high soprano voice. It sounded quite operatic, until in the middle Mary suddenly went into a jazzed up, syncopated rhythm that caused the crowd to stand and cheer. "I thought everyone was getting up and leaving," Mary said. "So I was stunned a few seconds later to see they were giving me a standing ovation." People climbed on chairs, shouted, whistled, and yelled "Bravo!" Within ten minutes Mary's future had changed. "Apparently the people there that night had never heard anybody swing classical music," she said, "and it wowed them." Mary's former playmate, Virginia May Milmo, was at the Trocadero that evening and watched with pride as her friend enjoyed a triumph. "I was so thrilled I didn't know what to do," Milmo said. "That was an exciting night for both of us."

The next morning Mary's long-silent telephone began ringing early, as one movie studio after another called to set up an appointment with her. Twentieth Century-Fox sent a car for her. "That car let me out at the front office," Mary recalled, "and another one drove me to the talent office, which was only across the street." Agents old and new were on the phone all of a sudden vying to represent her. The Trocadero hired her for a short engagement as featured singer, sharing a bill with comedian Joe E. Lewis, and radio and movie offers began pouring in. But the offer that appealed to Mary most came from Lawrence Schwab, an influential New York producer who happened to be in the crowd the night she scored at the Trocadero. After hearing her sing again, Schwab realized the range of Mary's talent and the magic of her stage presence. He offered her the lead in a Broadway musical he was producing that fall called *Ring Out the News* and agreed to pay Mary's way and Mildred's to New York. Mary was so down on Hollywood by then that she eagerly signed a two-year contract with Schwab and welcomed a change of venue. The producer agreed to pay her $150 a week and suggested that she get her teeth capped.

The divorce from Ben had become final with a minimum of bad feelings. Preston Martin arranged everything by proxy. Mary was given custody of Larry, and she wanted him with her as she

prepared to go east. But Juanita insisted that New York was no place for a young boy and argued that Larry was better off with her. Larry and his grandmother returned to Weatherford, while Mary finished out her commitments in Los Angeles and cemented plans for what looked like an exciting debut in New York.

The extended separation deepened the tension between Mary and Larry and created problems that wouldn't be resolved for decades to come. "Larry was so hurt," Mary said. "He thought I had deserted him. That broke my heart, but I could do nothing. Mother wouldn't give him up, and I was afraid of destroying her life because she wanted this little boy so much." Ben meanwhile opened his own law office in Weatherford and hired a secretary, named Juanita, whom he eventually married.

When Mary left Hollywood, she swore she'd never be back. She had experienced so much rejection there that the pain had become indelible. Mary was savvy enough about herself by 1938 to know that movies would not be her best medium. "I was told at the studios that I was no good, and I believed them," she said. But she had demonstrated in diverse arenas how she lit up before live audiences, how she savored their love and returned it. She knew nothing about the New York theater, had never even seen a book musical except for *Bittersweet* at the Fair Park Auditorium in Dallas, but playing the lead in a new Broadway show sounded thrilling to Mary and she was ready for the challenge. Mildred, however, seemed dubious. She pointed out that New York was a tough town and that her gullible friend had never performed professionally on the stage. "I was firm," Mary said. "New York was going to be our oyster."

Then came word that *Ring Out the News* had been cancelled. Mildred thought the bad news was an omen, but Mary insisted that she had a contract with Schwab and must go to New York, show or no show. Besides, everyone in Weatherford had heard that she was going to Broadway, and half the town was waiting to greet her when she and Mildred made a stopover in Texas on their way to the Big Apple. "I pretended everything was okay," Mary said, "and I went on to New York." Preston drove Mildred and his daughter to Galveston, where they boarded a cattle boat. "It really had cows

on it," Mary said, "and was the first boat Millie and I had ever been on."

They arrived in New York on September 13, 1938. Lawrence Schwab greeted them at the dock and assured Mary that something would turn up for her soon. He put the newly arrived Texans in a cab, and Mary claimed the taxi driver couldn't understand her southern accent and took them all the way to Hoboken before he realized that they wanted to go to the St. Moritz Hotel. "I didn't know any hotels in New York," she said, "so we picked that name out of the phone book. It sounded swell." She and Mildred spent the next few days seeing the sights—the zoo in Central Park, Fifth Avenue, the Empire State Building. Within a week Lawrence Schwab had found an apartment for them on Fifty-fifth Street, and the producer instructed Mary to find an accompanist and be prepared to start doing auditions, an ordeal she had learned to dread.

The chance of a lifetime occurred for Mary when June Knight, who had been rehearsing an upcoming Cole Porter show called *Leave It to Me* with Sophie Tucker, Victor Moore, and William Gaxton, decided to marry a rich oil man from Houston and left the cast. Knight had been a big hit in *Take a Chance*, which Schwab had co-produced in 1932, and she thought the silly little part she had been assigned in *Leave It to Me* was beneath her. Besides, the company had been in rehearsal for three weeks and the song she had been promised hadn't been written yet. Vinton Freedley, who was producing the Porter show, had known Schwab at Harvard, and after a long conversation Freedley told Schwab to send the kid from Texas over to the theater to read a few lines.

So Mary got into a taxicab and told the driver in her thick southern accent that she wanted to go to the Imperial Theatre. "I didn't know where I was," she said. "We drove and drove and drove, and finally we were back at the pier where I had come in. The driver thought I'd said 'Pier 13.'" Mary arrived for her audition forty-five minutes late. "There was a dull thud in the theater when I got there," she remembered, "because the director, the producer, and the writers were waiting." The house was dark except for one light burning up on the stage. Since Mary had never been in a

legitimate theater before, it all seemed terribly strange to her. When she came on stage, the man who was to read with her sensed how inexperienced she was and said, "Whatever you do, say it as loud as you possibly can because they must hear you in the gallery." Mary asked, "Where's that?" The bewildered actor said, "You don't know where the gallery is?" Mary told him, "I don't know where anything is. I don't even know where this theater is." The man repeated, "Just say it loud," and he handed her some pieces of cardboard with words scattered here and there and dots in between. He read a few lines and then stopped. Mary glanced at the cardboard she was holding and virtually shouted, "I'd like to renew my subscription," her character's first line of dialogue in the play. Somebody walked down the aisle to the orchestra pit and said, "That's it. Okay, be here tomorrow." Mary discovered later that the man who had read lines with her was William Gaxton, one of the show's stars.

Next, she was sent to audition for Cole Porter in his apartment in the Ritz Towers. The composer had suffered a crippling accident the year before when a horse he was riding on Long Island shied, reared up, and fell over backwards. Porter had not been able to extricate himself from the stirrups, and the horse broke both of the songwriter's legs in multiple places by rolling on them. Mary arrived to find the renowned Broadway composer in bed with a piano keyboard suspended over him from the ceiling. She thought, "This is the oddest audition I've ever had. Oh, well, I've auditioned everywhere else, I might as well sing for someone in a bed with a piano over it." The room was crowded with people, sitting around in a circle. Mary brazenly announced, "I'd like to do four songs. And if I can't sing all four, I'd rather not sing." She'd learned enough about auditions by then to know that she needed to demonstrate that she was capable of handling different kinds of material. Porter from his bed smiled and said, "Well, carry on—on all fours."

Mary sang in her soprano voice and followed that with a blues song and a hot rhythm number. She ended with "The Weekend of a Private Secretary," making it naughty but sweet. "If I hadn't sung that song, I would not have gotten 'My Heart Belongs to Daddy,'"

she said later. "If they'd stopped me after my high soprano voice, they'd have said, 'Thank you very much,' and I'd have been out of there." Among the throng gathered at Porter's apartment that day were producer Vinton Freedley and Sam and Bella Spewack, the authors and the director (Sam) of *Leave It to Me*. Bella, who had a tendency to frighten people with her growl, asked Mary if she had ever been on the New York stage. When Mary replied that she had not, Mrs. Spewack asked why she thought she could do this show. Mary drew herself up and boldly answered, "Try me."

And try her they did. With only two more weeks of rehearsal before the musical went on the road for tryouts, Mary was given the part of Dolly Winslow in *Leave It to Me*, not the lead, but she was told that she would have her own song. Mary was delighted. "Good, bad, or indifferent," she said, "at least being in the show would buy coffee and cake for Millie and me. And it was a New York show with three outstanding musical comedy stars." Nobody asked her whether she'd ever been married or had a child, so Mary didn't mention Larry to the people she worked with. Most of the company treated her as a naïve kid fresh out of the Texas scrub country. "No one knew my background," Mary said, "and I wasn't about to tell them. I was afraid I'd lose the job."

Mary had only ten days of rehearsal with the cast before the musical went to New Haven and Boston for tryouts, and she claimed that she didn't know what the plot of the show was about for months since she'd not read the whole script. Mildred went to the theater with her every day, but the seasoned members of the company quickly assumed a protective attitude toward her. William Gaxton, known to have a full vocabulary of expletives, didn't utter a foul word whenever Mary was in earshot, and Sophie Tucker, a former vaudevillian, became her second mother. Once "My Heart Belongs to Daddy" was written, Tucker gave Mary sage advice on how to sing the saucy lyrics. Mary was still innocent enough not to realize just how risqué the song was, and she maintained that it took her weeks to figure out whose mistress she was in the show. After observing Mary's utter simplicity, Sophie Tucker came up to the novice during a rehearsal and said, "Kid, do you know what

you're singing about?" Mary indicated that she did. "You know that Daddy in the song isn't your real daddy," Tucker persisted. Mary said she knew that, but Tucker continued: "Every time you get to a naughty line, you just look straight up to heaven and say it. Never look at the audience on a naughty line." So in the next rehearsal Mary did as Sophie Tucker had instructed, and the cast members watching went into hysterics.

Tucker later wrote that she knew from the start that Mary was going to be a knockout in the show. "She had so much on-the-ball eagerness, charm, and real ability," the veteran performer said. "She just couldn't miss. Everyone in the company was crazy about her." But Gene Kelly, one of the dancers who backed up Mary in her "Daddy" number, said, "We never dreamed she would be *such* a smash. We knew she was going to be a hit, because up in Boston, where the 'Daddy' number was put into the show, we saw that she was darn good. Still, I was too inexperienced to anticipate that she'd just take New York City by storm."

Leave It to Me was a top-flight show with few expenses spared. Not only did it boast songs by the illustrious Cole Porter and a book by the highly literate Sam and Bella Spewack, the musical was also produced and carefully supervised by Vinton Freedley, a man of sophistication, wealth, and taste. "Freedley had many love affairs during that period of his life," Mary recalled, "but I knew nothing about those until later. He never ever made a pass at me—I think because I was so dumb." Freedley's wife used to come to the theater and sit in the back during rehearsals. The producer personally oversaw Mary's costumes and at the dress rehearsal had her in a bonnet with ostrich feathers all over it. During a break Mary went out in front and sat down to see what the stage looked like. "I had this dress and hat on," she remembered, "and Freedley's wife looked at me and said, 'Oh, I see you're one of Vinton's favorites. He always dresses people in ostrich feathers that are his favorites.'" Mary couldn't understand why the woman seemed angry with her, since she had barely spoken to her husband.

Robert Alton, Broadway's senior dance director, was the show's choreographer, and it was his brilliance that helped make "My

Heart Belongs to Daddy" a success. The number started out as an adagio dance with Mary wearing a fur hat and a hip-length lynx jacket with flesh-colored tights underneath. "Every time the boys would start to lift me up I'd slide off," Mary said, "because the fur wouldn't hold." Alton saw that the number didn't look right and suggested that she do a mock striptease, with Mary getting down to pink teddies as she sang the insinuating lyrics to a rumba beat. He added a few dainty bumps to the routine, which were more humorous than sexy, and had Gene Kelly and four other boys gathered around her, dressed as Eskimos, feeding her lines and gestures. The scene was set in a Siberian railroad station, with Mary performing around a trunk. "I never knew why I was in Siberia," she said. "I'd started out in New York and suddenly I was in Siberia." Nor did she understand why the man Dolly Winslow was having an affair with wanted her out of the country. "All this was terribly funny," Mary said, "because everyone could see that I didn't really know much about what I was doing. . . . I didn't have any idea what finnan haddie [in the song] was, for example, until somebody told me it was fish." She simply sang the suggestive lyrics the way Sophie Tucker had coached her and thought the whole thing was fun.

Mary remembered how she and Gene Kelly were always the first to arrive at the theater. "We'd both come in and perform on either side of the stage before the show ever started." But during rehearsals, when not needed on stage, Kelly would be seated out front reading. One day Cole Porter came to the theater in a wheelchair and noticed the studious boy with his nose in a book. "What's that boy over there reading?" Porter asked Robert Alton. The choreographer introduced the composer to Gene, who told him he was reading Huxley's *Point Counter Point*. "We started to chat about the book," Kelly said, "and we struck up a friendship."

The cherubic Victor Moore, who played the American ambassador to Moscow in the show, became Mary's pet. "He was adorable," she said. "Never did I go on that stage that Victor didn't stand in the wings and watch. I'd see him out of the corner of my eye." She in turn watched Moore night after night in awe of his perfect

timing in comedy. "He was the best comedian in the business," Mary said. "He and Billy Gaxton taught me all I know on that score." Moore and Gaxton had been a team in many shows, during which they had refined their comedic exchange to a fine art. In *Leave It to Me*, Gaxton played a malicious newspaper correspondent trying to discredit Moore, while Sophie Tucker played the ambassador's overpowering, exultantly vulgar wife. Dolly Winslow was the sweetie of the aging diplomat, a girl who liked to make eyes at young men. When she said, "I'd like to renew my subscription," Dolly really meant that she was ready to resume her affair with the newspaperman seated behind the desk.

Leave It to Me opened at the Imperial Theatre in New York on November 9, 1938, a few months after Hitler convinced British prime minister Neville Chamberlain that there would be "peace in our time" and that the only additional land he wanted for Germany was the Sudetenland. Although the show's stars seemed nervous about the opening, Mary said she was "so darned green I couldn't wait to get out there in front of the audience just to see what would happen." She didn't have enough experience in the theater to face the audience when she said her first line and just kept looking at Billy Gaxton. Finally, he took her face in his hands and turned it out toward the audience and held it there.

The spoof, a musical version of the Spewacks' earlier *Clear All Wires*, was an immediate success, and Mary stopped the show cold with "My Heart Belongs to Daddy." Almost every word of the song had a double meaning, and she played against the lines, doing the striptease as nonchalantly as though she were hanging up laundry. With that one song in the second act, Mary became a star "overnight." Her coy delivery of the impish lyrics combined with her vivacious personality, heart-shaped face, and shapely legs to prove an absolute sensation. After three years of rejection in Hollywood, the "Weatherford Whiz" had at last found her place in show business. The opening night audience laughed, then cheered as the applause at the end of her number persisted. The next day critics turned verbal cartwheels. Definitely not the show girl type, Mary delivered Cole Porter's sophisticated verses chastely. Her combination

of comedy and gangly sex appeal and her forthright sweet vocal lustiness proved irresistible. Columnist Walter Winchell pronounced her "the find of the season."

"Mary Martin, on this her first appearance in New York, hits the bull's-eye with an edifying strip tease executed on the Russian Steppes," a critic for *Theatre Arts Monthly* wrote. Brooks Atkinson of the *New York Times* found *Leave It to Me* "a handsome carnival" that contributed "something constructive towards the merriment" of the current Broadway season. "There is a broad piece of ribaldry entitled 'My Heart Belongs to Daddy,'" the distinguished *Times* critic wrote, "which Mary Martin sings in the capital style of an inspired honky tonk." Later, Atkinson added to his appraisal: "For revelry of the flesh, there is Mary Martin whose mock innocence makes 'My Heart Belongs to Daddy' the bawdy ballad of the season." One wag later commented that Mary's number in the show wasn't so much a strip as a fur sale. "She'd toss away her mink and her ermine and her muskrat," the reviewer said, "but never actually got down to Martin."

There was a party at El Morocco after the show's New York opening. When Mary walked in, the orchestra struck up "My Heart Belongs to Daddy," and the crowd stood and applauded. She awoke the next morning to find herself the proverbial toast of the town. Her name went up in lights outside the theater, and there were endless requests for interviews. Earl Wilson did one of the first, and the New York journalist remembered arriving for the appointment to find Mary with her head in the oven. She had washed her hair and was drying it. Once she settled down for the interview, she was effervescent and instantly likable, and her unaffected, friendly manner promptly made her the darling of newspaper reporters. Someone asked Mary what the best part of her sudden fame was. Without hesitation she answered, "Feeling grateful."

She recorded "My Heart Belongs to Daddy" first with Eddy Duchin's orchestra, in the key she had used onstage, but that was only one of many versions of the song she recorded over the decades ahead. The number quickly dinned its way onto the Hit Parade charts, although the Porter lyrics couldn't be sung on the air in

the 1930s. Mary was invited to appear as a guest on several radio programs, and she soon made the cover of *Life* magazine. Newspapers across the country carried her picture time and again, and before long Hollywood began bidding for her services with salary figures running into four figures a week. She was nominated for the best musical comedy performance of the year, and by then it was obvious to producers that little Mary Martin was capable of far more than the contagious patter song that had brought her to the attention of the show world.

Stanley Marcus, head of Dallas's fashionable Neiman Marcus, had been in the audience when *Leave It to Me* opened in New York, and he went backstage to see Mary afterward. Marcus told her that they were from the same part of the country and took her to dinner a few nights later. "I noticed that she didn't really have the clothes of a Broadway star," the store owner said, "so the next day I sent her some nice clothes with a note saying that I just wanted to be part of her success." The two became lifelong friends.

Mary said that her success with the "Daddy" number presented her with two problems. The first was how to explain to the folks in Weatherford why she was doing a striptease on stage. Mildred finally composed a letter to the Martins saying that Mary was doing a part that called for her to poke fun at a striptease artist. Mary claimed that Preston Martin never knew that "My Heart Belongs to Daddy" was anything more than a kind of Father's Day tribute. Mrs. Yeager, Bessie Mae Sue Ella's mother, saw *Leave It to Me* on a visit to New York and said she couldn't understand what Mary Martin was doing in a show like that.

The other problem created by Mary's rapid success her father had anticipated. A babble of voices from friends, associates, and professional critics surrounded the budding star, giving her praise, criticism, and advice. She was counseled to do this and not that, scores of things that either made no sense to her or added to her confusion. "I tried very hard to listen to that echo within me," Mary said. "But there were times when it was difficult." Fortunately, she discovered that Helen Founts Cahoon, her teacher in Fort Worth, had moved to New York and was teaching at a studio in midtown

Manhattan. Mrs. Cahoon had also seen *Leave It to Me* on opening night and was shocked to find her former pupil up on stage singing naughty lyrics and taking her clothes off. When Mary came to her again for instruction, "we started working on developing tones," Cahoon said, "getting back her high register that had suffered so with those years of what I call singing in the cellar." The former concert singer was again impressed with Mary's remarkable ear, sure as a tuning fork. "She's never off key," Cahoon said.

Mary and Mildred found themselves a nice apartment, and Mary began going to parties and Manhattan's fashionable nightclubs, escorted by a number of beaus. One was Winthrop Rockefeller, the most dashing of John D. Rockefeller's sons; another was Frederick Drake, publisher of *Harper's Bazaar*. Meanwhile, Mildred seemed to grow quiet and a little aloof, not altogether approving of her friend's unexpected popularity.

A month after *Leave It to Me* opened in New York, sixty-six-year-old Preston Martin suffered a cerebral stroke in Weatherford. Juanita called to inform Mary that her father was sinking rapidly. Over Vinton Freedley's objections, Mary arranged to fly home the following weekend. She did two shows on Saturday and boarded a plane for Texas at midnight to spend Sunday at her father's bedside. Preston was in a coma when she got home, but he opened his eyes upon hearing his younger daughter's voice. With a show to do that night, Mary sped back to New York on Monday without much sleep, but bad weather grounded the plane in Washington, D.C. With a blizzard raging along the East Coast, Mary called the theater to tell the stage manager that she might be late, since she would have to take a train into Manhattan. The producer arranged to have a police escort at the station awaiting her arrival, and she was rushed to the theater in time for the second act.

Mary phoned home every two hours during the days that followed to check on her father's condition and was told that he was progressing nicely. But on Tuesday, December 20, Mildred called the theater with word that Preston had died. The company decided not to break the news to Mary until she'd finished her song that evening. The cast watched in the wings as she sang her "Daddy" number

and became so moved that the show continued with difficulty. Sophie Tucker was waiting to break the bad news when Mary came off the stage. Tears came to her eyes, but like a real trouper she brushed them aside and said that she'd perform at the Wednesday matinee as usual. She said it was her job and what her father would want her to do. The press learned about her father's death before she did, and she returned to her dressing room that evening to find it full of photographers. When Mildred called to say that reporters were also waiting outside their apartment building, Mary decided to spend the night in a hotel. Headlines the next day announced, "Daddy Girl Sings About Daddy as Daddy Dies." Years later, Mary acknowledged that not being present at her father's funeral left her with a great deal of hurt.

Until Preston became ill, the Martins had intended to bring Larry to New York to spend Christmas with his mother. Juanita and Larry did come a few weeks later than planned, and the two of them saw an afternoon performance of *Leave It to Me* from a box. Afterward, Larry met Sophie Tucker and Victor Moore but didn't say anything about the show. Finally Mary asked her son how he liked it. He said, "Oh, I liked it." She then asked how he had liked her in it. "I don't know," Larry answered. "Why did you take all those clothes off in front of all those people?" Mary explained that it was a dance and she was doing what the choreographer asked. "I just don't know why you did that," Larry said. Mary told him, "Well, maybe you will someday." Years later she found it amusing that the boy who grew up to play the dastardly J. R. Ewing on television was so embarrassed by her meek striptease.

While *Leave It to Me* continued to attract packed houses, with a large number of standees at every performance, Mary agreed in January 1939 to do one show a night at the swank Rainbow Room atop Rockefeller Center after she'd finished at the theater. Among the celebrities to reserve tables for her New York nightclub debut were Robert Taylor, Vera Zorina, Noel Coward, Douglas Fairbanks, Jr., and a host of upper-bracket socialites. Backed by an orchestra and Eight Men of Manhattan, who sang and danced with her while decked out in white ties and tails, the act was a classy one that included a

variety of songs from "Il Bacio" to blues numbers. For eight weeks Mary raced from the Imperial Theatre to the Rainbow Room for a midnight show, which ended with her walking among the tables singing directly to people. "Mary was a peach," said future movie star Van Johnson, one of the Eight Men of Manhattan. The two performers became friends, and Mary encouraged young Johnson to try his talent in movies, convinced that he had the necessary charisma. With no apparent need to hog the limelight, Mary generously told the management, "The red-headed kid sells the act. Give him more to do!"

Mary by then had had any number of movie offers herself and had turned them down, content to remain in New York. Then Paramount talent scout Arthur Jacobson talked her into making a screen test at the studio's facilities in Astoria. Jacobson said that Paramount was specifically interested in hearing her high soprano voice, since a director at the studio was looking for a lead in a picture called *The Great Victor Herbert.* Mary arrived for the test wearing her "Daddy" costume and, to show off her high soprano, proceeded to sing "Caro Nome" from Verdi's *Rigoletto.* Unsure of the right movements, she began slipping off her clothes as she sang the aria, just as she did eight times a week in *Leave It to Me.* On the high C she was down to her teddy. Paramount offered her a contract at a fee too good to refuse.

Leave It to Me played in New York until the end of July 1939, then went on the road. Just before the company left for its tour, Mary Martin was replaced in the show by a nineteen-year-old New Yorker named Mildred Fenton. Mary returned to California early in July to begin work on the Victor Herbert picture, although she still was not convinced that movies were right for her. Lawrence Schwab had encouraged his twenty-five-year-old discovery to give the Paramount musical a try and released her from their contract to make the one movie. But he wanted her back in New York by the end of the summer to star in a Broadway show he was preparing called *Nice Goin'.*

CHAPTER 3

Paramount Star

Paramount had the reputation in Hollywood for being the country club of studios, since the atmosphere there was relaxed and jovial. The twenty-six-acre lot had lawns and patios and a row of dressing rooms that looked like English mews. Despite its frivolity, Paramount developed a record for turning out well-crafted films and boasted a stable of stars that placed the studio on a par with Warner Bros. and Twentieth Century-Fox and only a step below the illustrious Metro-Goldwyn-Mayer. The company's theater chain grew to over two thousand houses, while its flagship, the Paramount Theater in New York, built in 1926, stood as a deluxe showplace at the base of a Times Square skyscraper, with art and artifacts from around the world on display in its lobby.

Mary found herself in the summer of 1939 ensconced in one of the studio's dressing rooms reserved for stars. Next to her was Paulette Goddard, a frequent leading lady in Cecil B. DeMille spectacles, and Patricia Morison, a young contract player who would later prove a sensation in the original Broadway production of Cole Porter's *Kiss Me, Kate.* Down at one end in the row of dressing rooms the occupant was Bing Crosby, while Bob Hope was at the other end. Mary returned to Hollywood in July and registered at the Roosevelt Hotel, where two years before she had sung in the

bar. "I'm terribly grateful to the 'Daddy' song and all it did for me," she told reporters, "but I hope I never have to sing it again! I think four or five thousand times is enough to sing any tune."

Mildred Wood was jubilant at the prospect of returning to Los Angeles and had gone to California ahead of Mary to find a house for them. She eventually leased a place in Bel Air, and Mary went to work on *The Great Victor Herbert.* Although Paramount was giving Mary star buildup, she continued to harbor doubts about her appearance in movies. Still, she was eager to show studio executives that she had talent and deserved the attention they were giving her. Mary had accepted the part in the Victor Herbert picture by long-distance telephone, and her elation over finally winning a Hollywood contract was shortly dashed when she discovered that she had been cast at the insistence of director Andrew Stone over studio head William LeBaron's strong opposition. Sensing that she was on probation, Mary confided to Mildred that their time in Hollywood might be brief.

LeBaron had wanted to borrow Irene Dunne for the Herbert picture and had delayed production on the musical in the hope of securing Dunne's services. Failing in that, Paramount wanted Stone to use Muriel Angelus as the female lead, since the studio had the English actress under contract. But the director thought Angelus was too cold and stiff for the part, and he was desperately seeking an alternative when choreographer LeRoy Prinz suggested Mary. Prinz had seen Mary's recent test and thought she had the looks, personality, acting ability, and voice for the role in the Victor Herbert picture. Stone ran the test, agreed with Prinz, and presented the idea of hiring Mary to LeBaron. "Everybody's turned her down," the studio executive complained, but he eventually reconsidered rather than suffer further delays on starting production. Still, LeBaron's reservations about Mary were strong enough that he told Muriel Angelus to learn the part and the numbers and be ready to go into the picture once "Stone's folly" proved a disaster.

Mary sensed the tension surrounding her casting and found it difficult to maintain a positive attitude, particularly when makeup artists kept complaining about her pug nose and costume designers

talked about how they had to camouflage her less than perfect figure. "Before I went to Hollywood," Mary said, "I didn't think I was too painful to look at, but the way the studio acted, anyone would have thought me one of the most unattractive girls anywhere." She readily admitted that she was no glamour goddess but thought she'd come off best by simply being herself. Yet studio hairstylists draped her face with hairpieces, claiming that her neck was too long, while a team of experts pondered how to turn this Texas daisy into a Hollywood beauty. "They even tried to make me look sexy," Mary said. "But most of the time I just looked sick." She was sent to a coach to get rid of her southern accent, and the studio worried that her voice was too good for the film, since she was to play a hometown girl in *The Great Victor Herbert* with a high voice, but not a particularly good one. To help devise a singing style that studio executives thought was right for the role, Paramount borrowed songwriter Jule Styne from Twentieth Century-Fox to work with Mary.

The Great Victor Herbert was not a biography of the famed composer of operettas, but the story of a boy and a girl whose lives are affected by Herbert and his music. After lengthy negotiations to secure the rights to a batch of Herbert songs from the composer's daughter for the modest fee of $10,000, sixteen numbers were created for the film, including one sequence in which Mary and her costar, Allan Jones, sang excerpts from eight of the songs. Mary, wearing ruffles, hoop skirts, and layers of petticoats, had to age in the movie from nineteen to thirty-eight, and toward the end she has a fourteen-year-old daughter, played by soprano Susanna Foster. "Susanna was the one with the great voice," Mary said.

Allan Jones had been a star at MGM, but he had left the more prestigious studio when he realized that he would always be competing there for choice roles with the better known singer Nelson Eddy. Jones came to Paramount for two pictures with more clout, enjoyed the studio's casual atmosphere, but quickly saw that Paramount did not have the money to put into movies that Metro did. He found Mary a joy to work with, wholesome and down-to-earth, and she later claimed that Jones was the man who taught her everything she ever knew about performing for the screen. "I

was mighty green about making pictures," she said, "and Allan did everything he could to give me the best of it, see that my camera angles were right, do retakes to give me the advantage, and a dozen things to make it easier on me." Character actors Walter Connolly and Jerome Cowan were also generous during the making of the picture, pointing out to Mary where she should stand when a light was supposed to be on her. "I didn't know anything," she said, "and I never learned very much. I was forever missing my marks." Yet she proved better in the rushes than William LeBaron had any cause to expect, good enough that the studio later signed her to a seven-year contract.

What Mary hated most about making movies were the long waits between scenes, while the cameraman and his crew set up the next shot. "You'd get up at 5 A.M., get in makeup by 8, and not film a shot until 6 in the afternoon," Mary said. "Making pictures was a bore." Yet Andrew Stone, who began making motion pictures during the silent era, had a reputation for working fast and being more concerned with the clock than he was with the value of individual scenes. For a sequence in *The Great Victor Herbert* set in a theater, the production manager had allotted a full day. "A whole day!" Stone screamed. "We can do it in an hour." Finally, the director compromised and agreed to devote half a day to getting the details right. "Andrew was a good businessman," Allan Jones recalled, "but he didn't care how the scene went. He watched his stopwatch. You can't make a picture that way. Seeing the director standing there timing you ruins the naturalness of your performance."

Mary may not have been comfortable performing for a movie camera, but she was perfectly at ease strolling around the Paramount lot. In record time she knew the name of nearly every file clerk, grip, and gaffer at the studio. She made no attempt at playing the star, and any deference to her as such struck the novice as funny. To all and sundry she met crossing the lot, it was, "Hi-ya, Hon," and she remained essentially the same gabby girl from Texas she had always been. Once while eating lunch in the commissary, she noticed a still photographer taking pictures of a stock player.

Mary jumped up, rushed over to the girl's table, and proceeded to get a better effect by fixing the girl's hair herself.

Mary was too busy trying to learn motion picture technique to pay much attention to Mildred. All she knew was that her friend came in every morning to wake her and made sure that she got to the studio by 6 A.M.. "At length it began to percolate through my head," Mary recalled, "that Millie wasn't just getting up then herself. She was coming *home!*" When she realized that Mildred's private life had taken a more active turn, Mary asked her companion what on earth she was doing staying out all night. Mildred's answer came as a jolt. She had married shortly after coming back to California. "He's the boy I was going with when we left for New York," Mildred told her friend.

When Mary recovered from the shock, she decided to bring Larry and her mother out to Hollywood. Juanita soon bought a house for the three of them at 1287 Holmby Avenue in Holmby Hills, a highly fashionable neighborhood between Beverly Hills and Westwood. Larry was enrolled in Black Fox Military Institute, where the sons of Bing Crosby, Edward G. Robinson, and Charlie Chaplin were classmates. Although Juanita liked living in Hollywood, she refused to visit the studio, saying that the hubbub there made her nervous. She drove her own car and was content to run the house and look after Mary and Larry.

The Great Victor Herbert wrapped on September 30, 1939, and was scheduled for release the following December. Two weeks after completing the picture, Mary began rehearsals on Lawrence Schwab's new show, *Nice Goin'*, in New York. A musical version of *Sailor Beware*, and originally called *Hold Your Hats*, the show had a score by Ralph Rainger and lyrics by Leo Robin. Mary was to be the star of the musical, and she looked forward to returning to Broadway and playing before live audiences. Carol Bruce, six years younger than Mary and herself destined for Broadway success in Irving Berlin's *Louisiana Purchase* the following year, was also in the show and had an opportunity to observe Mary's talent and generosity of spirit. "Mary was a lovely lady," Bruce said, "and I mean a lady all

the way. She couldn't have been more wonderful to me. She made us all feel that the show was a cast endeavor. That went right down to the chorus kids, who adored her."

Bruce was given two songs in the musical, one of them a zany but appealing number called "Would You Like to Be a Panamama?" Her costume for the routine had two avocados over her breasts, and Bruce's delivery of the song stopped the show. "Now here was the star of the show allowing this to happen," Bruce said. "The star doesn't usually permit another performer to have that kind of exposure, but Mary was so encouraging to me." The two performers spent hours in Mary's dressing room chatting, although never about anything really personal. "Mary was always warm and friendly," Bruce said, "and I could have been a threat to her. But I don't recall any temperament. She was always willing to rehearse and willing to go along with changes. She was just a charming, gracious, conscientious lady."

But critics shredded *Nice Goin'*, and the musical closed after three weeks of tryouts in Boston. "Mary worked her butt off in that show," Bruce said, "and continued working right up to the day we got a closing notice. I was heartsick that the show had failed, but Mary accepted the fact and assured me that I was gifted and said there would be other shows. I've never forgotten her kindness."

With Mary suddenly free of her obligation to Schwab, Paramount arranged for her to make a personal appearance tour in conjunction with the release of *The Great Victor Herbert*. She and Allan Jones were presented onstage at the Paramount Theater in New York for a week, beginning December 6, and a few days later Mary flew to Texas. Her mother, Larry, Mildred Woods, and an accompanist joined her in Dallas. Before leaving for the southwestern premiere of her film in Weatherford, Mary spent the night in Dallas at the Baker Hotel. The next day she posed in a snow-white lynx fur jacket beside a Christmas tree in Neiman-Marcus and got her hair done in Neiman's beauty shop while she ate a chicken sandwich. Then her entourage was driven to Weatherford. An escort met the caravan of cars at the city limits, while school kids lined the streets of the business district and shopkeepers displayed

"Welcome home, Mary Martin" signs in their store windows. Mary called out greetings to old friends as she passed by and posed for pictures in the open car as the high school band, playing "My Heart Belongs to Daddy," led a parade twice around the crowded town square. The procession continued on to the Martins' old home, where Mary, her mother, Larry, and Mary's sister, Jerry, spent the night and quietly commemorated the anniversary of Preston Martin's death.

By 1939, Weatherford had two movie theaters, the Palace and the Princess, both owned by Willard Sadler. When Sadler learned that Mary was making a movie, he wrote Paramount officials asking for the honor of having the regional premiere of the picture in Mary's hometown. "If you can send Bob Burns to Van Buren, Arkansas, for a premiere, you can surely let us have Mary Martin and her picture," Sadler had written. Paramount agreed to simultaneous showings of *The Great Victor Herbert* at both Weatherford theaters on Friday evening, December 22. Mary appeared twice on the stage of the Palace, equipped for radio broadcasting, and once at the Princess. West Texans had ordered blocks of tickets well in advance. Seated in the front row at the Palace were Ben Hagman and his wife of three months, Juanita. "There's no quarrel between Mary and me," Ben assured the press. "She wanted a career, I wanted a home. She has the career and I have the home. And if Mary hadn't got the career, I wouldn't have got Juanita. Everybody is perfectly happy."

Mary caught a train out of Fort Worth later that night for San Antonio, where she appeared with the picture on Saturday evening, and returned to Fort Worth for a similar appearance on Sunday. Christmas Day she spent with her family in Weatherford, coming back to Dallas for four appearances at that city's Palace Theater on December 26. On each occasion she sang a short recital, which included "My Heart Belongs to Daddy," "Listen to the Mockingbird," "My Prayer," and a swing version of "Caro Nome" from *Rigoletto*. The *Dallas Morning News* critic, John Rosenfield, wrote the next day: "Mary Martin is one of the most stimulating, amusing, provocative, and delightful personalities in the world of entertainment. . . . The girl is simply a prodigy of theatrical talent—looks, grace, voice,

musicianship, and that wonderful instinct for making each spectator in a crowded theater think she is performing directly at him."

Rosenfield contended that *The Great Victor Herbert* was a dream vehicle for Mary's film debut. "Miss Martin surprises movie audiences with the best cinema warbling this side Jeanette MacDonald," the veteran Dallas critic wrote, "and she has the Victor Herbert music to do it with." He also felt that Mary handled the picture's heaviest dramatic scenes with freedom and competence. B. R. Crisler of the *New York Times* agreed that Mary was thoroughly likable in her screen introduction and showed "unexpected resources in the role of an actress, as well as that of a frivolous chanteuse."

Early in Paramount's publicity campaign for Mary, the studio had arranged for her to be photographed shaking hands with a trained bear that happened to be on the lot for a picture. Mary thought the idea was rather tasteless and didn't suit the character she was playing in *The Great Victor Herbert* at all. She remembered that the last thing Lawrence Schwab had told her before leaving New York was, "Now, Mary, they're going to ask you to do every crazy thing on earth for publicity. Don't do anything foolish because you don't want to start out that way." Studio publicists assumed that her reticence to greet the bear stemmed from a fear of getting too close to the animal, unaware that the fearless Mary had grown up preferring boxing gloves and baseball bats to dolls. "This will make every newspaper in the United States," the publicist who dreamed up the stunt told her. "The trainer will hold the bear while we take the picture. The bear will put out his paw and you shake hands with him." When Mary continued to object, the publicist told her, "Miss Martin, you can't start off this way or you'll have trouble through the entire time you're making this picture." Feeling that she had no choice, Mary agreed to pose for a photo while she shook the paw of a big brown bear. But as the picture was being snapped, instead of shaking hands, the bruin grabbed Mary around the waist and down on the ground they went. "The bear was on top of me," she remembered, "and everybody was trying to pull him off. I could hear girls screaming all over the place. The bear didn't hurt me, but it scared the daylights out of me."

The secretary of Paramount story editor Richard Halliday happened to be walking across the lot at that moment and saw the bear lock Mary in a hug and knock her down. Amused and aghast, the girl rushed back to the office to describe the incident to her boss. "There's a young girl who's just arrived," the secretary began, "and the studio is trying to make a star of her." After hearing details, Halliday asked the girl's name. When he was told it was Mary Martin under the bear, he shook his head in disgust. "There is nothing that girl will not do for publicity!" he told his secretary.

Halliday had seen Mary in *Leave It to Me* in New York with his mother, his grandmother, and his aunt but had been unimpressed with her performance. "He was grumpy that night and went to sleep during my number," Mary said later. "His mother and aunt were having a ball, and Richard was sound asleep." Halliday, it turned out, had the flu at the time and felt awful. The next day he left for Florida with his sister to recuperate. But his assessment of Mary Martin remained negative, and he felt the "Daddy" number had been a cheap way to gain attention. When Mary's screen test arrived on the Paramount lot, Halliday had joined William LeBaron in voting no on casting her.

Later, during the making of *The Great Victor Herbert*, the story editor and Mary met at a small dinner party given for screen star Jean Arthur, who had become Mary's closest friend in Hollywood. Halliday sat across the table from Mary but spent the whole evening talking to Arthur. He was a handsome man, tall and thin with curly black hair, and dressed impeccably. Halliday ignored Mary through most of the evening, infuriating her. As the party was breaking up around midnight, the agent who was supposed to drive Mary home was late in arriving to pick her up, so Halliday offered to drop her off instead. They ended up sitting outside Mary's house talking about their careers until 3 A.M.

Weeks went by without Halliday asking Mary for a formal date, but their paths crossed frequently at the studio and at parties. If hosts needed an extra man to balance out the seating arrangement at dinner tables, the sophisticated Halliday was often their choice. "I thought he was the best-looking, most divine man I had

ever seen in my life," Mary said. But Halliday was also escorting Rosalind Russell, Madeleine Carroll, and Patricia Morison around town, and whenever he and Mary ended up at the same function, they always came and left in separate cars. "There was no romance," Mary said, just a cordial attraction. While she was making public appearances in theaters to hype *The Great Victor Herbert*, Halliday wrote her occasionally but said nothing more intimate than "Wish you were here to make a fourth at bridge," in notes dictated to his secretary.

After the publicity tour was over, Mary visited Lawrence Schwab and his wife in Florida to relax and then returned to Hollywood, where she and Richard Halliday began dating. Halliday, the son of Jack Hammond, a well-known newspaperman, was born in Denver on April 5, 1905, and christened John Hope Hammond. His mother, Hope Hammond, an interior decorator, was the daughter of William H. Harvey, author of the popular free-silver tract *Coin's Financial School* and a close friend of three-time presidential candidate William Jennings Bryan. Richard's parents had divorced when he was quite young, and the boy had grown up in an environment of fine antiques and culture and had absorbed his mother's flair for design and beauty. He attended Washington and Lee University, where he produced college shows, and then went to New York as a reporter for the United Press. During 1927 and 1928, Halliday was drama critic for the *New York World-Telegram* and a film critic for the *Daily News*. Then he began writing movie reviews for *Liberty* magazine and published a novel, *Fanfare*. In 1932 he became a story editor for Paramount Pictures in New York and transferred to Hollywood shortly before Mary arrived at the studio to make *The Great Victor Herbert*.

Whereas Mary was vivacious and exuberant, Richard was quiet and reserved. He had lived most of his life in a series of elegant apartments with his mother and sister. Mary made up her mind to thaw this patrician gentleman, even though his worldly demeanor made her feel inadequate. When he told her that his home in the East was full of antiques, Mary admitted that she hated antiques. They didn't seem to agree on much of anything. Richard complained

about the way she dressed and seemed as critical of her appearance as the department heads at Paramount were. "Mary was a Texas hick when I met her," Richard said later, but he soon recognized her extraordinary talent and appreciated her eagerness and willingness to improve.

Soon the two were going to parties together regularly, with Richard picking Mary up in his car. At one costume party she went dressed as Peter Pan, her favorite character, and it was after a progressive party given by Elsa Maxwell that ended at Pickfair, Mary Pickford's baronial estate, that Richard kissed Mary for the first time. Finally, he gave a party for her at his home, where everyone except Mary wore evening clothes. "I particularly remember Madeleine Carroll standing by the fireplace," Mary said, "wearing sapphires once owned by a member of the Russian royal family. I stood in the doorway, unable to speak." That was the night she met Richard's mother, who was visiting from the East. "When I first met Mary in Hollywood," Hope Hammond said, "she was a frustrated motion picture star, as nervous as a Mohammedan mullah."

Mary claimed that she no longer hated Hollywood, but still preferred the stage. Her second movie, *Rhythm on the River* with Bing Crosby, went into production in 1940 and was one of her better pictures. Directed by William Schertzinger, himself a musician and a graduate of the University of Brussels School of Music, the story had Mary and Bing ghostwriting songs for the character played by Basil Rathbone. "Making movies with Bing almost made Hollywood worthwhile," Mary said. "He was the most relaxed, comfortable, comforting man." She confessed to Crosby that she couldn't read a note of music, only to discover that he couldn't either. Whenever they met with songwriters, Bing would say, "You sing the melody first, Mary," and she'd say, "No, you're the star, you sing it first." Usually, they'd ask the composer to play the song for them before either would attempt it. Once the tune was established, neither had any trouble joining in. "Bing's phrasing was so special," Mary said. "He was very shy with ladies and to me seemed more of a man's man."

She didn't mention the night she and the crooner had met at the Casanova Club, but one day on the set between takes Mary went

over to a piano and started to sing "Shoeshine Boy." Crosby confessed that hearing the song made him sad. "One night I sat up until all hours listening to a girl sing that number," he said. "The next day I went to a lot of trouble arranging a screen test for her. Then I went back to the joint where she was working to tell her the big news. She was gone and nobody there could tell me how to get in touch with her. I often wonder what happened to her." Mary told him, "You're looking at her right now."

While they were making *Rhythm on the River*, Mary sang with Bing on his weekly radio show, *Kraft Music Hall*, several times, and they did a version of "Blues in the Night" together one evening that was such an instant hit that requests for a repeat poured into the network. Mary also performed on several other radio broadcasts that emanated from Hollywood, including the *Good News* program on a regular basis with Dick Powell, Fanny Brice, and Meredith Willson's orchestra. She and Bing both recorded for Decca, and her album of Cole Porter songs sold especially well.

When *Rhythm on the River* was completed on June 15, 1940, Mary was happier with the results than she'd been with the Victor Herbert picture. "Here is a light and tuneful bundle of excellent entertainment," a reviewer for *Variety* wrote when the film was released. "The picture provides Mary Martin with unlimited opportunity to score effectively both in the singing and acting departments. It will pay her big dividends for future box office rating." Bosley Crowther of the *New York Times* pronounced the film "one of the most likeable musical pictures of the season," and the critic said that Mary was "ever so comfortable to look at and sells a very nice song."

The rising Paramount star's great friend Bessie Mae Sue Ella Yeager saw *Rhythm on the River* but didn't like it. "Mary didn't photograph well," Bessie Mae said. "She didn't come across in movies as Mary. I was amused when I saw her with Bing Crosby, because he was singing and Mary was in the background sitting down, poking her head around one side of him and then the other to make sure she got into the picture. I just didn't think movies were right for Mary. You had to see her live to appreciate her warmth."

Most of the nine films Mary made at Paramount were only mildly successful and all are eminently forgettable. The glamour treatment the studio insisted on didn't fit her, and fan magazine writers found her drab, carping nastily because she had shown up at a dress-up affair in a sports suit. The Hollywood folderol seemed unreal to Mary, and working on films struck her as so impersonal, so technical and episodic, that she was never comfortable. Yet movie gossip columnist Hedda Hopper, who could be vicious, admired Mary's gullibility and wrote about her glowingly. Mary Martin, Hopper said, "sees, hears, and speaks no evil" and is "friendly as a kitten."

Y. Frank Freeman took over as head of production at Paramount early in Mary's tenure at the studio, replacing William LeBaron. Freeman was a longtime movie exhibitor from Georgia who had been a partner in Coca-Cola, but he knew little about making pictures. He was gentle and easygoing, and Mary got along well with him. "Even though the studio has a new management," she said, "I do feel a little strange about being here. This is the place where they told me I was too ugly for pictures." With that stinging analysis etched in her mind, it was impossible for Mary to feel secure, and she dreaded every option period when her contract would be subject to evaluation and renewal, yet almost hoped the studio would fire her.

With *Rhythm on the River* finished, Mary was put into *Love Thy Neighbor* with Jack Benny and Fred Allen, a picture directed by Mark Sandrich, one of the studio's better craftsmen. The film capitalized on the four-year-old radio feud between Benny and Allen, and Mary was assigned a couple of songs in it to break up the comic banter. The dialogue included the customary exchange between Benny and his man Friday, Eddie (Rochester) Anderson, but it all seemed like a rehash of what audiences heard weekly on Sunday night broadcasts. "I thought I was so awful," Mary said. "I couldn't stand the pictures I was in and wept every time I saw one."

Richard Halliday listened sympathetically as she poured out her reservations about Hollywood. One evening he invited her to dinner at his house, and for once the two of them were alone.

Richard's mother had returned to the East. He and Mary sat down to eat around 8 o'clock and didn't leave the table until 2 A.M. "During those intense six hours," she said, "we felt we had solved our problems for life." Richard suggested that they drive to Las Vegas and get married. Overwhelmed, Mary accepted his impromptu proposal. "Richard immediately put in a long-distance call to his mother," Mary recalled. "It was five in the morning in New York, but that didn't faze him." They drove over to Mary's house, woke her mother up, and told Juanita that they were going to get married.

The couple spent the rest of the night driving to Las Vegas, where they checked into a motel, changed clothes, and headed for the courthouse. They had to stand in line at the registry office, and when Richard signed his name on the marriage application, Mary looked surprised. She had thought his name was Holiday! After eating lunch together a few weeks before, Richard had bought them matching friendship rings in two tones of gold, clasped hands with a ruby heart in the middle. They had admired the design in a jeweler's window, and Mary's ring now became her wedding band. The fledgling Paramount star and the erudite story editor were married in a civil ceremony on May 5, 1940. After the brief cere- mony, they got back in the car and returned to Hollywood. Mary insisted that they go straight to the house her mother had bought so she could tell Larry that he had a new father. "Richard and I took the big chance of marriage without knowing each other very well," she later said.

The newlyweds began looking for a house to buy and decided on a French provincial cottage in Bel Air with a lovely garden. The place had once belonged to Hollywood stars Jeanette MacDonald and Gene Raymond. Richard had his furniture shipped out from New York, and Mary set about trying to turn herself into a home- maker. They disagreed on décor and lifestyle and for a time their arguments seemed never-ending. One night Richard stormed out of the house while his wife was in hysterics. Mary conceded that she wasn't much of a housewife, and in tears one morning she called Richard's mother in New York and begged for her help. Hope dropped everything and flew to California. She took over the decorating of

her son's home, hired a cook and servants, and tried to teach her daughter-in-law the fundamentals of supervising a household.

Richard had made a long practice of buying nightgowns and negligees for his mother, his sister, and his aunt, and he promptly announced that he didn't like any of the clothes Mary wore. He insisted she throw everything out and took her to I. Magnin's and bought her a new wardrobe. "He made me over," Mary said, "a whole new image. Even my hair was done differently." Richard later claimed that Mary always had innate class and good color sense, but that she had simply never developed the sense of style befitting a star. "I didn't know anything about taste," Mary said, pointing out that her mother, who had excellent taste, had made most of her decisions. But once she married Richard, he spent the rest of his life, Mary said, "editing me."

Although his control caused tension, Mary essentially surrendered to Richard's judgment. "I love him," she told Lawrence Schwab, "and he knows what's good for me." Yet there was little display of passion in their early months of marriage, since Mary was busy at the studio and Richard was preoccupied with managing his career and her. She would come home exhausted after long hours before cameras or in costume fittings to find her husband engaged in story conferences and business meetings. "Practically the only time we saw each other was when we met in different cars going in opposite directions past a traffic light," Mary said. "Life with Richard was never simple, but it certainly was never dull."

After working diligently to lose her southern accent, Mary was cast as a southern belle in Paramount's *Kiss the Boys Goodbye*. Based on a farce by Claire Boothe, the movie was again directed by Victor Schertzinger, whom Mary adored, and costarred Don Ameche. Critics found the film thin entertainment, even though Mary came off extremely well. "Miss Martin provides plenty of musical sock with her delivery of four songs," a reviewer for *Variety* wrote. She sang one cute number in the picture while doing a corny strip-tease, shedding her hoopskirt with mock refinement, then diving into a swimming pool in a streamlined bathing suit. Mary's ability at clowning seemed part of her natural talent.

Kiss the Boys Goodbye was completed on February 27, 1941, and Mary almost immediately went into *New York Town,* a comedy with Fred MacMurray and Robert Preston. Mary's role in the picture called for straight acting. She thought the script was dull and disliked the director, Charles Vidor. "Nothing was ever right for Charlie Vidor," she said. "He had Fred MacMurray and me in a taxi until ten o'clock one night doing the same kissing scene over and over." When they finished, the director walked over to his two stars and said, "It's been a pleasure working with you." MacMurray snapped, "I wish I could say the same," and walked off. Mary had to restrain herself from doing the same. "Vidor was the only man I worked with at Paramount that I truly disliked," she said. "I wanted to shoot him."

Meanwhile, the Halliday marriage remained far from bliss. Mary likely reckoned within a few weeks that Richard was predominantly homosexual. His whole personal and aesthetic orientation might be interpreted as gay, and he could be vicious in his outbursts, especially when he drank. Richard demanded perfection, and Mary was still the unrefined, superficial girl from West Texas, who loved people and viewed life with sugary simplicity. Their bond was a shared ambition, yet it was a marriage of oil and water and the mingling involved pain. Sometimes the strain was so great that Mary would walk into a room and Richard would walk out.

Finally, she couldn't stand the bickering any longer and fled. Mary wrote Richard a note: "I've left home. Don't try to find me." She went to a ranch near Victorville, in the desert east of Los Angeles. Richard spent a week looking for her. He drove to Palm Springs, then to Arrowhead, and finally at four o'clock on a Friday morning he reached the cottage where his wife was secreted. He stood outside a window and called softly, "Mary?" When she answered, it was in a plaintive, little girl's voice. "I just want you to know," he said, "that when you're ready to come home, I'll be there waiting for you."

Two days later Mary returned to Bel Air, having thought things through. She decided to concentrate on her career, let Richard mold her into whatever he thought best, and enjoy the companionship of a man she had come to love and admire. She turned over the business aspects of her work to Richard, let him make the

important decisions and handle all of their financial matters, things she neither understood nor cared about. From that point on, Richard became Mary's organizer, her protector, and her swain. "We knew if our marriage was going to last we would have to be in business together," she said, "and we wanted to be together." Richard fell in love with her talent and the alter ego he was creating. Mary's affection grew into worship of a trusted friend. Later, she maintained that she owed her husband everything. "Richard thinks things through more clearly than I do," she said, "and he knows what I can do better than I know."

With their turf established, the couple began to relax with one another. Richard made the decisions and fought their battles with the studio, while Mary was free to be the adorable gamin committed to positive thinking. In October 1940, they enjoyed a vacation yachting in the Pacific. That same month the American Association of Bachelors voted Mary the "ideal companion for the modern bachelor," an unexpected compliment. The group's West Coast president said, "We've been crazy about Mary ever since she first sang 'My Heart Belongs to Daddy' in New York." Life had grown sweet for the Hallidays. Richard was making $30,000 a year at Paramount, Mary in excess of $100,000, and she seemed resigned to helping the studio transform her into a movie star.

Early in 1941, Mary learned that she was pregnant. Although it was a difficult pregnancy because of Mary's Rh-negative blood type, the expectant mother continued to work until early June. She made another film with Bing Crosby, *Birth of the Blues*, and gave her costar a scare during filming when she fell off a wagon, since Crosby knew that she was expecting a child. The movie was something of a belated tribute to the Original Dixieland Jazz Band and hinted at the racial integration of American popular music. *Birth of the Blues* was one of the last pictures Victor Schertzinger directed before his premature death, and critics commended him on the smooth, easy-going pace he achieved. "Here is a film straight down the groove," Bosley Crowther wrote in the *New York Times*, "a blend of jump-and-jive music that should make the 'hep cats' howl." Crowther particularly liked the Crosby-Martin rendition of "Wait

Till the Sun Shines, Nellie" and a new number titled "The Waiter, the Porter, and the Upstairs Maid."

With a baby on the way, Mary agreed to invite Richard's mother to live in Los Angeles. Hope eagerly accepted the summons and rented a house near the Hallidays in Bel Air. Mary called Hope "Mammy," referring to her in print as "my mother-in-love," and from all indications the two women got along famously. Mary envied Hope's grace, her sense of style, and her ease with artists and intellectuals.

By August 1940, fearful of losing the baby, Mary and Richard rented a beach house in Balboa, where the expectant mother got her first real rest in six years. While idle Mary learned to pick out melodies with one finger on the piano and wrote a long letter to her friend from Texas, Bessie Mae Sue Ella, who by then had married and was living in Raleigh, North Carolina. "You have never heard from me in regard to our beautiful wedding present," Mary wrote Bessie Mae. "Honestly, I don't know where to begin, cause when you put it down in words it all sounds so ordinary and nothing could be as exciting as my life now." She described their beautiful home and the gorgeous flowers that grew in their garden and said that Bessie Mae simply had to come to California, where she would be waited on hand and foot, and see it all for herself. "I have practically a grown son," Mary told her friend, "that I didn't know could play the piano so well, and last but not least the most interesting man who I had breakfast with and *says* he's my husband." She told Bessie Mae about the new baby and insisted that her friend must bring her husband and spend some time with Richard and her. "All of this is at your disposal—well all but Richard," she said. "We could have such utter fun even though I would not be my usual beautiful chassis. You and I could have our first good visit since we were fifteen or sixteen. Please do think over all this very seriously as it will probably be my last vacation till heaven knows when."

When Bessie Mae wrote Mary that she, too, was pregnant, Mary replied that her friend could have her maternity clothes as soon as the Halliday baby was born. Since the prenatal child was extremely active during Mary's pregnancy, she and Richard decided before she was born to name her Heller, the term Preston Martin had

used to describe Mary as a girl. The eager mother was so certain her second child would be a girl that she refused to consider anything else. Sure enough, Mary Heller Halliday was born at Good Samaritan Hospital in Los Angeles on November 4, 1941. Jean Arthur and dramatic actress Judith Anderson were named the baby's godmothers.

Arthur and her husband, producer Frank Ross, had become the Hallidays' best friends in Hollywood, although Mary got to know movie actress Janet Gaynor and Nancy "Slim" Hawks, the wife of film director Howard Hawks, quite well. "Mary Martin is the only star I've ever known whose sweetness, purity, and naiveté are totally genuine," Slim Hawks wrote later. But Jean Arthur was Mary's special friend, an actress she had admired on the screen back in Weatherford, and the exact nature of their relationship has been a topic of much speculation through the years. In Hollywood it was rumored that the two were romantically involved, gossip that found credence in 1966 when Paul Rosner published a novel called *The Princess and the Goblin*. The book depicted the lesbian relationship between a singer from New York, who came to Hollywood in the late 1930s and returned to Manhattan a decade later to become the queen of Broadway musicals, and a publicity-shy movie star with an odd voice and a talent for playing comedy. The account was clearly a thinly masked exposé of the supposed liaison between Mary Martin and Jean Arthur. Even close friends vowed they didn't know whether the speculations were true and the exact nature of Mary's sexuality remains in question.

Besides her celebrity friends, Mary also had a group of a dozen or more young would-be actresses that she worried over and tried to encourage. She listened to their woes, worked with them when they rehearsed, lengthened their dresses if they were too short, and coached them on how to walk, talk, sing, and dance. One of these protégés was future MGM ingenue Jean Porter, another Texan who, like Mary, was studying voice with Dr. Stetson Humphrey in Hollywood. Mary even managed to get Jean an inconsequential part in *Kiss the Boys Goodbye*. "We just loved each other," Porter said. "Mary took me over to Paramount and introduced me around.

She dressed me up in my first pair of high heels and gave me a silver-fox jacket of hers to wear. I'd never had on a fur in my life, and she tried to make me look fancy and dressed up. She was marvelous and a total professional."

Pregnancy with Heller meant that Mary had to miss a chance to star with Bing Crosby and Fred Astaire in *Holiday Inn*, one of the classic Paramount musicals of the early 1940s. She reported back to the studio in February 1942, two months after the Japanese bombed Pearl Harbor. With the country at war, Californians particularly were nervous about the possibility of a shelling of the West Coast, and Washington had encouraged the movie industry to turn out films that would boost public morale. Mary sang one song, "Hit the Road to Dreamland," with Dick Powell in the wartime musical *Star Spangled Rhythm,* but the scene was merely an insert in an all-star comedy intended to relieve the antics of rambunctious Betty Hutton and mild-mannered Eddie Bracken, the movie's principal players. Mary is gussied up in 1940s plumage, designed by Edith Head, for her song with Powell, who is seated across from her in the diner of a train. Toward the end of the Harold Arlen–Johnny Mercer number, the two stars are joined by a quartet of black porters, and Mary looks quite comfortable being urged to retire for the night, although she is noticeably overdressed for travel. "Edith Head would always ask, when we looked at sketches of clothes she'd prepared for me, 'Are you comfortable in this? Do you feel the part?'" Mary remembered. Often she didn't know whether she felt the part or not, but she always said yes. "There were some things I really wasn't very comfortable in. When I was supposed to be glamorous, that threw me quite a bit."

Mary attended the Hollywood premiere of Cecil B. DeMille's *Reap the Wild Wind* in March, and the legendary filmmaker invited her to have lunch at his table one day in the commissary. "DeMille was always there with his entourage," she recalled, "and he sent me a note, asking me to sit with him. I just flipped my lid over that, I couldn't believe it." She was also impressed when Paramount assigned her a dressing room between the rooms of Claudette

Colbert and Ingrid Bergman, who was on the lot making *For Whom the Bell Tolls* in 1942.

Mary's sister, Jerry, and her young nephew paid a visit to Los Angeles that summer while Mary was making *Happy-Go-Lucky*, a Technicolor comedy that also starred Dick Powell, Betty Hutton, Eddie Bracken, and Rudy Vallee and was directed by Curtis Bernhardt. Mary told reporters that she wished the studio would make up its mind about the color of her hair before she went bald. So far in movies, her locks had been coal-black, platinum blond, red, chestnut, and in *Happy-Go-Lucky* sort of a dark blonde. When the picture was released in March 1943, Bosley Crowther judged the clowning "downright childish," although the critic said the film had "a couple of twinkling dance turns by Mary Martin" to its credit. Audiences found *Happy-Go-Lucky* enjoyable but little more.

Mary knew that she was capable of better things. Despite all of Paramount's efforts, she continued to hate the way she looked in movies, and Richard's vision of her was far different from what the studio foisted on her. "He used to just have a fit over the costumes," Mary said, "and some of them did make me look kind of creepy. But Richard, ever the perfectionist, thought most of them seemed dull and cheap, even though he adored Edith Head." Mary missed the excitement and rewards from a live audience. Making movies seemed so static and sterile to her. "You just sat around and waited for them to light the set," she said. "I didn't see any point in doing something I didn't find joy in." Richard missed New York and complained that Hollywood was a cultural wasteland. Finally, he said to his wife, "Let's quit. Let's go back to Broadway. You belong in the theater." But Paramount refused to release Mary from her contract.

She made one more picture, a bright, engaging little comedy called *True to Life*, directed by George Marshall, with Franchot Tone, Dick Powell, and Victor Moore as costars. Then, with five more years still on her contract, Mary went to Frank Freeman and told him she wanted a year's leave of absence. Freeman listened sympathetically while she listed her frustrations. Then the obliging production head said, "Mary, take a year. Take two years, or three, or twenty-five.

But remember, when you get over your Broadway complex and come back to Hollywood, you have a contract to finish out with Paramount." On that understanding, the Hallidays returned to the East toward the end of 1942.

Of their Hollywood period, Mary would later say, "We had been there three years and we both were miserable." Today the pictures she made at Paramount are largely forgotten. Mary felt that the studio was giving all the choice comedy parts to Betty Hutton and that even in the Crosby pictures, probably her best, she was little more than a pleasant accessory. "Hollywood was Boresville," she said. "I didn't learn a single, solitary, blasted thing out there." Under the terms of her contract she still owed Paramount six more pictures, but those would never be made, at least not with Mary. Richard was determined to create an entirely new image for his wife, one that would be elegant and urbane, yet retain Mary's simple, unaffected radiance. Years later she would write, "My Hollywood period is now almost nonexistent in my memory." Somehow it all seemed a huge joke to her.

"Mary has a capacity for love that not many people have," Bessie Mae Sue Ella maintained. "That great capacity for love, I think, is her most endearing quality." Despite her devotion to Richard, Mary needed something he was incapable of giving her—nonbinding, unconditional love. The great ardor in Mary's life would always come from audiences that returned the affection she showered so gleefully on them. Her love affair with her public was stronger than any romantic or sexual interest Mary Martin ever had. "I beat my brains out performing," she said, "and I like to hear the echo." That echo would be her ambrosia, her ecstasy, and her passion.

CHAPTER 4

Back on Broadway

Late in her life, Mary said she would have always had a career, but it would not have been the same without Richard. He charted and shaped Mary's route to international stardom and gave her the freedom to perform without the irritating distractions that harass less protected entertainers. Richard helped her sort through the advice and criticism she got, screened the people who saw her, selected her clothes and costumes, negotiated the contracts for her shows, paid the bills, decorated their homes, and took charge of supervising their household. Although Mary had drive and determination, emotionally she remained the vulnerable child. "Richard took over," Bessie Mae Sue Ella said. "Mary never really had time to grow up. Richard became her Svengali. Her life was as regimented as any infant's."

When the Hallidays returned to New York in the early winter of 1942, Richard made a difficult decision. He would give up his career to focus on Mary's. Theirs became a corporate partnership as much as a marriage. "In our business," Mary said, "marriage and career seldom work. Ours worked because we worked at it, because we had complete confidence in each other and respect for each other." Mary acknowledged that she had "not one inch" of business acumen. "I'm just delighted that I can write my name,"

she said. "Richard and I talked things out. There were times when I didn't believe in something but then would come around to it. And there were times when he didn't believe in something that I wanted. If I believed in it strongly enough, he'd go with it. But everything was centered on me as a performer." Richard viewed their marriage as akin to that of theater legends Alfred Lunt and Lynn Fontanne or Katharine Cornell and Guthrie McClintic. "I cannot believe the sexual aspects of these unions are of great importance," said Elia Kazan, who would direct Mary in her first starring role on Broadway; "that energy passes into their work."

Richard was determined to transform his Texas tomboy into a feminine, delicate creature who dressed alluringly and exuded poise and charm. Shortly after the Hallidays sold their home in Bel Air, Mary was given her choice of two upcoming Broadway musicals. One was the part of Laurey in *Away We Go*, the first collaboration of songwriter Richard Rodgers and lyricist Oscar Hammerstein II. The other was a show that had music by Vernon Duke and lyrics by Howard Dietz called *Dancing in the Streets*. Since Laurey wore nothing but gingham dresses and sunbonnets throughout the entire show, Richard thought accepting the lead in *Away We Go* would be a mistake. Besides, Rodgers and Hammerstein and the director, Rouben Mamoulian, saw *Away We Go*, based on Lynn Riggs's play *Green Grow the Lilacs*, as an ensemble piece, not a star vehicle. Mamoulian wanted to retain the simple folk quality of Riggs's play about cowboys and homesteaders and do away with the specialty numbers, chorus line, and dazzling paraphernalia typical of musical comedy. Instead, he intended to fashion something new, an integration of songs and dance within a drama that made sense.

All of this seemed dubious to Richard Halliday. He knew that the Theatre Guild was producing *Away We Go*, that the Guild had fallen on hard times, and had not had a success in some months. Oscar Hammerstein, too, was in a slump, having gone through eleven years of flops. In Halliday's judgment, the more traditional *Dancing in the Streets* was the better vehicle for Mary's return to Broadway. She would wear everything from a wedding gown to bathing suits in the show and have pleasing Vernon Duke melodies

to sing. The musical was being produced by the highly esteemed Vinton Freedley and would have scenery and costumes designed by the renowned Robert Edmond Jones. The combination seemed to add up to a Broadway winner, so Mary accepted the lead in *Dancing in the Streets* shortly after the Hallidays settled into a three-room apartment in the Gorham Hotel, a theatrical residence in midtown Manhattan.

Rehearsals on *Dancing in the Streets* began in New York early in 1943 and then the show went to Boston for tryouts, where it competed with *Away We Go,* also in tryouts—except by then that show's name had been changed to *Oklahoma! Dancing in the Streets* drew capacity houses, largely on the strength of Mary's fame in movies. But the show was not good, and Boston critics were merciless in pointing out its weaknesses. Consequently, the musical folded before going into New York. With two failures on the road—*Nice Goin'* and now *Dancing in the Streets*—Mary grew discouraged. "My dreams were nightmares," she said, "filled with visions of my sneaking back to Hollywood seeking Frank Freeman's sympathy."

Oklahoma!, on the other hand, with a cast of unknowns went on to break Broadway records during its protracted run, a total of 2,248 performances at the St. James Theatre, and its unique concept revolutionized the American musical theater, launching the "Golden Age" of Broadway musicals. For months after the Rodgers and Hammerstein show opened, according to Mary, "I got roses from Dick and Oscar because I had turned down their show. Had I accepted it, they said, they would have written a star part for me and probably ruined their integrated concept."

Richard Halliday had been down with viral pneumonia during much of *Dancing in the Streets'* tryout period in Boston. When the show closed, he, Mary, and Heller went to his sister's home in Connecticut so that he could relax and recuperate. They stayed there for two months, then rented a nearby farmhouse for the summer. While they were in Connecticut, producer Cheryl Crawford approached the Hallidays about the possibility of Mary's starring in a musical she was planning for Broadway the coming fall called *One Touch of Venus.* Based on F. Anstey's 1885 novella *The*

Tinted Venus, the show had been written for German star Marlene Dietrich. Crawford thought Dietrich was perfect for the title role and had many meetings with the exotic film actress in her home in Hollywood. The star promised that she'd be free of movie commitments by the time the musical went into rehearsal. But when Dietrich sang for the producer and composer Kurt Weill in the theater, they had trouble hearing her past the third row. "We knew then that if Marlene was going to do our show we would have to use a mike of some kind," Crawford said. Despite Dietrich's voice problems, the producer still wanted her for the part but grew discouraged when the sultry actress couldn't seem to make up her mind whether she wanted to do the musical or not. Finally, Dietrich told Kurt Weill, "I cannot play this play. It is too sexy and profane." She kept repeating that excuse in an increasingly stubborn way, while the composer and Cheryl Crawford tried to change her mind. "I have a daughter," Dietrich said, "and for me to get up on the stage and exhibit my legs is now impossible."

So Crawford and Weill began looking for alternatives. They considered Ilona Massey, who like Dietrich would bring a Central European flavor to the part. Then they turned to British star Gertrude Lawrence, who decided that she didn't want to do the show, and ballerina Vera Zorina, who balked at having to work with choreographer Agnes de Mille, known to be difficult. Next the producer, composer, and their associates auditioned singer Kitty Carlisle, but concluded that she was not right for their show. Crawford even indicated that if the choice came down to Carlisle, she'd rather not produce *One Touch of Venus.* "God knows, I don't think Kitty is ideal for the part," John Wildberg, the producer's lawyer wrote, "but if we have to sign her to a two-week contract until someone better comes along, at least we have got insurance." Then Crawford heard from agent Audrey Wood that Mary Martin was free. The producer had seen Mary in *Leave It to Me,* remembered how she had stopped the show with "My Heart Belongs to Daddy," but she had not seen any of Martin's movies. Crawford doubted that Mary possessed the star stature needed for *One Touch of Venus* but agreed to see her. The Hallidays came down from Connecticut, and Crawford,

Weill, and the rest of their production team met with Mary. "I tended to favor her," Crawford said, "but the others weren't sure." Mary left the meeting convinced that she had been rejected.

Crawford pointed out to her colleagues that Mary was a good singer and a lively performer and suggested that the part could be rewritten so that Venus coincided with Mary's thoroughly American demeanor. The script had already been through several revisions. Sam and Bella Spewack had initially been assigned to write the book of the musical, and poet Ogden Nash was chosen to write the lyrics. Nash had never written words to songs before, but he had a light touch and what Crawford considered "just the right social punch" for Kurt Weill's score. "The idea that had enticed me," the producer said, "was the irreconcilable differences between the world of mundane conventional human beings and the free untrammeled world of the gods." That theme had not been developed in the Spewacks' script, and they were taken off the project and replaced by S. J. Perelman, who agreed to write the book with Ogden Nash. When the literate, well-read producer saw their version, she liked it. "The conflict of two disparate worlds was now clear," Crawford said. Once the team settled on Mary Martin for the starring role, further revisions were made in the text to accommodate her singular personality.

Richard was all in favor of his wife's doing *One Touch of Venus*, but Mary thought the idea of her playing Venus was insane. "I was thinking of Venus de Milo," she said. "I thought it was a darling, wonderful script, but I knew they had written the part for Marlene Dietrich. I thought they had lost their minds when they came to me." Richard adored the idea of his wife's playing the goddess of love and urged her to accept Crawford's offer. "I can't," Mary protested. "I'd love to, but I'm five feet, four-and-a-half inches tall and I can't be Venus. I'm Miss Cornball from Texas." Richard argued that she could do anything she wanted to do. "I could learn to speak right," Mary said, "and sing right, but I can't get any taller."

Richard took Mary to the Metropolitan Museum of Art and showed her Venus in many forms. "We saw an awful lot of Venuses," she said. "Finally we saw one that wasn't large, and she had sort of

a larger can than she should have had. I said, 'You mean *that's* Venus?'" Richard assured her it was. "Well, if that's a Venus," Mary said, "I guess I could play her." So Cheryl Crawford arranged for Richard and Mary to hear the score in Kurt Weill's apartment in New York. It was a hot August night, but they both found his songs delicious. "When I heard 'That's Him,' I just flipped," Mary said. "I loved it so."

She still had concerns about her appearance, particularly her long neck. Crawford promised the reluctant star that her costumes would be exquisite and would resolve any problem with her neck. "It is possible I paid more for Mary's costumes than anyone had ever paid for costumes in a musical," the producer maintained. They cost between fifteen and twenty thousand dollars. Mary had fifteen changes in the show, and each of her entrances brought applause from audiences. Richard and Crawford wanted Mainbocher, the celebrated couturier from Paris, to design Mary's Venus gowns, but the designer had never done clothes for the theater and was doubtful. So Crawford arranged for Mainbocher to hear Mary sing the songs from the show at a production meeting in Kurt Weill's house.

Weill accompanied on the piano, while Mary went through the score. When she got to "That's Him," she spontaneously picked up a little straight chair, moved it right in front of Mainbocher, turned the chair around so that the back was facing the designer, and sat in it sideways as she sang the song directly to him. When she finished, the designer didn't say anything, nobody did. Finally Mainbocher told her, "I'll do your costumes if you promise you'll do the song that way in the show. Take a little chair down to the footlights, turn it just like you did tonight, and sing the lyrics directly to the audience. I'll make you the greatest negligee you've ever had in your life—all in lace." Mary did as he instructed, sang "That's Him" across the orchestra to the audience as if they were one person, and the song became the hit moment in the show.

Mainbocher solved the problem of Mary's long neck by simply putting a black velvet ribbon around it. Her first costume was chiffon in a shade the designer called "Venus pink," pale and glowing like the inside of a seashell. Another costume, which she wore at the

end of the first act, was a sleek black satin creation with a deep V front and low-cut in back. Mainbocher thought Mary had an attractive back and designed the gown to show it off. "All of a sudden I felt attractive," the star said. Several of her skirts had slits in them, a concession to the fact that Venus in statuary is seldom clothed. "So as often as possible," Mainbocher explained, "I exposed as much of Miss Martin as I could," particularly her great legs. To make her look taller, he made each of her costumes with long vertical lines.

The designer pulled Mary's long brownish hair back and said it should be worn up. He then sent her to the Saks Fifth Avenue salon, where her tresses were dyed pink. Mary preferred to do her own hair, and later in the run of *One Touch of Venus* she decided to apply the pink dye herself. "It turned out a funny shade of green," she said. "I played the show one night that way, and the cast didn't notice any difference. They were so used to seeing me as Venus that they didn't realize I had green hair."

Cheryl Crawford asked Elia Kazan, her old friend from the Group Theatre, to serve as stage director of *One Touch of Venus*, even though Kazan had never directed a musical before. He quickly discovered that Kurt Weill, S. J. Perelman, and Ogden Nash wanted their show directed as though it were a drama, with the songs a continuation of the dialogue, rather than in the traditional mode of musical comedy. Weill, who had had a big success on Broadway two years before with *Lady in the Dark*, seemed to dominate the collaboration, and Kazan told the composer in one of their first discussions that while he liked the songs, he thought the show's book was abysmal. Weill informed him that it would be his job to make the dialogue scenes carry their share of the weight.

Early in preparations Kazan found himself reduced in rank. "Conferences were being held without me," the director said. "The scenery that I'd planned with Howard Bay was attacked and, without my concurrence, replaced. . . . I'd become a sort of overpaid stage manager, subservient to everyone else." Yet Kazan discovered during the show's tryouts that Mary "could make an audience believe anything," and by the time the musical opened in New York the dialogue scenes didn't seem to matter.

Two exceptional women, choreographer Agnes de Mille and her principal dancer, Sono Osato, contributed markedly to the success of *One Touch of Venus*. De Mille had created the stunning choreography for *Oklahoma!*, and that triumph had given her tremendous confidence and temperament. Kazan remembered the choreographer as "the most strong-minded stage artist" he'd ever known. "She was absolutely sure of what she wanted to do and insisted that her wishes be precisely observed." She ordered the stage cleared of all scenery for her dances, insisting that she needed space. "Agnes didn't want me near her ballet," Mary said, "but she finally had to give in. When Venus came to life, the thing I had to do was be legato and go in and out, while Agnes' dancers raced around me and never stopped. Mainbocher's costumes made me look taller, and he told me to move as if I were from another world and look at these people rushing past me as if they had gone out of their minds. That first number set up the whole show."

Sono Osato, a tiny, good-looking woman of Japanese descent, was poetry in motion. "When she was on stage," Kazan said, "I couldn't look at anything else." Osato had been the premiere danseuse with the Metropolitan Opera ballet and the Ballet Russe de Monte Carlo. *One Touch of Venus* was her first appearance in musical comedy, yet Mary claimed that Osato taught her more about her part in the show than anyone else. During rehearsals the dancer told her, "Don't ever do anything in flat shoes. Get the highest heels you can find and learn to walk in them. Then think tall and you will be tall."

Before the show went into rehearsals, Cheryl Crawford set up a luncheon for Mary and Elia Kazan in the Oak Room of the Plaza Hotel. By then Mary had learned the songs and was becoming familiar with the book. The two talked and talked during the meeting, but it wasn't until late in their conversation that the director asked his star how she intended to play Venus. Mary admitted that she'd been afraid he would question her on that and replied, "I haven't the vaguest idea." She pointed out that she hadn't done much dramatically except films and didn't really know how to approach the part. Finally, she said, "I think in terms of how I will walk. If I can get that walk in my mind, then I'll know how the role should

be played." Kazan nodded agreement and said he thought Venus must move to a rhythm from another galaxy—the same point Mainbocher had made during Mary's costume fittings. Venus must seem puzzled by the mad scurry around her, with people showing no joy and appearing empty. Kazan said, "That concept is very exciting to me. Think of the role as a dancer. If you walk like a goddess, then I won't have to direct you." Mary said he and Mainbocher had given her the key to the part and she never had to think of anything else. After that discussion Kazan gave her complete freedom to flesh out her characterization with whatever details she felt were right.

Gradually, her concept of a mortal Venus began to come together, established by "I'm a Stranger Here Myself," the first song she sang in the show. Wearing stiletto heels and with her hair piled high on her head, Mary walked from one side of the stage to the other with a gorgeous, long pink jersey scarf around her neck. She stood with her legs apart and when she moved, it was in big, gliding steps, although slowly. "That made me feel like a goddess," she said. "Everything everyone had told me contributed to that image. I learned something from every single person. The only one that didn't like my entrance was Agnes de Mille. She said, 'That's Hollywood,' and claimed I looked like a Hollywood starlet."

Kenny Baker from radio and movies was cast as Rodney Hatch, the barber who brings a statue of Venus to life when he slips his fiancée's engagement ring on the goddess's finger. John Boles, also from motion pictures, played the art collector who buys the statue of Venus and has it brought to New York. But it was Mary who gave the show life. "She did everything asked of her better than any of us could have hoped," Kazan said. "She was also a completely devoted worker." The director soon learned that Mary's talent was "larger than life" and remembered her as "full of the love of being loved."

Mary found Kurt Weill a "strange little man" whom she adored. "I couldn't understand him too well because he had a German accent," she said. "He had a little ball of hair on his head and then tufts on each side." There was a remoteness about Weill and there was sadness in his enormous brown eyes, yet he approached his work and the production with undying enthusiasm. "He was fabulous to

me," Mary said. "He couldn't have been better and never demanded that I do a song any particular way."

One Touch of Venus was budgeted at a substantial $140,000, some of which Paramount Pictures put up. Rehearsals began on the show in New York in August 1943. Whenever possible, Mary liked to rehearse in costume, since that helped her feel the role. When she was onstage, Richard would watch from the back row. "Sometimes he would pace up and down," Mary said. "He'd be in the back lots of times, and I wouldn't even know he was there." Kazan noted that Richard seemed more like the star's manager than her husband. He was, the director deduced, "precisely what she needed to function perfectly, looking after her every professional and personal need."

Kenny Baker didn't mix very much with the rest of the cast members, but he proved perfect as the timid barber whom Venus promptly takes a shine to. Agnes de Mille threw some disruptive tantrums during the weeks of rehearsal and stubbornly refused to cut a single minute from her ballets. Her dancers never stopped working and had the dedication of fanatics. "I used to sneak away from my silly 'book' rehearsals," Kazan said, "to watch Agnes' girls and boys work by the hour." Even when the show left for tryouts in Boston, the director continued to find the script "foolish and boring." Perelman maintained that Kazan lacked a sense of humor. But when audiences in Boston also failed to respond to the wit of the dialogue, the book scenes were reduced to little more than bridges, mere introductions to the songs and dances, so that the show could move as rapidly as possible from one musical number to the next.

Shortly before the company left for Boston, Cheryl Crawford got a summons from an agitated Mary Martin. When the producer went to Mary's dressing room to see what was wrong, Mary said, "Cheryl, there's one line in the show that I simply cannot say. It's just too vulgar." Crawford asked which line was causing her trouble. Mary said, "It's that line where I say: 'Love isn't the dying moan of a distant violin; it's the triumphant twang of a bedspring.'" The producer was surprised that Mary's objection came so late. She thought the line was funny, hated to see it cut, and knew that Perelman

and Nash were already upset about other changes. The producer suggested that Mary say the line in the first performance at the Shubert Theatre in Boston and see how it went. "If you feel the slightest reaction from the audience that makes you uncomfortable," Crawford told the hesitant star, "I'll talk to the writers and see that the line is cut." Mary agreed and was so delighted with the way the audience laughed that she never mentioned cutting the line again.

One Touch of Venus had one of the all-time great show tunes, "Speak Low." Another winner was "That's Him," sung on a bare stage against a black backdrop, with Mary sitting in a tiny gold chair turned backward toward the audience, her arms resting across its top. Mary was dazzling in the production, casting an aura that was distinct, yet impeccably stylish. She glowed in Mainbocher's gowns, looking more like glamorous Rita Hayworth than the wifely Claudette Colbert that Paramount had tried to make her resemble in Hollywood. Yet she made Venus a creature of flesh and blood during the goddess's stay in this world, during which she pursues Rodney Hatch with frank and earthy passion.

Some of the costumes proved to be wrong in Boston, and the show had any number of ragged moments that needed correcting. A lot went wrong on opening night, but the biggest blunder came in the finale, which was choreographed around Venus, by then married to Rodney. She was seated center stage in the suburban cottage that Rodney had always wanted, but Venus was not happy and found the endless domesticity boring. Suddenly, dancers appeared, dressed as satyrs, nymphs, and dryads, and circled around Venus in a wild bacchanal before lifting her to their shoulders and carrying her off to Olympus. But when the scene started on the first tryout, Mary wasn't there. The dancers pranced in a circle around an empty chair. Eventually, Mary appeared and sat down, just in time to be carried offstage. The number was a disaster, and the curtain fell to weak applause. "We ran back to find out what had happened," Cheryl Crawford remembered. "Backstage, during the preceding blackout, a new stagehand had moved the flat containing Mary's change of costume to the wrong side. She had searched frantically

for her clothes, begging someone to find them. But the stagehands were too flustered to help. Mary had to run all the way across the back as the stage was in full light. Panting and nearly naked she finally located her costume."

The ending with the nymphs, satyrs, and dryads left the audience dissatisfied. It seemed disappointing for Venus to disappear, leaving poor Rodney all alone. A more upbeat ending was needed. Agnes de Mille came up with the idea of having Venus return to Earth as an ordinary human, dressed in a simple gingham frock and modest hat and carrying a straw suitcase, almost seeming like the country cousin of the love goddess. In the revision, the girl asks Rodney where she can register for the art course, and he asks where she's from. She tells him that she wouldn't think of living anywhere but Ozone Heights. He tells her that his name is Rodney Hatch. When she starts to tell him her name, he quickly interrupts: "You don't have to tell me, I know." He takes her suitcase, and they start to walk off, arm in arm, as the curtain falls. Oscar Hammerstein saw the show and said that Mary should always appear as she did in that last scene, like the corn-fed Texas girl she really was.

One Saturday night in Boston, Mary collapsed as she was leaving the stage. She rallied enough to finish the show, but a doctor discovered afterward that she had a fever of 104 degrees and insisted that she be hospitalized. Since there had been no time to select an understudy, a few performances had to be canceled. Meanwhile, Richard raced between the Ritz Hotel, where the company was staying, and his wife's bedside, making sure she had all the amenities she required.

By the time the show got to New York, reports had pronounced *One Touch of Venus* an enormous success, and the musical had an advance ticket sale of $100,000, one of the sturdiest in years. Long lines continued to form at the box office, where the top ticket price was $4.40. Mary was paid $1,500 a week, but the word from Boston was that Hollywood had not hurt her talent in the least. Still, there were naysayers in New York who doubted that the "Daddy" girl was capable of doing much more than singing her delightful little patter song, which required more personality than voice, while divesting

herself of articles of clothing. Few professional critics were ready for Mary's poise, her luminous good looks, her sure projection and total authority as a performer, and her lovely clear voice singing smart lyrics to a fetching score.

One Touch of Venus opened at the Imperial Theatre in Manhattan on October 7, 1943. Five years after she had stopped Leave It to Me with her playful rendition of "My Heart Belongs to Daddy," Mary returned to the same theater a Broadway star of the first magnitude, projecting a special magic that audiences found irresistible. She had warmth and sparkle and sang Ogden Nash's verses straight from the soul. "Mary Martin in One Touch of Venus," a reviewer for P.M. magazine wrote, "is the most captivating person I've ever seen on a musical comedy stage. She is beautiful and amusing, she moves with wonderful grace, and she sings hauntingly." Richard Watts, Jr., of the New York Herald Tribune said that, in his opinion, Mary gave the most sensational performance that New York had seen since Gertrude Lawrence's triumph in Lady in the Dark. "She can play an emotional scene touchingly," Watts said, "and a comedy scene with guile and humor. She has grace and lightness and style." Life magazine said, "Not since the late Marilyn Miller left the stage . . . has the theater boasted of a more radiant musical-comedy heroine than this pretty, vivacious girl from Weatherford, Texas."

The show also garnered rave reviews. "Life along Broadway is a bit more cheerful now," Lewis Nichols wrote in the New York Times. "After bumping along on the bottom for more weeks than it seemed polite to count, the theatre ten days ago pulled itself up to something nearer normal" when One Touch of Venus opened. Comparisons with Oklahoma! were inevitable, since both shows broke with musical comedy tradition. Time reported that the Kurt Weill–Ogden Nash production, like the Rodgers and Hammerstein groundbreaker, spurned "ready-made formulas, but where Oklahoma! took the smooth, pleasant low road of picturesque folklore, Venus takes the high road of sophisticated fantasy." Reviewers agreed that the book of One Touch of Venus was a disappointment, but most complimented Kazan on his fast-paced direction, Agnes de Mille on her inventive choreography, and the designers for their striking

modernity. "Whatever is wrong with it, *One Touch of Venus* is an unhackneyed and imaginative musical," the critic for *P. M.* concluded, "that has personality and wit and genuinely high moments of music and dancing." And the *New York Post* maintained, "It is a long time since we have heard a new and modern score in a musical comedy that struck us as something at once popular and unusually fine."

An opening night party was given for Mary in an apartment on Park Avenue, which Cheryl Crawford remembered was "about the size of Grand Central Station," with hundreds of elegantly dressed people invited. But after that, Mary limited her social engagements to conserve her strength for the show. She found quickly that even when she restricted her party going to Saturday nights, with no show to give on Sunday, she was worn out the following week and sometimes had to miss performances. Mary accepted that she had a responsibility to appear. "The audience doesn't come to see somebody tired or not be there," she said. "They pay to see you at your peak." Any time she could spare she devoted to singing for the wounded in military hospitals.

Mary grew a great deal during the nearly two-year run of *One Touch of Venus*, and the show solidified her stardom on the Broadway stage. She was still studying voice with Helen Fouts Cahoon in Manhattan and her vocal power and command of the stage increased noticeably. She made the cover of *Life* magazine again shortly after the show opened, and she was hailed as one of America's best-dressed women. Her performance in *Venus* earned her the Donaldson Award, the forerunner to the Tony Awards, and when British playwright Noel Coward saw the show, he was so impressed with Mary's talent that he came backstage, introduced himself to her, and asked if he could write a musical especially for her. Mary was so flattered that she said yes.

The Hallidays were still living in the Gorham Hotel when *One Touch of Venus* opened, with two-year-old Heller and her nurse spending most of their time in an apartment on the floor below. Richard had decorated his and Mary's quarters in "Venus pink" and brought in French Provincial furniture. It was a glorious time for them both. Mary suddenly found herself the darling of the

press, and she remembered that first year in *Venus* as one of the most thrilling periods in her life. "Oh, it is so good to be on the stage!" she told reporters. "I suppose you could say that I was success-ful in movies. But my heart was on Broadway, not in Hollywood. The stage is my parlor. The screen is just a screen."

There was still no air-conditioning in New York theaters during the Second World War years, only a fan and an ice system for cooling, with insufficient ice. *One Touch of Venus* played through the summer of 1944 with temperatures around 112 degrees onstage for something like a week. Mary would come into the wings after working under the hot lights, and an assistant stage manager would put ice on her wrists to cool her blood a little. Finally, the normally obliging actress complained so much about the heat that Cheryl Crawford brought the air-conditioning unit from her apartment to the theater and had it installed in the star's dressing room. "She played through the summer like a trouper after that," the producer said.

In August 1944, Juanita Martin died in Los Angeles after a gallbladder operation, and her body was sent to Weatherford for burial in the family plot. Mary felt that she couldn't leave *One Touch of Venus* to be in attendance at her mother's funeral. "No one would have wanted to see the show without Mary Martin," Cheryl Crawford maintained. Yet not being with her family was difficult for Mary, and she also had to make arrangements for Larry, her twelve-year-old son, to come to New York, so that he could live with her and Richard. It was a tense time for everyone concerned. "I would never see Mother until just before dinner, when she went off to the theater," Larry said later, "and that was it until the week-end. Then she'd be exhausted." Mary admitted that she was on stage all the time. "Larry had been the star at home," she said, "and here I was the star. That was the way it was, and Richard was in the middle. Oh, we had a rocky road." Richard offered to adopt the boy, but Larry, full of resentment, wouldn't have it.

Richard believed that Mary was one of the theater's great talents, and he would allow nothing to stand in the way of his wife's realizing her potential. He and Mary became inseparable, with Richard serving as her constant buffer. They talked not of "her career" but of "our

career." Whenever one spoke with Mary alone, it was always "we thought," "we decided," "we plan," or "we believe." She called her husband "Daddy," and he called her "Mommy." Richard insisted that his wife must learn strict discipline and get plenty of rest. He was impatient with anything that distracted from the career and begrudged having to deal with an active, unplanned adolescent boy who showed all the rowdy signs of early manhood. "He wasn't too fond of me," Larry said of Richard. "Nor was I a fan of his. He had to be in control of everything—an asset to Mother's career, but it made him a pain in the ass to be around if you weren't part of that little world." Besides, the boy was broken up over his grandmother's death. "I cried for days," Larry said. "She'd raised me through my first twelve years. . . . Without her, I was truly on my own in Richard's house."

By the time Larry came to live with the Hallidays, they had moved into an apartment on Fifth Avenue. Richard's mother had moved back to New York, so their world was centered on Mary's performing and the social life that Richard created and monitored. Larry liked Richard's sister, who, unlike her brother, was warm and loving toward him, but aside from that, living in New York was torment for the boy. Richard often blamed him when something went wrong. "Mother didn't know me," Larry Hagman wrote in his memoirs. "How could she? We'd never spent any time together." Finally, Richard's harangues became so great that the unhappy boy decided to run away. "I'd just read the novels about Huck Finn and Tom Sawyer," Larry recalled, "and I decided to head to the Mississippi and raft down the river. I packed a bag with sandwiches, milk, and cookies, bundled myself up because it was cold, and took my Schwinn bicycle outside. The Metropolitan Museum of Art was across the street, and I rode circles around the front. . . . I was trying to work up the nerve to ask someone where I could find the bridge to New Jersey." But after a few hours it began to get dark, and he went back home.

The year before his grandmother died, Larry's dad had given him a .22 rifle for his birthday. One night as Richard was taking Mary to the theater, the boy watched them walk to the car from his second floor bedroom window. "I happened to be cleaning my

.22," Larry remembered, "and a thought came to me—one shot, that's all I need. I sat down on the windowsill and drew a bead on the back of Richard's head. While picturing the bullet going right between his ears, I told myself, I could shoot the son of a bitch and nobody would think a twelve-year-old boy would do something like that." Fortunately, he talked himself out of doing anything foolish.

Larry was enrolled first in Trinity, an old-fashioned prep school that he rather liked. The students there wore jackets, ties, and flannels and called their teachers "Sir." Later he was sent to Woodstock Country School, a boarding school in Vermont. "I was delighted to escape Richard," Larry said. The boy was driven up to Woodstock in the Hallidays' Cadillac, with the backseat filled with his trunk. "Somehow despite my frustrations, I came to see Richard was simply a goddamned necessary evil," Larry wrote in his memoirs, *Hello Darlin'*. "Mother most likely wouldn't have had a brilliant career without Richard in her life. He and I would never get along, and it prevented Mother and me from having a real relationship until he died."

Socializing for the Hallidays while Mary was starring in *One Touch of Venus* mainly settled down to quiet evenings at home, sometimes shared with a few close friends. Mostly those were big-name theater people such as Katharine Cornell and Guthrie McClintic, Jean Arthur and Frank Ross when they were in New York, and later Richard and Dorothy Rodgers and Oscar and Dorothy Hammerstein. Their life was everything Mary had dreamed of, but far from a nourishing environment for children. Heller seemed to accept the world her mother and father made for her as normal, but Larry suffered and resisted.

Meanwhile, Mary reveled in a long run with a resounding hit that reeked of talent in every department. She fed on the love that audiences gave her and years later remembered the soldiers, sailors, and marines who waited at the stage door each night to greet her. "You were wonderful about it," Mary wrote Cheryl Crawford; "you would let us bring them in so they could see the show from the back." Mary was hailed as one of the brightest musical comedy stars to ascend in many a year. Whereas Marilyn Miller on Broadway

had represented innocent refreshment to audiences of the 1920s and brassy Ethel Merman had typified the rough-and-tumble 1930s, petite Mary Martin became the musical theater's lovable sweetheart of the 1940s and 1950s. "The gods were with me," Mary said years later, and "I thrived on a live audience." With *Oklahoma!* breaking records, *Life With Father* still going strong, and *One Touch of Venus* a smash hit, Broadway theater once again had regained the glitter and excitement of its legendary past. Yet the years ahead would be the golden age of female stars on Broadway, and for two decades Mary Martin and Ethel Merman were its queens, guaranteeing a show's profitability.

During the New York run of *One Touch of Venus*, the show had three barbers. Kenny Baker, a conscience objector to war, finished his contract and went back to Hollywood. The second Rodney Hatch had a beautiful voice but didn't last long. "He went off the beam," Mary recalled. "He walked off in the middle of a song with me one afternoon and nobody knew where he went. They had to close the curtain." One of the chorus kids, Geoffrey Warren, said, "I know the part. Don't worry, I've watched every move he made." The boy finished that matinee, and the cast members all flipped over his performance. "He was just adorable," Mary said. "He was blond and had curly hair and looked like a young boy out of Ozone Heights." The young man played the barber for the rest of the time the company was in New York and went on the road in the part.

The night after the matinee during which the second Rodney Hatch walked off the stage, Mary was in her dressing room making up for that evening's performance when the delinquent actor crawled through her window. He said that the physical strain of the show had been too much for him. Then he ran to his former dressing room and locked the door, maintaining that he wanted to go back onstage that night. Mary told him he was tired and needed rest. "Then he announced that the main reason he'd left the stage was because he was so much in love with Mary," Cheryl Crawford remembered, "and she was so much in love with her husband, Dick Halliday, that he couldn't face another performance with her." Eventually, Mary and her maid, Lena, managed to get the

distraught young actor placated and out of the theater with no further commotion.

At another performance, Mary lost her voice during "That's Him." The conductor, realizing what had happened, slowed the tempo for her, but no sound came from Mary. "She sat there in her little chair in a state of total shock," Crawford recalled. Finally, the star gestured to the audience and whispered, "Please sit, just stay. I'll stay and the voice will come back." They sat and waited for what seemed to Mary like an eternity, but probably was more like five minutes. Finally her voice returned and she finished the song. Later it was discovered that she was allergic to theater dust and that had caused her to lose her voice. Mary said the incident taught her that if a performer didn't panic, he or she could hold an audience.

One Touch of Venus netted a handsome profit and after 567 performances closed in New York. Mary was a bit reluctant to go on the road with the show, but Cheryl Crawford insisted that it was important in a theatrical career to build a national reputation. Lynn Fontanne and Alfred Drake, the star of *Oklahoma!*, also urged Mary to do the tour. "You will find the audiences enormously stimulating," she was told, "and those people will come to see you when they visit New York." So in February 1945 Heller was sent to Huntington, West Virginia, where her paternal grandmother was visiting, and Mary and Richard left for Philadelphia with the *One Touch of Venus* company. Mary found the tour hard but rewarding. "The road keeps me alive in a show," she said later. "There's the thrill of each new city and the challenge that every Monday night is an opening." Also there was satisfaction in bringing joy to others and having their affection expressed in thunderous ovations.

From the Warwick Hotel in Philadelphia, Mary wrote Cheryl Crawford a reflective thank you letter. "I *still* am amazed that you ever gave me the chance to play Venus," she said. "I'm so happy I didn't let either of us down. Now that I'm away from New York I know much too much happened too constantly. Already I'm getting a perspective, and I have a wonderful warm glow all inside and a good, deep grateful light all glittering with everlasting thanks to you. It hasn't all been perfect—but it's nice to grow up and find

that all *important* things aren't perfect—that most frequently a combination of ups and downs, good and bad, welds a much stronger, better, more lasting relationship. I'm happy that everything has been just as it has—and both Richard and I have loved knowing you."

Mary went on to mention that the experience with the show in Philadelphia had been "just unbelievable and continues to be exciting and satisfying and exhausting—and I love it." She thought it incredible that Crawford had been able to keep so much of the show together and even add to it. "You are to be congratulated on doing a durn mean job magnificently," she concluded. Their friendship would last for decades, with exchanges of gifts and frequent notes of affection.

The *Venus* tour was supposed to continue on to the West Coast. But in Detroit opera singer Grace Moore gave a party for Mary, at which Mary and Richard overindulged with champagne. After they got back to their hotel the Hallidays continued their indulgence, and Mary wound up pregnant. The company finished its performances in Detroit and moved to Chicago, where the show played to generous applause. "There have been many performances of your show that you would have loved," Mary wrote Ogden Nash. "Some of the audiences have been the best we've ever had—and responded to every line, every lyric. I just wish you had been with us last night when the cast, the stage crew, and the musicians gave John Boles and me a surprise party—and everyone did a take off of someone else's part in the show. . . . It was really fun and a *real* theater party."

But Mary was frequently ill in Chicago, and the pregnancy proved even more difficult than the one she'd had with Heller. Mary later claimed that she and Richard were delighted when they learned they were going to be parents again, but her violent illnesses forced the *Venus* tour to stop in Cincinnati. After four months on the road, Mary and Richard returned to New York, and Cheryl Crawford closed the show, since there was no one of equal star billing available to replace Mary.

The second Halliday child was expected in December, but Mary needed rest if she was going to carry the baby through to a normal

delivery. Shortly after her last performance in *One Touch of Venus* on May 12, Mary and Richard decided to visit Heller and Richard's mother at his grandmother's home in West Virginia. While they were there, Heller was severely bitten by a dog, and Mary reacted by going into a state of shock. Mary was rushed back to Manhattan, where the expected baby was stillborn, and a transfusion and penicillin were necessary to save her life. She remained hospitalized in critical condition for eight days, and it took several weeks for her to recover her strength and regain full composure. During her recovery she and Richard decided to buy a 175-year-old saltbox house outside Norwalk, Connecticut, an hour's drive from New York City. "We wanted Heller to grow up in the country," Mary said. The Hallidays also bought Richard's mother a smaller home near theirs. "For the next few years Larry, Richard, and I had a checkered career," Mary wrote in her memoirs. "There were moments of great joy and utter sorrow, tensions, times when we didn't speak, misunderstandings, anger, reconciliation, tears, everything."

For Richard, half of what he had set out to do had been accomplished: Mary was an established Broadway star. "The public is appreciating the richly exciting talent and personality of my wife," he said. But he was determined that Mary would grow as an artist. "I'll never completely change you," he told his wife. "You'll never actually be anything but a Texas hillbilly." He loved Mary's sparkle, her self-deprecating humor, and especially her incredible talent, yet he pushed her to expand and stretch her abilities beyond their natural limits. Unlike the effervescent Mary who found bliss in tranquility, Richard operated better under stress. "Theater people not only learn to live with emotional stress," he contended, "many of them depend on it for the extra drive and stamina they need." With that as his credo, Richard was resolute about steering Mary to her limit. "He believed in me far more than I did," Mary said. "Everything centered on me, and Richard showed me unbelievable thoughtfulness." Yet there were rocky times in their marriage and decisions that Mary regretted. Other decisions she viewed with mixed emotions. Two of those lay just ahead.

CHAPTER 5

Growing Pains

By 1945, Mary was receiving offers for starring roles from any number of Broadway and Hollywood producers. She had turned down the lead in *Sadie Thompson,* after Ethel Merman dropped out of the musical, feeling that the part of a reformed hooker was not for her. Besides, Mary had already experienced one failure in a Vernon Duke–Howard Dietz show, and she knew that Merman had dropped out of *Sadie Thompson* because all was not well with the production. June Havoc eventually played Sadie, but the musical opened in November 1944 to more unfavorable than favorable reviews and closed after sixty performances.

There was also talk that Mary would star in a Warner Bros. screen biography of dancer Marilyn Miller, with whom she was often compared in her early career, but that part ultimately went to blonde film star June Haver, whom Twentieth Century-Fox had groomed as a cover for the studio's biggest money-maker, Betty Grable.

In the summer of 1945, Mary and Richard decided after much deliberation that *Lute Song,* a play with music, would be the star's next Broadway vehicle. Written by Sidney Howard and Will Irwin and based on the fifteenth-century Chinese drama *Pi-Pa-Ki* by Kao-Tong-Kia, the show was an unusual choice for Mary. She would be playing the haunting heroine in a classic Chinese fantasy, a devoted

young bride who begs to save her husband's parents from starvation and sells her hair to give them a proper burial. When asked years later what it was about *Lute Song* that appealed to her, Mary answered succinctly, "Not much." Then she added, "That part scared me out of my wits. But it was a challenge, and Richard was all for my having all these challenges. We thought about it for a long time, and finally I got mad at myself. I thought, 'Well, I'm not *that* dumb. I got by with Venus; I can do this.' Besides it was a lovely movement part."

Up to that point, Mary had been viewed strictly as a musical comedy star, but the art-conscious Richard felt that she had the capacity to develop into a dramatic actress as well, on a level with Helen Hayes, Katharine Cornell, and Gertrude Lawrence. In the beginning Mary fought the notion, but Richard remained persistent. To Mary, movement was the beginning of any part she played. "If I know how I'm going to walk and how I'll stand onstage," she said, "then the part comes." For three months before *Lute Song* went into rehearsal, she attended ballet classes and worked twice a day with Yeichi Nimura, the show's great Japanese choreographer, on Chinese movements. "We started with the hands," she said. "The exercises I had to do were with each finger, then the whole hand." Nimura also taught Mary how to walk and posture for the role. At home she watched herself in the mirror, perfecting the movements Nimura showed her. In addition, she went to an exercise class every day to stay in shape.

Shortly before rehearsals began on the show, Mary and Richard made a brief trip to California for her to recreate her "Daddy" number in Warner Bros.' *Night and Day*, a highly sanitized film biography of Broadway composer Cole Porter. In the movie Mary has a cute scene with actress Jane Wyman, in which she is shown as a chorus girl fresh out of Texas, discovered eating watermelon, and picked to sing "My Heart Belongs to Daddy" when Wyman begs off. Although the sequence is fabrication, the *New York Times'* Thomas Pryor said in his review that "the incomparable Mary Martin" delivered "as only she knows how to put that suggestive ballad over."

While the Hallidays were in Los Angeles, they got together with Bessie Mae Sue Ella and her husband, Jac Austin, who was in the Marine Corps at the time and stationed in Santa Barbara. When the two couples met in Beverly Hills, Mary and her childhood pal hugged and kissed. "We didn't fall down," Bessie Mae remembered, "she *pulled* me down on the floor in laughter." For the occasion, Bessie had bought a dress she thought was pretty, but Mary didn't like it as well as some she had. So she had her friend select one of her designer gowns to wear, and Mary got down on the floor and basted up the hem, since she was taller than Bessie Mae. Then she decided to do Bessie's hair. "I thought it looked kind of funny when she got through," Bessie Mae said, "but Mary put a green orchid that Arthur Schwartz had sent her in my hair." Later in the evening when they ran into Schwartz, Mary exclaimed, "Oh, Arthur, I thank you so for this beautiful green orchid. If you hadn't sent it, I wouldn't have had anything to put in Bessie's hair!"

That was the night Bessie Mae and Jac first met Richard. "He was so sophisticated and so knowledgeable that I wondered how he and Mary were drawn to each other," Bessie Mae said later. "He was from a completely different world from hers. She had such admiration for him, and he had such love for her. Jac and I were both crazy about him." On the drive over to Jean Arthur's house, Bessie Mae and Mary chattered all the way. Bessie eventually whispered, "Mary, I like Richard." Richard overheard the comment and interrupted his wife's talk long enough to say, "I don't wear well." Yet through the years Bessie Mae continued to hold that Richard wore extremely well, and she appreciated the fact that he did "absolutely everything" for Mary and had awakened higher aspirations in her friend than Mary had for herself. The star often told Bessie, "Richard saw something in me I didn't know I had."

The longer Mary and Bessie Mae chatted, the thicker Mary's Texas accent became. Finally, Richard said, "Mary, if you don't stop talking like Bessie, I'm going to send Bessie home!" Even in advanced years, whenever Mary was in Texas or with friends from home, her cultivated stage voice disappeared and her Texas twang returned.

"I just adore the way Bessie talks," Mary said, "and I'd get down in Texas and be talking the same way within an hour."

Rehearsals for *Lute Song* began early in October in the ballroom of the Beaux Arts Building at Sixty-seventh Street and Central Park West. John Houseman, who had worked with Orson Welles in the highly acclaimed Mercury Theatre during the late 1930s, directed the show, his first theater work after a stint as a Hollywood producer. Mary found Houseman difficult. "He was from another school," she said. "As a person I adored him, but he had worked so long with repertory theater, where they can change whatever they do. So he'd set something one way and the next day he'd change it to another way. Every time something got set in our heads he would change it. He'd suddenly say, 'No, come in from the other side.' That was difficult for everybody. The dancers went out of their minds."

Houseman claimed that the nervousness in the company came from the Hallidays. "As a couple they were fretful and insecure," the director said, "constantly wondering whether Mary should be doing the show at all, till I began to avoid conversations with them, which I found demoralizing." In sharp contrast, Mary alone proved a "quick, receptive, hard-working, intelligent and flexible" performer, according to Houseman, in everything except her own songs, about which she had strong opinions. "In all else I found her most willing to adapt herself to a style of performance that was utterly different from anything she had ever done before," the director said.

Yeichi Nimura continued to work privately with Mary on her hand gestures and taught her long, liquid movements that suited the Oriental robes she wore in the production. During the planning Mary had wigs made for the role of Tchao-Ou-Niang, but in rehearsals she decided to dye her own hair coal-black and use just a matching fall, which she could later take off during the show's haircutting scene. She also shaved off her eyebrows to effect a more convincing Oriental look. "I must say," she confessed, "when they came back in they were rather sparse."

Throughout the preparations for *Lute Song*, the major problem centered on how to achieve a proper balance between drama and music. Even during out-of-town tryouts, Houseman never seemed entirely clear where the classical elements should yield to the musical aspect. "That was very challenging," the director said. The most critical moment came with Mary's big musical number, which was the climax of the first act, where the young wife stands in the marketplace and offers her hair for sale. "It was a good number," Houseman said, "and Mary gave it all she had—and it wasn't working."

For *Lute Song*'s score, producer Michael Meyerberg chose not an established musical comedy composer but Raymond Scott, a successful instrumental arranger. The lyrics were written by Bernard Hanighen, who had never done a Broadway show before. If the production was to work, a haunting mood and fluid tempo had to be established that was vastly different from the normal commercial musical. Much of the rehearsal for Mary's songs took place separately, sometimes in her home, with the composer at the piano.

To play Mary's husband in the show, Meyerberg had selected a balding, dynamic young performer of Russian-Chinese origin. The producer had seen him strumming a guitar and singing gypsy songs in a nightclub. His name was Yul Brynner, and *Lute Song* marked the future star's Broadway debut. "Neither the Hallidays nor Scott was enthusiastic about his voice, which was untrained and had a wavering pitch," Houseman said. "But he satisfied all other requirements, a sexy, exotic leading man with interesting speech and a vaguely Oriental look."

Brynner's part was actually larger than Mary's, yet the actor claimed that *Lute Song* was not a happy experience for him. "I did not like my part at all," he said. "I was playing a young lover and, like all the young lovers that I have had to play, he was badly written. He was a very flimsy young man and very weak. I had no respect for him as a human being. So it was extremely difficult for me to do him justice as an actor. And, of course, I had no skill as an actor— none at all." At the time Brynner was shy on stage and tried to hide his shyness by using a trick he'd learned while performing earlier. "I went back to what I knew of pantomime," he said, "and I

hid behind a very stylized performance that many people wrongly remember as quite remarkable, although it was not. Every performance of that show was painful for me and I hated my acting. I despised myself for playing such a weak character, and there I was stuck in a role I was ashamed of."

Yet Brynner projected special warmth and a male appeal that audiences hadn't seen before and found touching. Mary remembered the actor onstage as "grace itself, pure poetry." He wore a black toupee in *Lute Song* to make him look more Oriental and was absolutely liquid when he walked. "Yul Brynner moved more beautifully than anyone I've ever seen onstage," Mary said. "His movement with me was like water; the two of us moved right together." Although Brynner remembered his costar's enormous energy and shining stage presence, he did not think the role in *Lute Song* was a good one for her. "The show required a moody, sad creature, who is left behind and has to sell her hair," the actor said. "It was not the best vehicle for Mary at all."

During the final week of rehearsals, Robert Edmond Jones's unit set and lavish costumes were brought in. Jones was then the dean of Broadway designers, and his work on *Lute Song* stands as his final crowning glory. The show required many scenes varying from utter simplicity to overwhelming opulence. Despite failing health, Jones worked fourteen months designing the stage picture and the hundreds of costumes that were needed for the production. The set, which had beautiful hand-painted panels that moved in and out, was a thing of glowing beauty, while the costumes were dazzling in a Chinese style that Houseman claimed was "authentic in spirit if not always in historical detail." It added up to an extraordinary achievement in design, reinforcing the aesthetic and theatrical unity Houseman was striving for, but unfortunately Jones's mastery was not enough to carry the play, which continued to show enormous weaknesses.

With Robert Edmond Jones's set and costumes proving the extraordinary aspect of *Lute Song*, the Hallidays suddenly grew worried that Mary might not stand out and look her chic, adorable self in the production. Without consulting anyone, they asked the celebrated

Russian designer Valentina to redo her costumes in a more becoming style. "This act of treachery was not revealed until the final dress parade," Houseman said, "and it caused deep offense and unhappiness." Critics later sneered at Mary's character, supposedly reduced to beggary, wearing a gorgeous white silk gown designed by Valentina.

In this Chinese classic, the male lead ultimately finds himself torn between his love for his faithful country wife, whom he had mistakenly believed to be dead, and his feelings for the Princess, who has elevated him to a high rank at the Imperial Court. The Hallidays came to believe that it was improper for a star of Mary's magnitude to share her leading man. Richard harassed Michael Meyerberg until the producer agreed to change the ending, so that the Princess, amid popular rejoicing, generously returns her lover to his wife. Playwright Will Irwin protested the bowdlerized version of his script, and Houseman supported him. "Michael wavered," the director recalled. "But he was already more than $100,000 in the hole, and the Hallidays were adamant. So that's how we finally played it."

Before *Lute Song* opened in New York, the show went on the road for a seven-week tryout period in New Haven, Boston, and Philadelphia. The company arrived in New Haven on a Monday, and the set was loaded into the Shubert Theater, near the Taft Hotel, where the performers were housed. After the first run-through, Richard, backed by Raymond Scott and Bernard Hanighen, complained that Mary's big moment at the close of the first act still was not working. She was singing in the dark, and Richard insisted that to put the song over she needed a spotlight on her. Otherwise the whole number might as well be thrown out. "There was an arc in the theater," Houseman remembered, "and I agreed to let them try it—for that one number." The light was rigged, and on the next try the song worked far better. "Secure in the nimbus of light that followed her around the set, then slowly closed in on her till it formed a bright halo around her pale, tear-stained face," Houseman recalled, Mary raised her arms and loosened her long, black fall. With a sudden flash of the shears, she let the fall drop into darkness as

the song came to a close. Mary at last was able to make a dramatic climax of the moment that drew approval from onlookers.

All seemed satisfied with the change except Robert Edmond Jones, who had designed the lighting for the production, as well as its sets and costumes. "That's not my lighting," Jones grumbled. Houseman tried to explain to the designer that, since this was a musical number, the consensus was that Mary needed a spotlight to make it effective. "Not on my set!" Jones bellowed, and he darted up the aisle in a huff muttering "vulgarity." Houseman followed him into the lobby and tried to explain the rationale behind the adjustment, but Jones merely looked at the director in a reproachful way. "I realized there were tears in his eyes," Houseman said. "Not on my set!" Jones repeated. Then the designer turned and walked out of the theater and took the next train back to Manhattan. "I called him in New York," Houseman said, "but he wouldn't accept my calls."

Mary was still not comfortable in the role of the Chinese wife and not at all sure she should be doing the play. "I can't go into New York with this," she said. "I'll go on to Philadelphia, since it's booked there, but then you must get someone else." Playwright Thornton Wilder saw the show in New Haven and came up to Mary and Richard's hotel room afterward. "I'm not right for this," Mary told Wilder as she broke into tears. "You are, if you'll forget that you're from Texas," the distinguished playwright said. "Don't even have that in your head. Remember that you were born in China." And he proceeded to give Mary a two-hour lecture on concentration. "It was like Gabriel coming down," she said. "By the time we opened in Philadelphia I'd gotten the part into my head, and I never got it out until we had finished."

In Boston the director tried hard to get rid of a young actress Mary had met in Chicago when she was on tour with *One Touch of Venus*. At Mary's request, the girl had been cast in *Lute Song* as the Princess's flower-maiden. Houseman remembered the novice as "a pink-cheeked, attractive but awkward and amateurish virgin by the name of Nancy Davis." (Later, of course, she married actor Ronald

Reagan and became the country's First Lady.) Mary found out that Houseman was thinking of firing Nancy and intervened to save her job.

Since *Lute Song* received favorable notices in Boston and was doing good business, Houseman decided after the first week to freeze the show. He returned to New York, leaving an assistant in charge. The director had no sooner reached Manhattan than he received a frantic call from his assistant saying that all hell had broken loose in Boston. Houseman took the next train back, arrived at dawn, had breakfast with his assistant, talked to the stage manager, and then conferred with Mary and Richard. "It seems that the fiend that had lain dormant inside Michael Meyerberg had finally broken loose," Houseman said. The producer had been sick when the director left Boston and was spending a few days in the hospital. "Within two hours of my departure he had leapt out of his hospital bed, called the entire company to rehearsal," Houseman said, and "began to restage the entire production of *Lute Song*, beginning with Scene One. The cast had been too stunned to object."

Houseman went to the theater expecting a heated confrontation. The cast and crew were assembled and waited nervously for Meyerberg to show up. Then word reached them that the producer had suffered a relapse and was again confined to his bed. "He stayed there, incommunicado, over the weekend," Houseman recalled, "emerged the following Monday, visited the theater that night, and declared himself delighted with the show. No word was ever spoken—by me or by him—about his incomprehensible foray. But I took care to remain in residence for the rest of our Boston and Philadelphia runs."

Few changes took place in Philadelphia, although Mary and the songwriters continued to polish her numbers. The actress did have one suggestion that she wanted to make, but she hesitated to speak to Houseman about it since there had been so many adjustments already. When she mentioned her reluctance to find further fault to Lena, her maid, Lena saw fit to give Mary a stern talking to. "You're a star now," the maid said, "and you got to act like a

star. The show isn't right and you got to speak up and say so." Mary went to Houseman, who agreed to make the change she wanted.

Lute Song opened at the Plymouth Theatre in New York on February 6, 1946. Critics praised Mary for her courage in taking on such an improbable part and greeted Yul Brynner as a promising newcomer, but it was the beauty and delicacy of Robert Edmond Jones's sets and costumes that drew the major acclaim. "Visually, *Lute Song* is one of the most exquisite and exciting things I have ever seen upon a stage," wrote John Chapman of the *Daily News*. Yet the show itself seemed like a pose. "Good taste abounds," Vernon Rice wrote in the *New York Post*, "Pageantry, mood, and atmosphere are there, too. But over it all is the shroud of dullness." None of the reviewers were much impressed with the music, although most said that Mary sang the songs persuasively—particularly "Mountain High, Valley Low." Lewis Nichols said in the *New York Times* that the show had "many and distinctive virtues" and deserved respect. But respect did not result in lines at the box office, and *Lute Song* did no better than acceptable business in New York for about five months.

Nonetheless, there was a gala party for the cast at Sardi's after the opening night performance, and Mary felt satisfied that she had expanded her creative horizons. "In *Lute Song* I sure learned plenty about being dramatic," she said. Undoubtedly, it had been a risk for her to star in such an exotic, unorthodox piece, and she had risen to the challenge.

Yet life in the Halliday home showed no improvement during the run of the show—at least not for Larry when he was home from boarding school. The one time Mary and Richard and the two children were likely to be together was on Sunday evenings for dinner, and Richard usually turned that into torture for Larry and four-year-old Heller. "By five o'clock he was shit-faced," an adult Larry maintained. "By six-thirty he was shit-faced *and mean*. At the table he would lecture us about proper manners. 'No elbows on the table,' he'd snap. 'Eat with your mouth closed. Your fork goes in your left hand, the knife in your right. No talking at the table.' He tormented us with ridiculous head games. He would ask questions just to try to catch us contradicting ourselves so he could berate

us." Larry contended that Richard was verbally abusive—never violent, just constantly picking on Heller and him.

Mary slept most of the day when she had no matinee performance, getting up around four o'clock in the afternoon to get ready to go to the theater. She ate a light supper at home before leaving and on matinee days had the 21 Club send over her dinner between shows. After the Hallidays moved to Connecticut, Richard drove Mary to the theater along the Merritt Parkway and worked in the apartment that the couple leased in the Hampshire House, overlooking Central Park, while his wife performed. After the show Richard drove Mary back to Connecticut, except on Tuesdays and Fridays, the nights before she had matinees, when they stayed at their place in New York.

Lute Song was the first time Heller saw her mother on the stage, and Mary rather hoped that her daughter would decide she wanted a theatrical career for herself. Mary never became altogether secure in her Oriental role and said she could have played the part better a decade later, since by then she knew more about acting. Yul Brynner claimed that the show was not truly successful until it went on the road with German actress Dolly Haas replacing Mary in the lead. "Dolly Haas understood the part," Brynner said. "She had an affinity for it, and the play immediately improved. It wasn't at all that Dolly was a better actress. She was just better casting for the part than Mary." Even Mary admitted that *Lute Song* benefited from Dolly Haas's performance. "Dolly was really an honest-to-gosh actress," Mary said.

In Chicago particularly, the critics were highly enthusiastic about the play, and Brynner had girls in audiences there swooning over him. "I loved the part," Haas said. "*Lute Song* was actually a very primitive story, very simple, but very emotional and very lyrical. I love eastern women, the way they move and the way they dress." Since Haas had only six days to rehearse the role and John Houseman wasn't available to work with her, only the stage manager, Mary gave her replacement some pointers. "There are certain colleagues that are just not to be believed," the German actress said, "and

that darling, beautiful Mary Martin was one of them. She was so encouraging and such a dear human being."

Lute Song closed in New York after 142 performances. By then Mary was already committed to do *Pacific 1860* in London, an operetta that Noel Coward had written especially for her. Richard wasn't thrilled about the project and maintained that they should hear the score and read the script before his wife agreed to star in the show. But Mary was eager to see England and thrilled at the prospect of working with a man of Noel Coward's stature. So in September 1946, Mary, Richard, and Heller sailed for England aboard the *Queen Mary*, while Larry was placed under the supervision of Richard's mother.

Coward met the Hallidays in Southampton with the distressing news that a permit to repair the war damage on the Theatre Royal in Drury Lane, where *Pacific 1860* was booked, had unexpectedly been refused. Rehearsals would have to be postponed for a month, and the show was not scheduled to open until December 19. In London the Hallidays checked into the Savoy Hotel, and Mary and Richard soon heard the songs Coward had written for the show in the composer's mews house. "I thought every song he wrote was the most divine thing in the world," Mary said, "but I kept wondering who was going to sing them. They certainly didn't sound like me." Mary's part in *Pacific 1860* was that of an opera singer, Mme. Elena Salvador, and required her to use her high soprano voice. She also had to learn to sing in what Mary called "English" English, which meant that Coward had to spend hours teaching her the clipped, quick enunciation that London audiences were used to. During her first evening in the composer's home, Mary also met her leading man, Graham Payn, a graceful, easy-going young fellow from South Africa who was Coward's boyfriend.

Before rehearsals began the playwright took Mary and Richard to see Laurence Olivier in *King Lear* on the stage, and afterward Coward, Graham Payn, and the Hallidays had dinner with Olivier and his wife, actress Vivien Leigh. In mid-October, Mary spent a week in bed with a sore throat, but she recovered in time to travel

to Paris with Coward and Payn toward the end of the month. Early in November, rehearsals started on *Pacific 1860* with the playwright directing a company of nearly a hundred people. Almost from the beginning, things went wrong with the romantic operetta. The theater was freezing cold, since the heat wasn't working yet, and the hammering of carpenters and electricians constantly interrupted the rehearsal onstage.

Coward was not long on patience when dealing with people, hated any kind of self-indulgence, and could be vicious when provoked. Richard had perhaps even less patience and could be downright nasty. There was trouble between the two men from the outset. The main song Coward had written for Mary was "Alice Is at It Again." As Mary remembered the number, "Alice was really *at* it, with the birds and bees," and she didn't think it proper for a genteel lass from Texas to make her London debut singing that kind of salacious song. "I knew it was funny, terribly funny," Mary recalled in her memoirs, "and now I know that I should have sung it. It would have stopped the show every night." But she refused, and Coward agreed to write her a replacement. At that point the playwright felt charitable toward his star, even though her demands in cables from New York had irritated him. He found Mary quick and knowledgeable about her work. "She is the only star I have ever worked with who has a real sense of the balance of the show," Coward wrote in his diary. "She is generous about everyone else in the company and never tries to snatch."

The first big fight between the two occurred when designer Gladys Calthrop made a huge picture hat for Mary to wear in the show's opening scene. The hat tied in a bow under the chin, and Mary absolutely hated it. Richard flatly told Coward that his wife wouldn't wear something so unbecoming, arguing that her face was too small and "just vanished" in such a big hat. Coward replied that Calthrop, a long-time friend, knew a great deal more about the clothes of the 1860s than the Hallidays did, and from that point on things went downhill. When Calthrop and the playwright came to Mary's dressing room to attempt to persuade her at least to wear a wig that was appropriate for the period, Richard, who

Coward claimed had been drinking, started shrieking abuse at the designer and called her a bitch. "It was one of the most hideous, hysterical, and vulgar exhibitions I have ever known in the theatre," the playwright said. "Mary remained quiet but, with one spurt of temper, declared that she would never wear a hat, never, never, never."

Coward ultimately mandated that if Mary didn't wear the bonnet with the bow she would not set foot on the stage on opening night. Furthermore, he threatened to tell the press that the reason his show didn't open was that Mary Martin was "stubborn and impossible." Mary said, "We were almost hitting each other." Finally, she agreed to wear the hat but not the large organdy bow. "I had the bow removed," she remembered, "and we never spoke again for two years."

The star admitted later that she learned a lot about stagecraft doing *Pacific 1860*, even though the part was wholly foreign to her. "I was playing an opera singer who sang in eight languages, and of course I couldn't even speak 'English' English," Mary said. She was supposed to get angry with her manager in the show and hit him. "I couldn't do it," Mary said. "I just adored this man. He was just darling." But Coward insisted that the scene where she got angry needed a display of violence. "He kept rehearsing that moment and rehearsing it," Mary said, "and I finally got so mad at Noel that I hit the man playing my manager so hard I almost knocked his head off. Then I started crying and couldn't stop." Coward eventually showed her how to hit an actor without hurting him. "It was he who taught me two of the most important techniques of acting," Mary said: "first, how to really let go onstage; second, how to express emotion without feeling it so much that it absolutely destroys you."

The star dyed her hair red for Coward's operetta but continued to be unhappy with her songs, feeling that they were written in an old-fashioned operetta style. She found the show rather flat. "*Pacific 1860* sounded like a telephone number," Mary jested later. Meanwhile, the playwright grew worried that his show was going to be a "rousing flop." Early in the rehearsals Coward concluded that the fundamental problem with the show was that "Mary, charming

and sweet as she is, knows nothing about Elena, never has and never will, and that although she has a delicious personality, she cannot sing. She is crammed with talent but she is still too 'little' to play sophisticated parts." Coward's attitude toward Mary became increasingly rude, and he positively hated Richard. While the show was in rehearsal, the playwright's friend Hugh "Binkie" Beaumont informed Noel that Richard had a poisoned foot, to which Coward retorted that "some of his motives must have got into his socks."

As rehearsals progressed, the playwright redid Mary's first scene in the show. He spent an hour rehearsing her in it alone, eventually convincing his star that she must "play it full out for comedy." Mary finally did as she was directed, and Coward said, "The difference was amazing. If only she had done it before." Yet some of the playwright-director's friends accused him of encasing Mary in a straightjacket of his own determination and crushing her personality with his dictates. Mary remained edgy but improved, yet she still did not perform to Coward's complete satisfaction.

The Theatre Royal, England's oldest theater, had been bombed in 1940, and *Pacific 1860* would mark its reopening after the Second World War. Seats were put back into the auditorium only three days before Mary made her London debut. Plans for a full week of dress rehearsals on *Pacific 1860* had to be abandoned in order to get the theater ready, and it was not possible for the show to try out somewhere other than London since the provincial houses had already begun their season.

Pacific 1860 opened on a freezing night during Christmas season, 1946, and brought out the cream of London society, as well as fans who had spent thirty-six hours waiting in line to buy tickets for the unreserved seats. Mary won a warm ovation from the first-night audience, but Coward's operetta, despite a lavish production, was not well received by the critics, who called it dated, a thin piece of nostalgia reminiscent of *Bittersweet*, *The Chocolate Soldier*, and *The Desert Song*. "Not one good notice," the playwright wrote in his diary, "the majority being frankly vile." The word the *New York Times* had from London was that *Pacific 1860* failed "to add up to an entertaining evening." Yet Mary proved a real trouper and behaved superbly

despite the disappointing notices. She seemed artificial singing Coward's pale score, whereas her attempt at a British accent made her sound stilted. Nonetheless, the star attended the opening night party and was gracious and charming. Even Noel Coward noted that Mary's behavior throughout a difficult evening was "absolutely impeccable."

The second performance of the show, according to the playwright, "couldn't have gone worse. Nothing got any applause and the theatre was icy." Coward had drinks with Mary and Richard the following Sunday and confided in his diary that they were "very sweet." After the December 17 matinee, where the theater was only half-full and the audience proved unresponsive, Coward discussed reconstructing the musical's first act, then rebelled and decided that "if the critics and the public don't like the show, that's their affair."

While the playwright blistered under the cool reception of *Pacific 1860*, Mary waxed unbridled enthusiasm about the opening to friends in New York. "It was like a real dream come true," she wrote Ogden Nash. "There just is something about the Drury Lane Theatre that is different and exciting. And there certainly is something about Noel Coward that no other theatre-man has. And there certainly is something very exciting when you hear those gallery gods—way, way up there about six floors above you—shouting your name and their approval. And a reception afterwards given by the directors of the theatre in the big bar that runs the full width of the building—and everyone getting up, drinking toasts, and making speeches. And meeting people who had flown over from Sweden and Paris just for the opening."

But Mary admitted later that she was miscast as a crinolined diva in hoop skirts and felt that her costar, Graham Payn, had been favored by Coward more than she was. Although the advance ticket sales for *Pacific 1860* had been excellent, attendance fell off after the first few weeks. Heller, who was taking ballet lessons at Sadler's Wells during her stay in London, saw her mother's show with her father. At the point where the opera singer and her younger lover are getting together romantically on a mythical island in the South Seas, the four-year-old stood at her seat and exclaimed, "Doesn't

Mummy remember she's married to Daddy?" The audience sitting around her howled with laughter.

A royal performance was given for the King and Queen and Princess Margaret on January 23. (Princess Elizabeth was ill.) Coward sent flowers to Mary with a courteous note and went to her dressing room to wish her luck before the show. "She never mentioned the flowers," he said, "and was extremely chilly. The show went well but Mary was not good." The next night Mary made a speech to the company, thanking them for giving such a good performance for the King and Queen. "The company received this incredibly naïve impertinence in bewildered silence," the peeved playwright wrote in his diary.

Mary continued to perform doggedly in *Pacific 1860* for four months, but Coward persisted in his claim that she had been a disappointment. "Her charm and personality are not enough to put her over in a big theatre," he said. "She should be crooning through a microphone." A month into *Pacific 1860*'s run, the playwright still insisted that Mary and Richard were "not behaving well." On March 13, 1947, Coward went to see the show, after returning from a brief trip to New York, and recorded in his diary, "Company gave excellent performances. Mary awful. Fear that show, seen with fresh eyes, really is rather a bore." Audiences seemed glumly unmoved by his writing, and a critic for *The New Yorker* maintained that "the whole show has a curiously amateur flavor." When it closed, the production had lost 28,000 pounds.

On April 17, Winston Churchill gave a farewell party for the Hallidays, at which Coward put in a dutiful appearance. "Thank God they are leaving tomorrow," he confided to his diary. The playwright held Richard responsible for most of the trouble he had had with Mary, saying it was "dreadfully awkward and all over nothing." Of Richard he wrote, "He is a pathological case and is twisted with strange jealousies. I wish the silly ass were at the bottom of the sea."

On April 26 the Hallidays returned to New York on board the USS *America*, arriving two days late because of stormy weather at sea. Mary had loved the British audiences, but continued to harbor

remorse over the rows with Coward. "For two years we didn't speak at all," she said, "and I cried every night for those two years. Richard would hear me, and he'd say, 'You're crying because of Noel Coward, aren't you?'" Shortly after her return from London, Mary told costume designer Lucinda Ballard that she'd had a horrible experience in England. "Noel was the great darling of the world as far as I was concerned," Ballard said. "I just couldn't believe that something so wrong had happened. But apparently Noel had bawled Mary out in front of everybody onstage."

For Coward, the rehearsals of *Pacific 1860* ranked among the unhappiest experiences he'd had in the theater. Years later, director Joshua Logan remembered being shocked when he, Anita Loos, and Helen Hayes dined with Noel Coward at Club 21 soon after Mary's London debut. "She's not very good, you know," the playwright had said of the star he'd fought with while preparing *Pacific 1860*. "She hasn't much talent." Logan recalled that he was so bowled over by Coward's comment that he couldn't look at Hayes, who knew Mary and admired her ability. After the British playwright left the table, the three Americans agreed that if Mary Martin had not been a success, the trouble must have rested with *Pacific 1860*. They knew that Elia Kazan was so keen on Mary's talent that he had even suggested her for the role of Blanche DuBois in the original production of *A Streetcar Named Desire*, although the director admitted that it was "a reach in the dark toward a woman I admired." Perhaps wisely, Kazan's unusual casting thought struck "no chord of affirmative response" from *Streetcar*'s playwright, Tennessee Williams, or its producer, Irene Selznick. Yet Mary could feel validated by the nod.

CHAPTER 6

Stalwart Trouper

The Hallidays had seen Ethel Merman in *Annie Get Your Gun* at an actor's benefit on a Sunday evening shortly before they left for England. The Irving Berlin musical, based on the life and career of midwestern sharpshooter Annie Oakley, had received rave notices from the New York critics and proved a delight to capacity audiences. When Mary and Richard returned to their apartment after seeing the show, they were ecstatic. "Mary, dear," Richard said to his wife with a wry smile, as he handed her a knife, "cut your throat. This is exactly the kind of show we've dreamed about for you." Mary refused the knife and told her husband firmly, "I'm going to play that role someday." She knew immediately that Annie was ideal for her and claimed later that the part was the *real* her. She said to Richard, "I won't ever do the show in New York, but I'd love to do it on the road. I love the road, and I don't see any reason why I can't take that show on a national tour. Merman was great, but I won't play Annie anything like she does."

Until Mary did *Annie Get Your Gun*, she was viewed by Broadway denizens either as the sex kitten who warbled "My Heart Belongs to Daddy" in a short fur coat or as the stunning, amusing love goddess of *One Touch of Venus*. Mary knew that the Berlin show, with its rich score and hillbilly sharpshooter, could change her image and

broaden her reputation. So she and Richard proposed to Richard Rodgers and Oscar Hammerstein II, the producers of *Annie Get Your Gun*, that she head the production on a long tour across the country. But Mary cautioned from the outset that she would only do the show if she could audition for it.

One weekend at author Edna Ferber's house, Mary was prevailed upon to sing a few songs after dinner. Rodgers and Hammerstein, Irving Berlin, and director Joshua Logan were among Ferber's guests, and to their surprise the two songs Mary chose to sing were "Doin' What Comes Natur'lly" and "You Can't Get a Man with a Gun," both big numbers from *Annie Get Your Gun*. She bellowed them out in a rowdy hillbilly style that nobody in New York had heard from her before. "What an explosion there was!" Logan remembered. "The walls reverberated." When she finished, Mary asked, "Do you think I'm too demure?" Berlin, Logan, Rodgers, and Hammerstein readily confessed their surprise at how raucous she could be. "I used to be a hillbilly singer," Mary told them. "I was the Crazy Girl at the Crazy Water Crystals Hotel in Texas."

While Mary was in London doing *Pacific 1860*, she received a cable from Rodgers and Hammerstein asking if she would stay in England and star in the London production of *Annie Get Your Gun*. By then the friction between the Hallidays and Noel Coward had soured Mary on England and she was homesick. Richard got *Annie*'s producers on the telephone that evening, and Mary told them, "No, I won't do the show in London, but I'd like to come back and do it all over the United States. I'd like to open in Dallas, which is near my hometown of Weatherford." Rodgers and Hammerstein voiced surprise since most Broadway stars of Mary's standing, Merman included, hated lengthy tours. The grind of traveling was punishing. "Let Dolores Gray play Annie in London," Mary told the show's producers. "She can sing the daylights out of the part, and let me come home and play it on the road."

In April 1947 an announcement was made that Mary Martin would star in an eleven-month national tour of *Annie Get Your Gun*, opening October 3 at the State Fair of Texas in Dallas. Mary told the press that she was looking forward to appearing in her home

state, remarking that it would be her first visit to Texas in nearly ten years. Five-year-old Heller would also be in the show's cast, playing the part of Nellie, Annie Oakley's kid sister. The tour would be one of the first times that a major musical comedy star went on the road in a part that somebody else had created and become identified with in New York.

That summer, Mary told Larry she was going on tour and asked him to join her. "There're a couple of small parts in the show," she said. "Heller's going to have one. I'd love to have you in it, too." Larry claimed that he went numb. "I had no aspiration to be onstage," he said. "Worse, the thought of being with Richard for a year on the road made me dumbstruck." The boy informed his mother that he really wanted to be a cowboy. "The thought had never entered my mind before," an adult Larry Hagman recalled, but he told Mary that he wanted to go back to Texas, live with his father, and become a cowboy.

Ben Hagman, Larry's father, had been a major in the American army during the Second World War and had spent a week or so behind the German lines during the Battle of the Bulge. Larry later described his father as "a two-fisted, drinking, good old Texas boy," who slept with a .45 under his pillow from the day he came home from the war. Since Larry had left Weatherford with his grandmother, Ben and his second wife had had a son, and they quickly agreed that it was probably best for Larry to be with them. So when school ended in 1947, Larry boarded a train bound for Texas.

Although Mary described her son as "all man, like his father," his peers in Weatherford initially viewed him with suspicion. "It was like entering a new world," Larry said. "I didn't look anything like a fifteen-year-old from Texas. I wore a Brooks Brothers suit and tie, had thick glasses, and my hair was done up as was stylish in New York, in a big wavy pompadour." The Texas kids made fun of him until school started again in the fall and Larry took up boxing.

That September, Mary began rehearsals on *Annie Get Your Gun*. Originally, the score was to have been written by Jerome Kern. The producers had succeeded in luring Kern away from Hollywood, and the distinguished composer had come to New York to work

with Herbert and Dorothy Fields, who were writing the musical's book and lyrics. But soon after Kern arrived in Manhattan, he collapsed on the street and died of a stroke. That's when Irving Berlin was brought into the project. Oscar Hammerstein and Richard Rodgers told their book writers, "We have the most wonderful idea, but it means that Dorothy cannot do the lyrics."

Since Berlin always wrote the words for his songs, Dorothy Fields, the daughter of Lew Fields of the comedy team Weber and Fields, graciously consented to limit her work to the show's book. "You just don't say that you want to do the lyrics if you can get Irving Berlin!" she said. "Dorothy had the most lovely nature," Lucinda Ballard, the production's costume designer, said. "Herbert was a pain in the neck and interfered with everything, but Dorothy was a dream and one of my favorite people." Irving Berlin spent a weekend thinking over Rodgers and Hammerstein's proposal, while the producers and their book writers nervously bit their nails. Then on Monday Berlin said, "Yes, I'll do it." As it turned out, *Annie Get Your Gun* was the greatest success the songwriter ever had.

Rodgers and Hammerstein made sure that no expense was spared on the national company of *Annie* and oversaw every detail. Both were perfectionists, yet each could be highly amusing. Rodgers, a natty dresser, was a rather cold, aloof person during production meetings and rehearsals and seemed the harder businessman of the two. Hammerstein was quieter and gentler, although many sensed that he was the force behind the team. "I really loved Oscar," Mary said. "He was like my father. But I loved Dick Rodgers, too. We all lived close together in Connecticut and became great friends."

Working with such powerhouses as Irving Berlin and Rodgers and Hammerstein, Richard Halliday was more restrained in his demands than usual. He was always on hand to represent Mary— to the point that a friend once commented, "You don't really know where Mary leaves off and Dick begins." Yet there were none of the outbursts on *Annie Get Your Gun* that had marred the Noel Coward experience. "*Annie Get Your Gun* was really such a happy show," Lucinda Ballard remembered. "Mary was absolutely enchanting, and Dick Halliday was all right then. I never knew anybody

who was or had been an agent that was really all right. But he was acceptable."

Joshua Logan, who had directed the show with Merman, was retained as stage director of *Annie*'s national company. A man of enormous energy and contagious enthusiasm, Logan approached his craft with the same meticulous care that Rodgers and Hammerstein exhibited. He understood a feed line and a laugh line and was adept at building up to the next laugh and making it work. "To stage the touring company and allow for the differences between Martin's and Merman's interpretation," Logan said, "I found myself making a change, albeit an almost infinitesimal change, in just about every line and phrase of the production. Only the very broad strokes and the actual tempo of the music remained the same." The director found Mary an engaging personality but a limited actress. "She could do certain things impeccably," Logan said, "but Merman was a much stronger actress. Still, I loved Mary Martin more."

As a college student at Princeton, Logan had dropped out of his senior year and gone to Russia to watch Konstantin Stanislavski's rehearsals. "I observed Stanislavski take these rather stiff, unpolished music students and force them to act," *Annie*'s director said. "When the music was played repeatedly, the young actors were able to shift their emotions as the music shifted. That impressed me deeply. I'm sure that's what started my whole directing career." Logan developed a rule in his shows that became known among his friends as "Logan's Law": before the final curtain fell, there must be discernible growth in the central character. If the curtain came down on a nobler or wiser protagonist, the director believed the audience would be satisfied and the show would be a success.

Annie Get Your Gun was a perfect example of Logan's philosophy. Annie and her future husband, Frank Butler, were constantly at each other's throats, since they were rivals in shooting matches. But Annie was in love with Frank and kept losing him because of her superior marksmanship. So Sitting Bull, the Sioux chief who adopted Annie in the musical, saw her miss a shot at a clay pigeon with a gun that had been tampered with. "That's good," Papa Bull

tells Annie. "Lose contest, win Frank. Win contest, lose Frank." Annie gets the idea and walks up for her next shot, with the orchestra playing "You Can't Get a Man with a Gun," misses the shot, and turns triumphantly to Papa Bull. "Before we know it she has Frank by the ears," Logan said.

Mary responded well to such strong direction. Sometimes Logan acted out things for her, overplaying the moment to help his actors get the point. He could be flamboyant, sometimes made impossible demands, but at his best he was masterful. Mary grasped quickly what Logan was getting at and followed his lead. "She was a bit younger and more romantic in the role that Ethel was," the director said, "so the show became much more of a boy-girl romance. Mary took a chance with this tour, but she was a smash hit in *Annie*. She was so enthusiastic and, of course, was always talented beyond compare."

Mary's biggest problem in *Annie Get Your Gun* was sustaining the loud singing the role required. In that regard, the trumpet-voiced Merman had the edge. Vocally, the score was tough and required unusual stamina from the star, who was onstage most of the time. Mary had to lower her voice for the songs, which ultimately caused her to lose her high notes. "I stripped all the gears in my throat belting the big songs," she said. "I don't know how many numbers there are in *Annie*, but it's just an unbelievable amount. That was the longest time I had to sing, ever, in the theater." Some of the keys had to be changed for her, and often the songs were done with a modified rhythm. Mary's rendition of "I Got Lost in His Arms" became more of a lovesick young girl's statement than Merman's version, and she moved about during the second chorus instead of sitting on the steps of the Wild West Show's wagon. Mary especially liked "Moonshine Lullaby," which she sang to the children and made sweeter than Merman did. Berlin came to many of the road company's rehearsals and looked on with approval. "He'd sit in the back and watch," Mary remembered, "but he never gave any opinion."

Lucinda Ballard had designed the costumes for the original production of *Annie*, and she did them again for the national tour. "Naturally I did research on Annie Oakley," the designer said,

"and she always wore the most boring shirtwaists and long skirts. So I had to invent Annie's costumes for the stage. To me a costume should help an actor feel the part as well as look the part." Ballard liked to talk to performers before she designed anything for them. "If somebody thinks that they look absolutely terrible in pink, or if it's unlucky to wear green, forget it. Because if an actor isn't happy with their costume, no matter how well it looks and how well it fits the story, that can ruin the effect "

Ballard knew that Mary and Noel Coward had fought over a hat in England, and she had been warned to be cautious. The designer invited Mary and Richard to have lunch with her at Club 21. "They both kept exclaiming how sweet I was to ask what Mary would like to wear in the show and how she felt about this, that, and the other," Ballard recalled. "They told me about the trouble over *Pacific 1860*, but they told the story quite differently from what I'd heard." Merman wore a broad-brimmed hat that framed her face with her sharpshooter's outfit in *Annie*, but Ballard designed a petite Stetson of leather with a brim that turned up on the sides for Mary. For some of the costumes there was practically no change, although Mary did ask that her ball gown be blue rather than white, which Merman wore, maintaining that blue would make her look more feminine. "And I didn't have to hide Mary's legs in the black velvet leotard the way I had Ethel's," the designer said. "Merman had really beautiful legs and feet, but they were too slim for her torso. . . . Anyway when we got through, Mary was quite happy with her clothes, and we became great friends. Mary was such fun in those days."

Annie Get Your Gun proved almost a perfect musical. The book was exceptionally strong and the songs were brilliant. The story was set in a mythic West and yet it became believably human. The characters seemed real, and the role of Annie Oakley fit Mary like a dream. She could use her Texas twang and effect a rough-hewn quality that audiences found adorable. "Ethel Merman wasn't a corny person," Mary said, "she wasn't a backwoods type at all. But it didn't matter when Merman did *Annie*. She did Annie Oakley like Merman, which had nothing to do with the part. I think of all

the things I did in the theater, *Annie Get Your Gun* was one of the three most enjoyable."

The day before the national company left for Dallas, Mary and her cast did the show for Merman and her company at the Imperial Theatre in New York. "That was a tough thing for Mary to do," said actor Tom Ewell, who was present for the occasion, "because *Annie Get Your Gun* was one of the biggest hits of Merman's career." Ewell was working for Rodgers and Hammerstein at the time in *John Loves Mary*, which the songwriters also produced, and the actor remembered the curtain call at the end of Mary's performance. "Merman, who had been sitting in the front row, went up on stage and hugged and kissed Mary," Ewell recalled. "Then the two of them sang 'There's No Business Like Show Business' together, which was one of the most exciting things I ever saw."

Three decades later, Ewell maintained that he had witnessed "one of the great performers of our time" in a show that had "every kind of detail lavishly attended to by its producers." Everything about the national company of *Annie Get Your Gun* was top-grade. "The costumes cost a fortune," the actor said, "and everything was the very top creme de la crème. I remember the terrific ovation that Mary's company received from that audience of theater people. It was a marvelous, magical moment." All Mary remembered of the performance was Merman sitting down front and clapping with white gloves on. "I could see you clapping and I could hear your laugh," she wrote her Broadway colleague. "But I wanted to shoot you. Why did you wear those white gloves?"

The national company arrived in Dallas early in October, and the sets were moved into the State Fair Auditorium. Mary and Richard came to Texas by train, arriving at Union Terminal, and stayed in a suite at the Baker Hotel downtown. Soon after she arrived, Mary received a call from Larry in Weatherford. Strained though their relationship was, Larry admitted that his mother gave him sensible advice. She told the boy that he should acquire his own wisdom, which would come from his own experiences. "She told me not to fear making mistakes," Larry remembered. "To take chances. Have

fun. Live. . . . She didn't tell me to be a great or successful actor. Nor did she tell me to be a good human being."

But Mary seemed more demanding of Heller, convinced that her daughter would opt for a career in the theater. Shortly after settling into her hotel suite in Texas, Mary and Heller paid a visit to Bessie Mae Sue Ella and her husband, Jac Austin, who by then had moved to Dallas. Mary was eager for Heller to show off what she had learned at Sadler Wells' ballet school, even though Heller preferred to play with the two Austin girls, about her age. "Mary was a great disciplinarian," Bessie Mae said, "not only of herself, but she expected her children and her dog to behave properly." So Mary took Heller aside and told her, "These are my close friends and you must dance for them." Jac put some appropriate music on the phonograph, and Heller danced. "It was agony," Bessie Mae recalled. "Heller was so tense that she was not dancing as well as she was capable of doing, and Mary was tense that Heller wasn't performing properly. We were all nervous. It was just a complete fiasco. Finally Heller ended in tears and ran into my daughters' room and cried."

Mary realized that she was wrong in forcing Heller to perform and promised Bessie, "As long as I live I will never again impose my will on *anyone*. But I can't understand a child who doesn't want to get up and perform." Bessie sensed then that a life on the stage was not what Heller wanted. Mary continued to push the idea, however. She often came into Heller's room at night and encouraged her daughter to dance with her. "We would dance to such music as *Swan Lake*," the girl remembered. "I always insisted that Mummy play the part of the man."

Months before the *Annie Get Your Gun* company arrived in Dallas, R. L. Thornton, the Fair's president, had hailed the show as "the greatest musical attraction ever presented by the State Fair of Texas." Thornton assured the public that the national company of *Annie* would be no weak copy of the Broadway production but a stellar recreation on the highest professional level. When Irving Berlin came for the opening in Texas, he confirmed Thornton's claim. "Rodgers and Hammerstein have produced the show as carefully as for a New York opening," the composer told the Dallas press.

A throng of celebrities were on hand for the festivities sur-
rounding the premiere: Rodgers and Hammerstein; Dorothy and
Herbert Fields; Joshua Logan; Lucinda Ballard; Helen Tamiris,
Annie's choreographer; and Jo Mielziner, the production's set designer,
among others. The lobby of the State Fair Auditorium was swathed
like a fall harvest for the opening, and busloads of people came
from Weatherford, Fort Worth, and Houston. Mary was excited that
her sister Jerry, Bessie Mae Sue Ella, Billie Jones, her family's former
maid and nurse, and folks in Weatherford would have a chance to
see her in such a terrific show.

Opening night in Dallas was truly magical. Mary, her shoulder-
length hair dyed a dark red, filled the stage with her inimitable
sparkle, winning hearts with her impish laugh, and using her voice
with abandon. She was coarse, she was tender; she was awestruck,
she was in control. The "I'm an Indian, Too" number, no longer
politically correct and omitted from recent revivals, she made into
a comedic lark and feast for the eyes. Mostly, she was touching, fun,
and romantic. "Miss Martin surprises us with a red-hot-mama style
of her own," wrote John Rosenfield, the respected critic of the
Dallas Morning News. "Her Annie thespically is a consistent, appealing
characterization." The critic went on the say that the girl from Weather-
ford was a distinctive personality, "not just a pretty warbler." Rosen-
field added, "She can croon or shout with the best of them."

Mary claimed that she never heard applause at a premiere, but
she did the night *Annie* opened in Texas. She ended the curtain
calls with some special lyrics that Irving Berlin had written for her.
Instead of "There's no people like show people," Mary sang, "There's
no people like my people." When she walked out into the auditor-
ium's foyer after the show, she seemed to remember everybody's
name, people she hadn't seen since she left Weatherford. "There
was nobody there to prompt her," Bessie Mae Sue Ella recalled.
"She just knew them herself!"

Stanley Marcus gave a celebratory party after the opening perfor-
mance, and *Annie Get Your Gun* went on to break attendance records
in Dallas, grossing $248,000 in two weeks. Mary was made an honorary
Texas Ranger, and the consensus was that her talent had grown

into something extraordinary. "That tour was really what made Mary Martin's career as a star," Josh Logan said. "Her performance made me a believer in the biggest way possible."

During the show's run in Dallas, Bessie Mae Sue Ella discovered something about her friend that she hadn't known before. "I learned that she rested almost as furiously as she worked," Bessie Mae said. "That was part of her discipline." Mary donned rubber ear plugs when she went to bed, a trick she learned in Dallas during the weekend of the TU-OU football game there, when the street between the Baker and Adolphus hotels became the scene of a noisy all-night pep rally and drinking bash.

Mary did manage to spend a little time with family members during her stay in Dallas. The star's cousin, Don Martin, saw *Annie Get Your Gun* during the State Fair and met Richard backstage after the performance. "He was too much of an artistic type guy for me to understand," Don said years later. "Richard never would come to Weatherford. He didn't want any part of a country town." Throughout their marriage Halliday consistently refused to visit Mary's hometown, although he seemed to enjoy socializing with Jac and Sue Austin.

Toward the end of the engagement in Dallas, Richard called the Austins and invited them to have supper with Mary and him. While they were talking, Mary made an endearing comment to her childhood friend, and Bessie Mae replied, "Well, darling, I could never have kept in touch with you if you hadn't approached me first. It wouldn't have been appropriate." Mary, not fully understanding what her friend had meant, said, "Well. Bessie, you haven't changed either." According to Bessie Mae Sue Ella, the star was still "Mary Martin from Weatherford, Texas. Not that these other things haven't thrilled her, and they certainly have been part of her life. But she has remained exactly as she always was. There's been growth, definite growth, but Mary's innate heart and thinking and values stayed the same as they were when she was a little girl."

"Any star," Joshua Logan maintained, "who has to carry a show on his or her shoulders has built a protective covering." If Mary seemed free of that façade, Richard was not, and he took delight

in parading a star's temperament. When Cheryl Crawford, Elia Kazan, Kurt Weill, and lyricist-playwright Alan Jay Lerner proposed a meeting with Mary and Richard while *Annie Get Your Gun* played in Chicago, Richard wrote Crawford a gushy yet haughty letter. The producer, director, composer, and writer wanted to discuss the possibility of Mary's starring in an upcoming musical they were preparing called *Love Life*, which the collaborators thought would be ideal for her. "What fun to have such a *legitimate* excuse to see you all in Chicago!" Richard replied to their request. "And how generous of you all to make such a big effort. It would be . . . such fun, so exciting, such an emotional strain—*so* important to each of us—that we should try to be intelligent too—and *try* to plan the get-together at the best moment."

Then he went on to detail how successful *Annie* had been in Dallas and said that Mary would be "legitimately exhausted" by the time she reached Chicago and would need to conserve her energy. "She is having fun with the part," Richard told Crawford. "Imagine taking in just a few dollars short of $50,000 for the four performances over last weekend," breaking every record. He pointed out that the opening week in Chicago would be hectic and insisted that "the first chance Mary will have to catch her breath, to *start* to catch up is Sunday, November 9th. She is going to bed Saturday, the 8th, and stay there and sleep and read and rest until the show Monday, the 10th." Richard mentioned to Crawford that Hollywood was beckoning again for his wife's services, this time to star in a movie version of *One Touch of Venus*. "Don't worry," he wrote the producer, "we have said no—thanks." Then he ended his letter by saying, "We're going to see you. Yippee!" And he saw fit to explain that "Yippee" expressed "the gladest anyone can be."

Crawford obviously passed Richard's letter on to Weill and Lerner, since they wrote the producer a mocking response a few days later. "We just got the letter from Dick and it all sounds *absolutely* wonderful," the composer and lyricist began. "The only thing is that Marion and Lenya [their wives] have been doing two shows a day in New City, four shows a day in Pomona, eight shows a day in Suffern and *no sleep in between*. Traveling all day from New City to

Pomona can be *so* tiring, as well you know, or don't you? Besides that, we (Kurt and Alan) have not been working at night lately and you know what that means to Marion and Lenya. *However,* if we could all make it in Chicago, wouldn't it be *fun?* Such fun! So exciting! So emotional! And so full of shit!"

After playfully reminding Crawford what a joy show business could be and how it allowed one to meet such thrilling, sweet people, Weill and Lerner's sarcasm grew even more pointed. "Tell Mary and Dick we'll be just too delighted to see them in Chicago at any time that's convenient to them, providing it's one o'clock on Sunday and *not a moment* later. Also, we'll *absolutely* guarantee that Mary will be back in bed to read and rest by five o'clock *that* afternoon, of course. Oops! There's that Hollywood call again! Such excitement! But we won't tell you about it—now, anyhow—or maybe ever." The two concluded by writing, "We're going to see Mary and Dick! Yippee!" Then they defined for Crawford their meaning of "Yippee," which was "Balls." Finally, they added a postscript: "We just broke every record—over each other's head!"

Clearly, Richard's demands and puffed-up attitude were greeted with exasperation and mirth within show business circles, yet he remained Mary's guardian. Detractors maintained that Mary made the bullets that Richard shot, and there is likely truth in the statement, particularly as her career progressed. But undoubtedly, Richard was the greater prima donna, the more demanding personality, and the one Mary's colleagues found most difficult to satisfy. Richard's growing alcoholism made his petulance worse, until Mary herself became less relaxed and more stubborn in professional disputes.

Privately, she remained unaffected and upbeat. "I have rarely seen Mummy depressed," Heller maintained. Mary had an enduringly positive philosophy of life and held few illusions about herself. She always came across in publicity sessions as obliging, straightforward, joyously content with a dreamlike career, with a ready capacity to laugh at her own inadequacies. That was the real Mary— at least until some threat to her star image became involved. "To be a star of the first magnitude," Broadway dancer Gretchen Wyler contended, "you've got to be a killer." Others in the business

agreed with the assertion, insisting that the star of any production must make sure to remain the focal point of attention, and some have been quick to list names of Broadway barracudas to illustrate the point. "What about lovable Mary Martin?" seemed a logical rebuttal to the argument. "Surely she was no killer." Among those in the know, the answer to that query was always the same: "Mary didn't have to be; she had Richard Halliday."

Mary and Richard did meet with *Love Life*'s team of creators and heard the show's songs on a Sunday afternoon in Chicago. The play was about what happened to marriage over a period of time, beginning with the colonial era in America and continuing through the breakdown of home life in contemporary modern society. It was rather avant-garde and both dramatically heavy and vocally demanding. The one song Mary really liked from the score was called "Susan's Dream," written for a black woman to sing during an interlude in the production. The words were quite touching, but the song was inappropriate for a white person to perform. Consequently Mary decided against doing the show. "I felt that *Love Life* was a little beyond my talent frankly," said Nanette Fabray, who starred in the musical opposite Ray Middleton when it opened on Broadway in the fall of 1948. "But I was thrilled and flattered that Cheryl Crawford, Alan Jay Lerner, and Kurt Weill asked me to do the show. The theme of the play was heavy-handed, and it didn't quite work." Although *Love Life* proved something of a disappointment, the musical ran for 252 performances in New York. According to Crawford, the show had "no heart, no passion," and audiences "couldn't get emotionally involved" in the marital problems of its characters.

Mary needed vehicles that audiences could readily identify with, and throughout the tour of *Annie Get Your Gun* full houses did just that. From Dallas the company went to Kansas City, where an overflowing audience one night had to wait until 11:30 for the performance to begin. A concert had been given in the theater that afternoon, and the scenery for *Annie* couldn't be put in place until the pianist had finished playing. The curtain didn't come down on that performance of the Berlin musical until 3 A.M.

Heller developed a crush on the seven-year-old boy who played her brother Jake in the show. "Ours was a romance of extremes—either playing like mad or fighting like mad," an adult Heller remembered. One night while the two children were waiting in the wings, the boy yanked Heller's pigtails. When she turned around to say something mean to him, he socked her in the eye. "Despite my tears I went on," Heller said, "because Mummy always taught me that the 'show must go on.'" Mary recalled that her daughter chased the boy playing Jake shamelessly and that he bit her on the arm one day, then sent her flowers afterward to make up for the wound he'd inflicted. "I must have taken after my mother," Heller said, "because I was outgoing as a child and made friends easily."

The girl liked being in the show, loved traveling, and enjoyed the friends she made. "But most of all," Heller said, "I loved it because Mummy, Daddy, and I were together." Yet when her daughter started horsing around backstage and disturbing the cast during rehearsals, Mary called the company together. "Heller is no different from any of the children here," the star told cast members. "If she gets out of line, let me know. I won't have a spoiled child." According to Heller, Mary stopped right in the middle of "Doin' What Comes Natur'lly" at one rehearsal, took the unruly girl backstage, and gave her a spanking. "Don't ever test your mother's warning," Mary told her daughter.

Omaha followed Kansas City on the *Annie Get Your Gun* circuit, and on November 3 the company opened in Chicago for its longest engagement. Already some of the soprano comeliness had gone out of Mary's voice. "But I just loved every moment of the show," she said, "every moment of screaming my lungs out and ripping my throat apart. By the time we ended the tour I had very little voice left, but it didn't matter."

Critics seemed not to notice the star's declining range. In June, when the company opened a two-week run in Pittsburgh, the reviewer for the *Post Gazette* said, "Pistol Packin' Mary Martin was fired to new heights by *Annie Get Your Gun*. Nearly three hours aren't half enough of Miss Martin's Annie. It could go on and on, at least until malnutrition sets in."

The tour ended in California during the summer of 1948. Movie director George Sidney had seen Ethel Merman do *Annie* in New York, liked the show, but didn't think it had motion picture possibilities. "Then I saw Mary Martin play the role in Los Angeles," Sidney said, "She played the story so that you knew there was a character there, and the love story worked with her." Sidney later directed the film version of *Annie Get Your Gun* for Metro-Goldwyn-Mayer with Betty Hutton in the lead.

Oscar Hammerstein and Richard Rodgers were in Los Angeles for the opening of *Annie* there, while the team was on a short respite from trying to meld two stories from James Michener's *Tales of the South Pacific* into a satisfactory libretto for a forthcoming musical. The two tales they had in mind were quite diverse, and the songwriters were struggling to find a way to make them complementary. "All this was against the accepted rules of musical-play construction," Rodgers said. "If the main love story is serious, the secondary romance is usually employed to provide comic relief." But in this case both of the tales had complications and the potential for tragedy.

Seeing Mary again in *Annie Get Your Gun* convinced Rodgers and Hammerstein that she would make an ideal heroine in the show they were working on, which they intended to call *South Pacific*. The songwriters phoned Mary while she was playing *Annie* in San Francisco to ask if she would costar in their next musical, which they assured her would be something special. The weary star immediately wanted to know who would be in the show with her and was distraught when told that her costar would be Metropolitan Opera basso Ezio Pinza. "You want two basses in your show!" Mary exclaimed in disbelief. She pointed out that her voice was just destroyed after appearing in *Annie* for eleven months. She knew that it would require weeks of diligent work to get her high notes back, if that was even possible. She couldn't imagine singing in the same theater with the great Pinza, who had already been signed for the Broadway show. But the composer promised Mary that he'd guarantee that she and the opera star would never sing together in *South Pacific*. Between final performances on the *Annie Get Your Gun* tour, Mary read *Tales of the South Pacific* in her hotel

room in San Francisco. She didn't think the part of Nellie Forbush was particularly interesting and couldn't imagine doing an entire show dressed in a navy nurse's uniform. But she told Rodgers and Hammerstein that they would talk more when she and Richard returned to Connecticut.

"I cried when the tour of *Annie Get Your Gun* ended," Mary said. "I was sure I'd never get another show like it." The Hallidays, with Heller missing a front tooth, drove back east after the show closed in San Francisco. The night they arrived home, they went to Richard Rodgers' country place and heard music from *South Pacific* for the first time. Neither Mary nor Richard slept much that night. They both knew the musical was going to be a landmark in Broadway history and a show Mary simply had to do.

Masterful Navy Nurse

Mary knew that *South Pacific* was for her when she heard Richard Rodgers play and Oscar Hammerstein bark the lyrics of "Some Enchanted Evening," even though she was told that she wouldn't sing the song in the show. But that melody, with its Puccini-like feeling, haunted her all night after she'd left the songwriters. "Richard and I just kept thinking of that fabulously beautiful song and what Dick and Oscar had done with it," she said. Having heard three songs from the score, none of them Mary's, the Hallidays accepted Rodgers and Hammerstein's offer for her to star in their forthcoming musical, convinced that it had the earmarks for success. But Mary quickly reminded the songwriters that her voice was about six tones lower than normal from belting out the raucous numbers in *Annie Get Your Gun*. She needed time to rework her voice and to rest. Rodgers assured her that they still had considerable work to do and that she would have the entire fall and winter to recuperate.

Through hard work and the exercise of endless discipline, the luster in Mary's voice began to return. "I had to work like crazy," she said, but most of her upper register came back. Meanwhile, she turned down the lead in Cole Porter's *Kiss Me, Kate*, even though she and Richard both recognized that the show's score was brilliant. "I simply could not have sung Cole's songs at that moment," Mary

said. Any spare time she had during the last months of 1948 she devoted to Richard and Heller and to overseeing the remodeling of their house in Connecticut.

The Hallidays had bought six acres in Fairfield County. They turned the tiny-roomed farmhouse near Norwalk into a charming, spacious home. The walls of three small rooms were ripped out to make a living room–dining area forty feet square that overlooked green countryside and Long Island Sound in the distance. Upstairs, windows were added to give more light and maximize the view of the Sound. Richard supervised most of the work, and under his watchful eye a weather-beaten farmhouse was transformed into a picturesque home of elegance and comfort. The furnishings were predominantly antiques and family pieces, while the house's exterior was painted a deep, cool green to blend with the surrounding landscape. French doors opened onto a wisteria-covered terrace. Richard, who had a green thumb, ordered trees moved around to improve the view and added plantings of evergreens to the rolling lawn. Two ceramic roosters, a gift from Jean Arthur, were set in the gateposts, and clasped-hands made of stone lined a path winding around the house and grounds. A former barn was converted into a playhouse for Heller, although it was sometimes used for family parties. Its walls were draped with red and white curtains, and the main room was filled with toy animals. A pool, made from the brook that ran through the back of the property, was given a sand cove for sunbathing and relaxing, and Mary often spent leisure hours out there resting.

She always credited Richard with being the force that held the family together. Both Mary and Heller relied on him for advice and understanding. "Daddy manages my mother's career," Heller said, "runs our household, arranges our lives—and occasionally becomes the buffer between Mummy and me." The slim, gray-haired Richard was still boyish-looking, yet he possessed a will of steel, particularly where Mary's career was concerned. Whereas he was the connoisseur of antiques and fine décor, and even chose most of his wife's wardrobe, Mary remained the affable, delightfully uninhibited charmer with little or none of the expected affectations of stardom. "Her

friendliness exceeds her joy in beautiful things, even clothes which she adores," Richard's mother said of her daughter-in-law. "Her taste is quite restrained." Even Heller remarked, "Mummy likes trees better than diamonds."

Christmas in their Connecticut home in 1948 was possibly the most fun the Hallidays ever had. From all reports, *South Pacific* was shaping up into something extraordinary, a meaningful play in which popular music was used with operatic skill. Rodgers and Hammerstein, working closely with director-playwright Joshua Logan, were fashioning a musical with a powerful dramatic mood, one in which the characters were defined in song. Mary's numbers would have a completely different flavor from those of her costar, Ezio Pinza, since she would be playing a youthful, unsophisticated navy nurse and Pinza a middle-aged French planter with two half-Polynesian children. Mary knew, as she heard the songs being written for her, that *South Pacific*'s score was going to be a milestone in theater history. The longer Rodgers, Hammerstein, and Logan worked, the more everyone realized that here was a musical with substance and sound dramatic structure.

Hammerstein was a man of unusual perception. He believed that a lyric should be like a one-act play, containing a statement, a development, and a recapitulation. A veteran of countless Broadway shows, Hammerstein knew about play structure, about how to introduce characters, about clarity and rhyme, and how to avoid false rhyme. A person of integrity, the lyricist-playwright contended that an artist must be true to one's self and use the creative instinct to express whatever vision of the world he or she held. Hammerstein and his *South Pacific* collaborators were sensitive to racial intolerance and made that theme the spine of their show, yet incorporated social comment without becoming heavily didactic and without spoiling the romantic, high-spirited nature of the musical. Rodgers and Hammerstein knew about intolerance and had felt its sting in their own lives. "Being Jewish in a fairly non-Jewish society was subtly difficult," said Mary Rodgers, the composer's daughter. "There were social undertones that made life a little hard. But the theater is where people care what you do, not who you are."

Hammerstein, working in conjunction with Josh Logan, succeeded in combining two of James Michener's stories, "Our Heroine" and "Fo' Dollah," into a compelling script. Ensign Nellie Forbush, Mary's character, falls in love with Emile DeBecque, the Pinza character, on an island in the South Pacific during the Second World War, but she flees from him when she discovers that the deceased mother of his two children was Polynesian. Nellie, with her Arkansas background and instilled prejudices, is at first unable to accept her worldly lover's past biracial marriage. Likewise, Marine lieutenant Joe Cable, in the show's subplot, falls in love with Liat, an innocent Tonkinese girl, but fears that the difference in their skin color will ruin their chances for a happy union. The two stories are joined when Cable goes off with DeBecque on a dangerous reconnaissance mission and is killed.

Rodgers and Hammerstein's aim was a perfect blend of drama and musical comedy. There would be no chorus line in *South Pacific*, no ballet troupe, just singing actors, with every performer onstage playing a distinct character. Hammerstein usually wrote the lyrics to their songs first, working slowly and painfully, with every syllable carefully deliberated. A big man with a pitted face, built like a football tackle, Hammerstein frequently wrote standing at a lectern. He'd agonize for hours over a single word, unwilling to compromise, determined to lift his sentimental predilections to a higher level. From the outset, Hammerstein and his partners envisioned songs that delineated character and advanced the drama rather than numbers suited to individual performers that generated applause. "That's always been Dick Rodgers' passion," Josh Logan said, "to dramatize with songs," and Oscar Hammerstein was in full accord.

Once the meticulous lyricist delivered his completed verses to Rodgers, the composer wrote music for them with amazing speed. Rodgers spent a great deal of time thinking about a song before he actually went to the piano, getting the rhythm and mood clearly in mind. So when he finally got to the piano, he seemed to compose almost in the amount of time it took to play the song. "In truth," his daughter Mary said, "there was often a lot of thought that went into the writing ahead of time." Rodgers' strength as a composer

lay in the richness of his melodies, his harmonic genius, and his ability to come up with the unexpected. "I've always been fascinated by his beginnings," said Mary Rodgers, herself a composer, "what seem like simple, uncomplicated, obvious little melodies, and then they go somewhere peculiar. After they go there, you realize the absolute musical correctness of what he wrote." The composer could be playful in dealing with performers in his shows but he could also be tough, and he was a firm taskmaster where his music was concerned, insisting that it be sung exactly as he had written it.

Michener's *Tales of the South Pacific* had won the Pulitzer Prize for fiction in 1948, and the musical based on it found Rodgers and Hammerstein at the peak of their creative powers. Since the show appeared soon after the Second World War ended, its subject was immediate. *South Pacific* had suspense, humanity, and consistent believability. One of the tasks the collaborators faced was how to present the Cable-Liat story without its becoming too much like *Madame Butterfly*. They also took characters, most notably Luther Billis, from some of the other tales in Michener's collection. The challenge was to pull all of the components together into an integrated musical drama with humor, passion, sentiment, color, and intimacy.

The casting of DeBecque came about when Edwin Lester, the long-time head of the Los Angeles Civic Light Opera Company, approached Rodgers and Hammerstein about taking over a contract he had with Ezio Pinza. After twenty-one seasons with the Metropolitan Opera singing Boris Godunov, Don Giovanni, and Don Basilio, the internationally renowned basso had decided to give up opera and wanted to appear in a musical comedy. "The trouble is," Lester told Richard Rodgers in a telephone conservation, "I haven't been able to come up with a damn thing that's right for Pinza, and if I don't find something in a hurry, I'm going to have to pay him $25,000. Do you and Oscar have anything cooking that might be suitable?"

By happenstance, they did, although *South Pacific* at that point was still in the early planning stages. "Some Enchanted Evening" was written with Pinza in mind. Then came the problem of finding a suitable song for him in the second act. It took a while for

Rodgers and Hammerstein to devise "This Nearly Was Mine." Mary had never seen the basso perform in opera, but she liked him enormously once the two met. "Ezio was so romantic, so *male* in person," Mary said. Since English was not Pinza's native language, the constant changes of lines and scenes during rehearsals confounded him for a while. Also, he was used to moving slower in opera than what was required on the Broadway stage. "I won't say that I immediately took to musical comedy like a duck takes to water," the former opera singer said. "I spent my evenings at home going over the day's new lines while Doris, my wife, helped me with the English pronunciation. At the next rehearsal I would find everything changed again. Eventually this began to get me down."

Rehearsals on *South Pacific* started on February 2, 1949, in the Belasco Theatre in New York. Mary arrived five minutes before the appointed hour the first day, and Pinza came in shortly afterward with an entourage that included his manager, agent, secretary, accompanist, arranger, lawyer, wife, and several others. Rumor had it that the opera singer had been waiting outside until Mary showed up on the belief that the most important star should arrive last. Jo Mielziner unveiled a model of his settings for the show, and the cast began to read.

Mary knew already that her songs were the exact opposite of Pinza's, reflecting a lively, colloquial quality appropriate for the brash, unvarnished young nurse from Little Rock. The actress resurrected her southern accent for the role and had no trouble projecting an authentic air of feisty innocence. Her opening number, "A Cockeyed Optimist," established Nellie's character, and the opening lines of "A Wonderful Guy"—"I'm as corny as Kansas in August, I'm as normal as blueberry pie"—made the self-description whole. "Twin Soliloquies" was the only time Mary and Pinza sang the same song, each rendering the melody, but not together and standing a distance apart as they expressed their hesitant, doubting love. "This was the moment when for me the show became great," Joshua Logan said. "But the song stopped too quick; the music had to continue to strengthen the passionate, almost sexual, feeling." It was left to Trude Rittman, who did most of the show's underscoring, to supply the

musical continuation needed. It was the moment, Logan maintained, where the audience felt the emotion along with the actors and became truly absorbed in the drama.

A week before rehearsals began, Mary had her hair shaped into a poodle cut and dyed dark blonde. Struck by how quickly her short hair dried at home after a shower, she suggested to Logan that she actually wash her hair onstage. "It might be fun for the audience," Mary said. So the director conferred with Hammerstein, who immediately came up with the idea of "I'm Gonna Wash That Man Right Outa My Hair" as Nellie's number when she determines to break off with Emile. Together they decided that Mary would soap her hair, sing the song stage center in an improvised shower, copied from a snapshot a glider pilot in the company had made in Normandy, and then dance about flicking a towel and bubbles at the other nurses.

Mary quickly got into the mood of playing a sunny all-American girl and worked to make Nellie cute without being coy, sweet without becoming saccharine, pained without being tragic. The role required her to dance, sing songs with a variety of moods, fraternize with the robust military personnel on a remote island, play straight dramatic scenes without letting down, and show evidence of inner growth. To a great degree the open, wide-eyed character she played in *South Pacific* was Mary herself, yet her Nellie became a finely chiseled creation, a new figure in American musical theater, a heroine who captivated audiences, amused them, and communicated a touching lesson in acceptance. "I loved her," Joshua Logan said of his star. "I loved her for her generosity of spirit, for her complete professionalism."

Logan let Mary choreograph her own dances. For the "Honey Bun" number, a vaudeville-type interlude, part of the show-within-a-show the camp staged at Thanksgiving, Mary chose the same soft-shoe steps she had taught her pupils in Weatherford. "It was so corny it was right," she said. With Nellie dressed in an outsized sailor suit, the pants long in the crotch and the sleeves so big they covered her hands, "Honey Bun" was destined to stop the show. When Mary heard the deliberately trite lyrics Oscar Hammerstein wrote for the number, she shrieked with joy. "It was my kind of

song, my kind of singing," she said. "Of all the fun moments Josh staged for me in theater, dancing and singing 'Honey Bun' was the most." Mary demonstrated her comic ability as never before and even worked Bessie Mae Sue Ella's name into the sequence, which made the routine still more personal. Nellie announces to the appreciative service personnel gathered about the makeshift stage that the barrel roll had been done by "Lieutenant J. G. Bessie May Sue Ellie Jaeger," signaling for their applause. The star had used her friend's name in some of her movies and would work it into her later Broadway shows as a good-luck token.

Luther Billis, played originally by Logan's college friend Myron McCormick, shared the stage with Nellie during the "Honey Bun" scene. McCormick appeared in the number with coconut shells for bosoms and had a sailboat tattooed on his stomach. At one point in the hilarity, while Mary made a costume change, McCormick rolled his belly so that it looked like the ship was sailing through waves. It was a riotous progression, one enjoyed by audiences and entertainers alike. "From the time we started rehearsals on that show," Mary said, "everybody, every Seabee, couldn't wait to get to the theater and perform. When we'd finish we'd say, 'No, let's continue working.' I don't think there was ever a cross word from anybody in that cast."

Mary decided that it would be appropriate for Nellie Forbush, with her coltish high spirits, to make a crossover from one side of the stage to the other doing cartwheels, something she'd learned to do as a child. Performing the cartwheels during rehearsal one day, the star was blinded by a spotlight, overshot the stage, and landed in the orchestra pit, knocking out Trude Rittman, seated at the piano, and striking a glancing blow to the conductor, Salvatore Dell'Isola. Fortunately, no one was seriously hurt, but Mary sent Rittman and Dell'Isola football helmets filled with flowers as an apology. The cartwheels were subsequently eliminated.

Mary had an aversion to profanity consistent with her homespun demeanor. The strongest expression anyone ever heard from her was, "Oh, plop" or "He's a son-of-a-bear." *South Pacific*'s co-producer,

Leland Hayward, however, drove the star to distraction with his constant use of four-letter words. "You've got to straighten up," she'd tell him. "I just can't listen to this." Otherwise, she adored Hayward, as he did her. Negotiating with Richard Halliday, on the other hand, proved the toughest part of the producer's job. "If Mary Martin wanted something," Hayward's wife, Slim, recalled, "Dick Halliday made sure she got it." That even included khaki uniforms made by Mainbocher for her attire as Nellie Forbush, uniforms that could have been bought at a PX. But Richard insisted that his wife felt comfortable only in Mainbocher clothes.

The biggest problem Pinza presented was to make the singer's diction understandable in his dialogue scenes. "He was a delightful man, and he enjoyed acting enormously," Josh Logan said. Pinza worked hard and got along famously with Mary. "Unlike the usual star," Logan said, "she had no jealousy; she wanted Pinza to succeed. She knew that if the audience loved Pinza, they would know why Nellie Forbush did." The two stars' rapport was reflected in their performances. At the end of "Twin Soliloquies," Pinza started toward Mary with two brandy snifters in his hands. "The chemistry between us was fabulous," Mary mantained. "It was unbelievable. I've played *South Pacific* with many people, but never to the degree that I did with Ezio. If ever anybody was born for that part, it was Pinza."

Logan, by no means a secure man, gave his leads considerable latitude in their performances, extracting depths from them they didn't know they had. Rumors circulated that Pinza was thinking of leaving the show because he felt Mary's role was becoming more important than his. Yet placing the elegant basso next to a vibrant example of American vitality showed both stars to an advantage. Mary claimed that she learned something about breath control from Pinza every time they performed together. His voice was beyond compare, but the opera singer also proved to be a sensitive actor. "Pinza and Martin did something almost unbelievable," Richard Rodgers recalled. "They each wanted a very high percentage of the gross, and we told them that it wasn't possible and that

if they wanted to work together, which by that time they did, they would both have to take a salary and percentage cut. They did and were very good about it."

Rodgers recalled no display of temperament on the show, saying that all went smoothly and fell into place. But Richard Halliday was constantly on hand to protect his wife's interests and seemed to expect Logan to focus exclusively on her. Mary herself could be strong-willed and tough minded, but she seemed "deeply concerned," according to Rodgers, "that whatever she did be in the best interest of the production as a whole." She watched from out front while the director staged "There Is Nothin' Like a Dame," in awe of Logan's skill. "Josh knew how to move those boys," Mary said. "He'd take a group and say, 'Follow me.' They'd go this way and then another way. The whole number was staged within five minutes and it never changed. We all watched in the theater while this happened and just screamed and yelled. The momentum of those boys pacing back and forth in different directions was absolutely thrilling."

Logan introduced movie technique into the stage production, using a "dissolve" in the scene where a plane takes Cable and DeBecque away on their reconnaissance mission. "It was just a scene in one," remembered actor Reid Shelton, who later played Daddy Warbucks in the original Broadway production of *Annie*, "but the audience felt they were on the air strip, and it all happened as the curtain wiped across the stage and opened on another scene."

The only two roles in *South Pacific* that proved difficult to cast were Cable and Bloody Mary, Liat's avaricious mother. William Tabbert, who finally created Cable, was vocally right but didn't look the part until he'd lost weight, firmed up his physique, and Mary and Richard had given him a G.I. haircut. Juanita Hall, a mulatto singer with an Oriental appearance, came to her audition, took off her shoes and stockings and, according to Logan, "struck a squatting pose that said, 'I am Bloody Mary and don't you dare cast anyone else!'" Hall got the part, had a laugh that rang with humor, and made the haunting "Bali Ha'i" a musical highlight of the show.

Mary remembered Tabbert, Hall, and Betta St. John, who played Liat, practicing their finger work for the "Happy Talk" number endlessly. "Every time you'd look up they'd be in the wings working on that," Mary said. "They worked on that for hours and hours. Josh wanted it perfect, and it took a while to jell." Tabbert and St. John turned the "Younger Than Springtime" scene into a sensual coupling, beautiful and rapturous without nudity. Initially, Cable and Nellie did a song together, but when the show proved too long, the number was dropped. (Later it was restored, with no particular distinction, in the movie.)

During the last week of rehearsal in New York, things began to take proper form. Pinza remembered Richard Rodgers going up to Mary Martin after something she had done exceptionally well, throwing his arms around her, and saying, "Darling, I love you so much I could give up Joshua Logan's percentage of the show!" Mary maintained that the company still didn't know what they had for sure when Logan announced that they were going to do a run-through with just boxes, tables, and chairs for props. "I want you to perform the show as if you were performing it on opening night," the director told his company. "We're going to have just enough lights for us out in the audience to see your faces." When the cast started performing, they heard laughs from out front, but the house was too dark for them to see who was there. "We had an idea that there were more people out there than they were telling us," Mary said, "although they had told the onlookers not to applaud. When the lights came up, we saw all these people in the balcony, everywhere. Everybody in theater who knew we were going to do this run-through was out there. It was a terrific idea because we went to New Haven with a little more confidence."

Mary felt that Logan had been in top form until the company left for four weeks of tryouts in New Haven, but once the show opened there the director started to go down psychologically. "He was terrified," the star said. At the first performance in New Haven on March 7, two of Mary's big numbers didn't work. "Josh walked the streets that night crying," she said. "Nobody could find him. When they finally did, he said, 'I just ruined Mary. I ruined her whole career.'"

Pinza arrived in New Haven scared, but on opening night he scored such an enormous hit with "Some Enchanted Evening" that the show couldn't continue for several minutes. To everyone's surprise, neither "I'm Gonna Wash That Man Right Outa My Hair" nor "A Wonderful Guy," both in the same scene, went well for Mary. Richard was livid, and Rodgers and Hammerstein were so distressed by the failure of their songs that they avoided looking at Logan. "I felt like an amateur," the director said. He had instructed Mary to rub her head with soap and water just as she started the refrain of "I'm Gonna Wash That Man Right Outa My Hair." But what he hadn't anticipated was that the audience would be so shocked by the physical act of Mary's washing her hair onstage with real water that they didn't hear the song. When the number finished, there wasn't a handclap. The solution proved simple enough. Mary sang the song first and *then* went into the shower and began lathering her head. "During the loud music that had been composed for the dance," Logan said, "Mary washed her hair and romped about, flinging soap and suds." Once that change was made, the number ended to a roar of applause. Later her costume for the scene was sprayed with Scotch Guard so that Mary could finish the act in dry clothes.

Everyone had assumed that "A Wonderful Guy" would be a showstopper. Mary heard the song first in Josh Logan's apartment in New York at 2 AM and got so excited that she fell off the piano bench. The director staged the number as a clowning piece, with the other nurses on the beach catching Nellie's glee and joining her hackneyed comic antics. But on opening night in New Haven the celebration fell flat. "The audience enjoyed the music and the lyrics," Logan said, "but the corny clowning was just cornball—or rather, embarrassing." After much thought and a talk with Mary, Logan decided that the other girls should not be onstage during the song and that Mary should sing the number as a soliloquy. Hammerstein adjusted the lyrics slightly, and after the first chorus Mary did an exuberant little dance with Emile's hat, then circled an upturned boat with one foot on the boat and the other on the ground, and finally did a few waltz clog steps on top of the boat.

For a finish she pulled the hat over her eyes as she sang the last note. Once its staging was revised, "A Wonderful Guy" became the smash hit the song was intended to be. "The ovation continued through the reentrance of the girls," Logan said. "From then on, the number was our highest peak."

To the director's surprise, Mary seemed unperturbed by the failure of her two big numbers on opening night in New Haven. "Maybe it was the way I did them," she said. "I'll get applause tonight. Don't worry." But it took several days of feverish work to get the staging right. The company was still rehearsing every morning, and the writers were making changes after most performances. "We just worked like fiends," Mary remembered. Playwright Emlyn Williams was on hand in the Taft Hotel to confer with the collaborators, and eventually forty-five minutes were taken out of the show—two songs and words here and there.

Despite all the changes, Rodgers and Hammerstein kept reprimanding Logan for being so discouraged. "Josh," the composer said, "you don't seem to know we have a hit." Critics had thought so from the beginning. "It can't miss," Variety reported after the New Haven opening. "The show isn't quite a smash yet—but it's gonna be." And despite the problems with staging her big numbers, Mary received immediate rave notices. "She does everything in the book and does it all terrifically," the writer for Variety continued. "She hits all the stops, from sobs to solos, from humor to hoofing." Never before had Mary shown her talent for outrageous comedy with such captivating skill, nor acted with such persuasion.

Pinza was judged superb in his first musical comedy. The dignified, gallant, gray-haired former opera singer suddenly found himself hailed as a national sex symbol. At the Met he had earned a reputation as a great lover, and the girls in the cast of South Pacific had many humorous stories to tell about his unsuccessful pursuit of Mary Martin and the pinches they received on their way to and from their dressing room. Yet onstage Pinza proved as irresistible in his mature, cultured way as Mary did playing an effervescent Arkansas hick.

Shortened and polished, South Pacific went to Boston for more tryouts. Already, word had reached New York that the show had a

book of unusual literacy and was a treat to look forward to. Broadway playwright-director Moss Hart saw *South Pacific* during tryouts and quipped upon returning to New York, "The show is doing so well they're shipping the money in by barge from Boston down the East River." Few productions in theatrical history ever attracted so many New Yorkers to out-of-town performances. "It was absolutely terrifying to have such a hit out of town," Mary said, since there was always the possibility that the show would be overrated in early publicity and then seem disappointing.

Mary came to a rehearsal one day to find Pinza working at a piano with his accompanist. That was when she discovered that the opera singer couldn't read music either. "He had to hear the melody," she said. "That's the way he learned all those operas. I never brought it up, but I knew what he was doing." She also remembered Robert Russell Bennett, Rodgers and Hammerstein's arranger, bringing sheets of music to the theater with a cat perched on his shoulder. "He was a tall, good-looking man," she remembered, "but he always had that cat, a real one."

South Pacific opened at the Majestic Theatre in New York on April 7, 1949, to the biggest advance ticket sale Broadway had ever known—nearly a half-million dollars. Although expectations ran high, the show amply fulfilled them. Howard Barnes of the *New York Herald Tribune* called the musical "a show of rare enchantment." Not since *Oklahoma!* had Rodgers and Hammerstein worked with a book of such merit or produced such a satisfying score. "*South Pacific* is one hell of a funny, moving, lyrical, and absorbing play," a reviewer for *Theatre Arts Monthly* wrote. Its dances appeared to be captivating improvisations, the songs deliciously hummable, but it was the fusion of music and drama that impressed critics most. *Time* called *South Pacific* a "musical play" in which "story moves on equal terms with song."

New York had nine major daily newspapers at the time, and the consensus among them was that Mary had given the performance of her career. Her personality filled the Majestic Theatre on opening night. "For a long time everyone has known that Mary Martin was exceedingly expert and charming in the ways of musical

comedy," Richard Watts, Jr., wrote in the *New York Post.* "But nothing I have ever seen her do prepared me for the loveliness, humor, gift for joyous characterization, and sheer lovableness of her portrayal of Nellie Forbush." Brooks Atkinson of the *New York Times* voiced total agreement: "Since we have all been more or less in love with Miss Martin for several years, it is no surprise to find her full of quicksilver, pertness, and delight as the Navy nurse." And a few days later Atkinson added, "Although Miss Martin is a prodigious performer, she has the grace to esteem the quality of a well-written character." Nellie grew during the course of the play and revealed a richness of understanding in the last scene that she did not have when the show opened.

Mary claimed that she had been sick at her stomach for weeks before *South Pacific* reached New York, but when opening night finally came, her stomach was fine. After the performance, the star hopped around her dressing room content as could be, as the room filled with ritzy well-wishers, baskets of flowers, gifts, and balloons. "It seems like Kentucky Derby Day being held in a floral shop," the *New York Post* said of the turmoil. An after-the-show party was held on the St. Regis Roof, a full-dress affair that lasted until the morning papers came out. Josh Logan remembered Sam Zolotow, the theatrical news editor of the *New York Times* rushing in with an armload of papers and exclaiming, "It's a great notice. Nobody has to worry—it's a great notice."

As *South Pacific* settled down for a prolonged run, four of its songs zoomed to the top of the Hit Parade charts. In April 1949, the most prized tickets in New York's theater district were those for *South Pacific, Death of a Salesman,* and *Kiss Me, Kate.* Within three months after its Broadway opening, and with available tickets in New York a rarity, plans were already being made to send out a road company of the Rodgers and Hammerstein hit. An outfit called South Pacific Enterprises was formed to produce *South Pacific* scarves, dolls, perfume, underwear, sheets, and pillowcases, an early effort at big-scale theater merchandising.

Meanwhile, Mary was declared one of the stage's truly great ladies. "She seems to feel what she is singing," Joseph Wood Krutch

said in the *Nation*. "The gestures seem inspired from within, and she communicates what seems to be her own genuine joy in doing what she can do." The editor of the *Saturday Review of Literature* wrote, "With Martin the corn is as high as an elephant's eye. She gets right to the kernel of the meaning." And the brilliant Broadway producer-director Harold Clurman saw *South Pacific* and declared in *New Republic:* "Mary Martin is our ideal, our dream, our faith. She is fresh, lively, humorous, useful, and very, very good company. . . . In addition to her shining bright personality, Mary Martin is a grand performer. Entirely without cheapness, stridency, stickiness, she is effortlessly deft. She sings, dances, flirts, and acts with a bouncing naturalness that is the happy marriage of hard work and talent."

A few days after the Rodgers and Hammerstein show opened, Mary appeared on the cover of *Life* magazine dressed in the sailor suit she wore during her "Honey Bun" number. The blind Helen Keller attended a performance of *South Pacific* and came backstage to visit Mary in her dressing room afterward. Passing her hands over the star's face, Keller said, "To me you are the spirit of eternal youth." When asked what she thought of Mary's performance, Ethel Merman reputedly shrugged her shoulders and quipped, "Oh, she's okay, if you like talent." Merman, who, after Gershwin's *Girl Crazy* in 1930, became the reigning queen of New York musical comedy, accepted that she had a worthy counterpart.

Mary was voted one of the country's ten best-dressed women, and her poodle haircut, which she had trimmed every two weeks and required a home permanent every three, started a national vogue. As the months went by, the star's portrayal of Nellie Forbush took on deeper hues. "I've always been able to yell good," Mary said, "but I've found that good singing is soft." And her affection for costar Ezio Pinza continued to grow. "Every time he started my way, with that face of his, that magnetism, that music, a spark came across like nothing that ever happened to me before," Mary told reporters. "When Ezio hugs me he almost breaks my ribs."

South Pacific won the Pulitzer Prize for drama in 1950, becoming the first musical to win the honor since *Of Thee I Sing* in 1931. The

Rodgers and Hammerstein blockbuster also won eight Tony Awards, including the award for best musical, best actress (Mary Martin), best actor (Ezio Pinza), best supporting actress (Juanita Hall), and best supporting actor (Myron McCormick). Meanwhile, ticket scalpers did a lively business, getting $60 for a $6.60 seat for the show. When asked how he managed to get tickets to *South Pacific*, Edgar F. Luckenbach, Jr., heir to the Luckenbach steamship fortune, replied, "Oh, I just swapped a couple of ships for them." And an enterprising cafeteria on Forty-fourth Street put a sign in its window proclaiming, "Our hotcakes are going like tickets to *South Pacific*." Some veteran playgoers argued that the musical was even better the second time they saw it. Publisher Bennett Cerf called the show "an absolutely perfect and unforgettable evening in the theater."

By the end of 1949, six renditions of "Some Enchanted Evening" had reached the Top 40 lists of recorded song hits. The show's backers had their money returned within the first four months of the Broadway run. "I will never have another *South Pacific*," Mary said decades later. "Everyone in the world came to see it. People came to *South Pacific* to get married, to get divorced, to get back together again. Presidents, kings, emperors came to see it."

A month after *South Pacific* opened in New York, Noel Coward came to see the show, and the British playwright and the Hallidays had a friendly reunion, after not speaking for years. "Mary was enchanting," Coward wrote in his diary. "It was really touching. Mary was genuinely in tears and truly happy and relieved that we were making up. I feel as though a weight has been lifted from me. I hate quarrels and feuds, and she had a bloody time in England and I have felt uncomfortable and unhappy about it." As Mary remembered the reconciliation, Coward knocked on her dressing room door, came in, knelt at her feet, and said, "It's over, isn't it? We're never going to fight again." She told him, "As far as I'm concerned, never." They remained friends for the rest of his life.

The Texas star stayed in *South Pacific* for twenty-six months on Broadway, washing her hair onstage eight times a week and missing only three performances during the longest run of her career. To have the energy needed for performing, Mary slept ten hours a

night. "I really didn't do anything else," she said. "I would stay home until four o'clock every afternoon," either in bed or out by the pool sunning. "I'd have a light supper at five, leave for the theater around six, vocalize, and get ready for the show. That was my life." It was Mary's firm belief that if audiences were going to pay hard-earned money to see her perform, she owed it to them to be in top form for every performance. "There were years in which I never even talked with friends," she said, "because I had to save my voice. Years in which I seldom went out, even for meals, seldom went to parties." Ernest, the Halliday's long-time chauffeur, drove the couple into New York each evening from Connecticut, except for matinee days when they spent the night before in their apartment at the Hampshire House. "We did most of our talking on the Merritt Parkway," Mary said.

Richard ran the household, gave instructions to the servants, took care of business affairs, saw that fan mail was answered, and did his wife's shopping for her. "Mary throws herself so completely into everything she does on the stage," Richard said, "that she needs all the rest she can get. Our home life is geared to an offbeat rhythm, but the pace is as consistent as we can make it." Between afternoon and evening performances, Mary took an hour's nap in her dressing room before time to go before the footlights again. After the show, she and Richard usually went to Frankie and Johnnie's, or some other quiet restaurant, for a late supper. The star seldom carried a purse and never wrote a check. One matinee afternoon during the Broadway run of *South Pacific*, Richard was ill and couldn't accompany Mary to the theater as he normally did. The Hampshire House doorman called a taxi for her, and when she got in the cab, she told the driver that she wanted to go to the theater where *South Pacific* was playing. When pressed for the name of the theater, Mary realized that she couldn't remember where she'd been performing for almost a year. She just depended on Richard to get her there.

After Slim Hayward, wife of producer Leland Hayward, taught her how to do needlepoint, Mary sat in her dressing room and worked on a needlepoint rug by the hour. That was her relaxation

between cues. When not doing needlepoint, she spent time back-stage reading *The Life of Gandhi* and Tolstoy's *The Kingdom of God Is Within You*, from which Gandhi had gotten much of his inspiration. As Richard's alcoholism worsened, Mary's inner strength seemed to grow proportionately. "She had enormous vigor in her and enormous inner energies that allowed her to remain that great, shining presence we saw on the stage," Yul Brynner said.

In June 1949, Bessie Mae Sue Ella and Jac Austin came to New York and stayed with the Hallidays for a week at the Hampshire House and in Connecticut. Richard arranged for the couple to see *South Pacific* not once but twice from house seats, even though tickets for the show had become impossible to get. "It was the first time I'd ever seen Mary on Broadway," Bessie Mae said. "I really was stunned. I expected to see her name in lights, but when we walked into the lobby of the theater and I saw great big pictures of her, it came as a surprise. I hadn't thought of that, and I was absolutely thrilled." Richard had told them on the drive from the airport, "Wait till you see her onstage." Bessie Mae agreed that Nellie Forbush was the ideal role for her friend. "Love that Nellie," the Austins wired Richard after they'd returned home.

Mary and Richard had spent as much time with their guests on their trip as possible. "No matter what, there is always some 'surprise,' 'emergency,' or 'something' that holds us [at the theater] a minimum of fifteen minutes," Richard wrote the Austins before their arrival. "It does seem as though no matter how much we try to keep the gal free, things happen anyhow." But the Hallidays cleared their schedule that week so they could devote themselves largely to Bessie Mae and Jac. The one commitment they did not turn down was an after-theater party at the Plaza Hotel, which the Hallidays thought their Texas friends would find fun. Mary had been asked to be the guest of honor at a benefit for the War Veterans' Entertainment Fund, and a lot of theater people were to be there. At the party Bessie Mae and Jac met Ezio Pinza and writer Edna Ferber, among others. After talking with the Austins for several minutes, Ferber tellingly observed, "Well, if Mary hadn't had a Bessie Mae Sue Ella, she would have had to invent one!"

A bit later in the party, Richard Rodgers sat at the piano and played while Mary sang. Eventually, the star had Bessie Mae Sue Ella come over and join her on "Sam, the Old Accordion Man" and songs they'd sung together as children. "I knew Mary was going to do that to you," Richard Halliday told Bessie Mae on the drive to Connecticut.

Bessie loved Mary's house. "It was just like coming home," she said. "Juanita Martin always had fresh flowers in everybody's bedroom, and Mary did the same. It was fun to see Mary in a very at-home setting." The star's seventeen-year-old son, Larry, who had been attending Bard College on the Hudson River in New York, was with the Hallidays in Connecticut for the week the Austins visited, preparatory to his making a trip to Sweden with friends. The tension between Richard and Larry was obvious. Richard complained that Larry had failed to let them know when he would arrive and grumbled that the boy required so much time and attention. "Although we've been planning this trip [to Sweden] for six months," Richard told the Austins, "and all the information had been sent directly to Larry—surprise, surprise, we find that he hasn't attended to one-tenth of what was supposed to be done."

The visit with Mary and Richard nonetheless was an exciting time for the Texas couple. Bessie Mae did an interview on Jinx Falkenburg's radio show, in which she discussed her long friendship with Mary. She and Jac saw *Kiss Me, Kate* and *Mister Roberts*, starring the Hallidays' neighbor in Connecticut, Henry Fonda, and Mary spent all of her free time talking with Bessie Mae and reliving old times. But the Austins did get a glimpse of the problems in the Halliday marriage, notably the antagonism between Richard and Larry and Richard's alcoholism. Even before they'd left home for the trip to New York, Marion Cazier, the Hallidays' secretary, had written Bessie Mae Sue Ella: "I'm sure that Miss Martin would be sending her love, but at the moment she's on the stage. Mr. Halliday I know would send his, but he's on the town—drunk."

Mary drew on her inner strength and found contentment in her work. She adored her role in *South Pacific* and continued to

approach it with untiring gusto. One evening she was heard walking through the alley to the stage door singing "Younger Than Springtime," which wasn't one of her songs in the show, at the top of her lungs. Mary claimed that illustrated the state of her feelings after a year in *South Pacific.* People were still waiting months after buying tickets to see the show and came to performances with high expectations. "Audiences are keyed up," Mary said. "The atmosphere in the theater is that of a festival."

Pinza left the cast on June 1, 1950, and was replaced by Ray Middleton. The former Metropolitan Opera basso had liked playing Emile but was not accustomed to doing eight shows a week. "Ezio loved to sing," Mary said, "so he'd sing full out. Then about the middle of the week he'd just wear out his voice and have to let his understudy take over. I played about sixty times with the understudy. Doing a Broadway musical was difficult for Ezio. He'd been trained to sing in a different manner." The only difficulty the two stars ever had was that Pinza, fearing he'd catch a cold, kept turning the heat up backstage and Mary kept turning it off. "One day I'd just had enough of that," Mary said, "so I brought pliers to the theater and removed the mechanism that regulated the temperature." Pinza thought her ingenuity was funny.

Early in Mary's second year in *South Pacific,* the Korean War broke out. "Immediately the show took on a sharp new meaning," she said. "Under the impact of events, it turned from a series of war recollections, softened by time and gilded by glamour, into a picture of grim contemporary reality." The star played Nellie Forbush 501 times before missing a performance and finished her Broadway run in the show in June 1951 without having performed to an unsold seat. When the curtain fell on her last Broadway appearance in *South Pacific,* the house was drenched with emotion. People brought her gifts onstage, while others cried. Richard Rodgers, Oscar Hammerstein, Leland Hayward, and Joshua Logan gave their star a diamond and pearl bracelet, and a big party took place after the audience left the theater. The next day the *New York Times* said, "Not in recent memory has an actress received such a farewell as that given to Miss Martin."

After Mary's final New York performance in the show, the Hallidays, including Heller, took a cruise up and down the north Atlantic coast on a chartered sixty-seven-foot yawl, but had to come home when the weather turned bad. Life for them in Connecticut was complicated by the fact that Larry had moved back in with his mother and Richard for a short while. "I was drinking pretty heavily at the time," an adult Larry confessed. "It was a skill I had picked up at Bard and honed in Dallas," where he'd spent two months doing theater on a break from school. When her son got alcohol poisoning, Mary faced him down. "If you drink like that, you can drink on your own," she told him. "Larry, I'm going to give you fifty dollars a week, and you can go find a place of your own. Visit me backstage when you can." Later, Hagman said that getting kicked out of the house in Connecticut was the best thing that ever happened to him. "I felt I was a misunderstood teenager, which of course I was," he said, "so I packed my one suitcase and I left without any hard feelings." He took a train into Manhattan and found a room at the old Knickerbocker Hotel.

While living with his father in Weatherford, Larry had decided that he wanted to be an actor. He had been in school plays at Weatherford High and upon graduation took a job baling hay to earn enough money for a bus ticket to Connecticut. "He turned up at our home one day, looking tall, strong, tanned, wonderful," Mary remembered. During Larry's year at Bard, a progressive college, students had January and February off from classes in order to get real-world experience, and since Larry was majoring in drama and dance, he decided to test his skill in a professional theater. With his mother's help, young Hagman had gotten an apprenticeship with Margo Jones's prestigious theater-in-the-round in Dallas. He appeared first in *My Granny Van*, a comedy by Texas author George Sessions Perry and Loren Disney, carried a spear in *Romeo and Juliet*, and had a small part in Sean O'Casey's *Cock-a-Doodle Dandy*. The boy lived at the YMCA in Dallas, drank in excess, but discovered that he enjoyed being onstage. After dropping out of college, he spent a summer with Margaret Webster's Shakespeare workshop

in Woodstock, New York, and resolved to launch himself as a professional actor.

Mary was surprised at her son's decision, since Larry had never wanted any part of show business, "That was because show business had taken me away from him," she said, "and he resented it without knowing why." But when Margo Jones gave Larry a job, all that changed. "I didn't see him in Dallas," Mary said, "but everybody said he was absolutely marvelous for somebody who had never studied. I asked him if he wanted to study, but he wouldn't."

With Martha Wright playing Nellie Forbush on Broadway and *South Pacific* destined to run in New York for a total of 1,925 performances, Mary was signed to reprise her role in the show in London, with Wilbur Evans as her leading man. The star told her son that there was a small speaking part open in *South Pacific* and that he could have it and also be in the chorus in London if he was interested. Larry jumped at the chance. He played a Seabee in the show and had one small scene with his mother. After his rebellious years and a total dislike for anything connected with the theater or an acting career, Larry settled down enough to do justice to a bit part in the West End production of his mother's milestone musical.

In the fall of 1951, Mary, Richard, Heller, and Larry sailed from New York to Southampton on the *Media*, a small passenger ship belonging to the White Star Line. Before rehearsals began, the family took a short vacation in the English provinces. "At one point we were at Castle Combe, a fine countryside hotel," Larry remembered, "and once again Richard was on my case." When Halliday saw Larry vault onto a horse outside the stables and ride off bareback, he complained to Mary that her son was misbehaving as usual, and the incident became an issue between them. According to Larry, "Richard was also busy planning [mother's] schedule, dealing with the producer and the press, and generally getting on everybody's nerves." The stress became even greater once they checked into the Savoy Hotel in London, and eventually young Hagman had had enough of the bickering and left. He told his mother that he had to get away from Richard. Mary assured her

son that having him in *South Pacific* was important to her and, without saying so, indicated that it was a way for them to have a relationship. But the hot-tempered youth was fed up. "I was on the street again," Larry said, "looking for a place to stay, when I got an offer from Archie Savage, the show's lead dancer." Savage was the only other American in the company, besides Larry, Mary, and Wilbur Evans, and had rented a place on Belgrave Square. Hagman had known the dancer, a gay black man, in New York and had once rented an apartment on Third Avenue from him. Larry stayed with Savage for two weeks, then moved in with a friend from college.

South Pacific was slated to open in London on a raked stage at the Theatre Royal on Drury Lane, the same theater where Mary had played *Pacific 1860* five years before. She looked back on the Noel Coward show as a "huge flop" and was nervous about redeeming herself with London audiences. The star had studied voice under Dino Borgioli during the run of *South Pacific* in New York, raised her voice from a frail high C to a cautious E flat, and arrived in England in top vocal form. Director Joshua Logan was to recreate his staging for the Rodgers and Hammerstein show in London, but he didn't arrive until ten days before *South Pacific* opened there. The songwriter's stage manager, Jerry Whyte, supervised rehearsals while the company waited for Logan to take over, although Whyte was reluctant to make decisive suggestions for fear Logan would come in and change everything. Oscar Hammerstein tried his hand at directing the company for a while but failed. When Logan finally came, he found that the play had been treading water for ten days and Mary was tense and frightened. "The result was a very slow, plodding, lethargic production," the director said. "I started working on each character, and I found that Mary was resisting me. She said, 'Please don't change anything, Josh, I'm too scared.'" Logan watched her go through the role she had performed for over two years on Broadway and couldn't believe his eyes and ears. "She was still charming, pretty, vivacious, but too carefully so," the director said. "She was strident and mechanical. She lacked her greatest gift—spontaneity." When Logan tried to talk to Mary, she shrank from him and her lips quivered.

Wilbur Evans as Emile exhibited an excellent voice and was extremely handsome, but he lacked confidence. "I knew that if the show went on this way," Logan said, "it surely would crash." He did his best to pump energy into the performers, tried to revive the show's vitality, but Evans continued to present problems and Mary was unnerved by even the slightest departure from the staging she'd done with Pinza. "The reserved and careful Mary Martin I was directing at the Drury Lane was not the Mary Martin I had directed in 1949," Logan maintained.

When Richard Rodgers arrived in London a few days before the opening, he expected to find a reasonable facsimile of the show's New York production and was shocked when he watched a dress rehearsal. "Apparently tiring of his original concept, Josh had so deliberately altered and rearranged the show that it no longer held together," Rodgers said. "I couldn't understand what he was trying to do, and during the intermission I made my feelings known. Josh, however, remained unconvinced." Desperate to pump vigor into the production, the director had rearranged things in an effort to achieve freshness, but the changes threw Mary into a panic. At the end of the rehearsal that Rodgers observed, she sat in her dressing room crying hysterically. Between sobs, the star told Rodgers and Hammerstein that if the staging wasn't put back the way it had been originally, she wasn't going to open in the show.

The night before the production was to premiere in London, Logan decided to talk to Richard Halliday about the situation. Halliday agreed that his wife was terribly stressed and apprehensive. "Not only does she have to get used to all these new people," Richard told Logan, "but don't you see, the last time she appeared in London—at the Drury Lane—was in Noel Coward's *Pacific 1860*, and it was not a success. And Noel complained about her. She's determined to show them tomorrow night, and terrified that she won't be good enough. But don't talk to her, Josh. If you have the slightest criticism she'll lose her nerve."

Logan couldn't imagine anyone playing robust, happy, uncomplicated Nellie Forbush while quaking with fear, so he turned from the conversation with Halliday and walked directly into Mary's

dressing room, pushing past the obstinate Richard. When Mary saw him enter, her face went white. "Now, Josh, really," she said, "I don't think I can listen to any more." Logan began calmly: "Mary, you are the greatest Nellie Forbush that ever lived. You created her, but now you've got her covered up with a veil. She can't quite be seen. She's draped in panic, in doubt. But it's a very thin disguise she's hiding behind. Mary, just let Nellie burst through it." Logan grew more forceful as he talked. "I've doubted this way," he said, "and I know how you feel. Listen to me, honey. William Blake helped me get over [my fear] with four short lines of verse. Mary look me in the eyes and let me tell you what he said." His voice grew quiet as he recited Blake's words:

> He who doubts from what he sees
> Will ne'er believe, do what you please.
> If the sun and moon should doubt,
> They'd immediately go out.

Mary stood looking at Logan for a long time, then came close, put her arms over his shoulders and placed her cheek next to his. Then she whispered into his ear, "Thank you, Josh. Let's rehearse."

There in her dressing room she went through every song in the show for him. "She sat at her dressing room table and sang 'Wonderful Guy' in her original unrestrained, quietly jubilant way," Logan recalled, while the director listened sitting on a little stool nearby. "I didn't have to comment," he said. "She could see by my eyes how I approved." Richard Halliday looked on, his face flushed with excitement, while Mary did all of her numbers, closing her eyes for a moment between each one. When she finished, Logan said, "Nellie Forbush is back with us, folks. Back with us!"

When the three of them exited the stage door a bit later, it was pouring rain. The Hallidays' chauffeur was waiting with an open umbrella, since their car was parked a block away. As they passed the front of the Theatre Royal, they saw a long line of people waiting in the downpour to buy tickets for unreserved seats to see the next night's performance. Some held newspapers over their

heads, others had umbrellas, a few sat on stools. The chauffeur told Mary that the people intended to wait there all night for the box office to open the next morning, when gallery tickets went on sale. Mary called over to the crowd, "Thank you for coming so early, but we're not ready with the show yet." People standing in line laughed, and one of them shouted back, "Sing us a song, Mary." In a clear, euphoric voice she sang, "I'm in Love with a Wonderful Guy" at the top of her voice. When she finished the crowd cheered, and Mary slipped her arm through Logan's and squeezed it. As the throng continued cheering and shouting, Mary tossed them kisses through the pouring rain, as she walked toward the waiting car.

South Pacific opened in London on November 1, 1951, to an audience filled with royalty, famous actors, and important British dignitaries. The theater in Drury Lane was larger than the Majestic in New York, but Mary's performance was intimate, joyous, and free. English critics weren't as enthusiastic about the show as Americans had been, but they thought Mary was terrific. "As the hick nurse, wide-eyed at life and eager," the review in *Punch* read, "she gives a performance of such charm, humor, and originality that while she is on nothing else matters." The British estimation was that the show's plot was slow-moving and dull and that its songs, while good, didn't bear comparison with those in *Oklahoma!* The emotional theme that midcentury Americans related to so easily— that a white woman would show reluctance to marry a white man she loves because he had fathered children with a woman of a different race—was an issue English audiences had trouble taking seriously. Generation after generation of young Englishmen had gone off to India and the East and married there, so *South Pacific's* point seemed remote if not downright racist to British theater-goers. While the reviewer for the *Spectator* liked Mary's "skipping and roaming around the stage" like a moonstruck fawn, he was confused by a musical romance that tried to be involved with an adult subject. "First, this 'musical play' is quite alien in tone and method to what we understand by 'American musical comedy,'" the critic said. "Secondly, its treatment is realistic, which at once precludes ballet and chorus-girls."

Before *South Pacific* opened in London, there had been so much talk, such massive publicity, and such tremendous anticipation, that the show was bound to suffer. The Theatre Royal was sold out for six months in advance, except for the gallery seats required by law to go on sale the day of performances, and the London opening of the Rodgers and Hammerstein musical had become the most eagerly awaited, most ballyhooed, first night in memory. Yet, for Mary Martin the return to the West End was an unqualified triumph. "Mary had a great ovation which she richly deserved," Noel Coward recorded in his diary. "She gave a superb performance and . . . is a great artist. Audience wildly hysterical." Time after time, the star was brought onstage for another curtain call—Larry Hagman counted at least two dozen—while the crowd showered her with shouts of "Mary, Mary!" As the *New York Times* reported, "The distinguished audience, glittering with diamonds and swathed in mink, that gathered at the Drury Lane Theatre to see the long-awaited opening of *South Pacific* seemed determined to never let her go."

Noel Coward, Laurence Olivier, and Vivien Leigh led the vanguard of admirers who flocked into Mary's dressing room after the show. A party at the Savoy to celebrate the opening followed, at which Olivier led Mary onto the dance floor while her son danced with Vivien Leigh. "Miss Cornpone" from Texas, as Mary liked to call herself, awoke the next day to find that she had stepped into the front rank of London's favorites. Ray Walston, who had played Luther Billis in the national company of *South Pacific* opposite Janet Blair, repeated his performance at the Theatre Royal. "I don't think anyone who ever played Nellie Forbush could be compared with Mary Martin," Walston said. "She was absolutely brilliant in the part."

Being in *South Pacific* for a year gave Larry a chance to see how much the theater meant to his mother. "She was so focused," he said. "It was the first time I'd ever watched her this closely." She always had a piece of needlepoint going, which she worked on between scenes in her dressing room. During the year in London she made Josh Logan a pillow with a pastoral scene, a setting sun, and a rising moon stitched on one side and on the other

William Blake's lines that the director had quoted to her before opening night.

During their stay in London, the Hallidays lived in a furnished flat, where they enjoyed a family Christmas that included Larry, with presents around a tree and a leisurely lunch. Gossip columnist Louella Parsons reported rumors from London that Mary would become a mother for the third time, but that information proved wrong. On Sunday, January 13, 1952, the *South Pacific* star did a benefit with Noel Coward at London's Café de Paris, a one-night stand that had considerable success and further healed the relationship between the two performers. "Rehearsed all afternoon at the Café with Mary and the orchestra," Coward noted in his diary on November 11. "Mary was really magnificent—she is a marvelous artist." And of their Café de Paris performance he wrote, "Really a triumph—Mary was superb—tore the place up."

After a year's run, the Rodgers and Hammerstein play was still filling the theater on Drury Lane, and English audiences continued to be in the grip of their love affair with Mary Martin. Mary felt that her interpretation of Nellie matured during that year, particularly in the second act. "I drew on the things Noel had taught me," she said. "He cautioned me not to overdo the last scene, where Nellie thinks she may never see Emile again, because then the audience won't care. So only at the very last of my soliloquy would the tears come, but not sobbing or anything. Josh had staged it so beautifully. Still, as long as I live I'll always contend that the only person who should have played Emile is Ezio."

Seasoned player though Mary had become, she still got nervous when she learned that a VIP was in the audience. The night ballerina Margot Fonteyn came to see *South Pacific* in London, the show's star fell off the rowboat doing the waltz clog in her "Wonderful Guy" number. "I just slipped right off!" Mary remembered. "I'd never done that before, never done it since. It was just that I wanted to be so right."

Ray Walston left the London cast a few weeks before Mary did and in September 1952 sent her an affectionate note. "How truly dear of you to write that heart-warming, heart-stimulating letter,"

she replied. "It will carry me through to the end—November 8th—just six weeks and seven performances more." A few days before Mary finished her London engagement, Josh and Nedda Logan flew to England. The director wanted to talk to Mary about *Kind Sir*, an upcoming comedy he had in mind for her, and another musical, *Fanny*, which they had discussed earlier. "Josh is here at the moment," Mary wrote Walston. "I've never seen him so well and full of good, exciting ideas. It's fun having him here."

The Hallidays planned a long period for rest and refueling after Mary finished her third year in *South Pacific*. "Richard and I are getting on a slow boat to Jamaica right after November 8th," Mary wrote Walston. "Then plans call for us to fly to New York, where I'm supposed to do a scene with Rodgers and Hammerstein and sing a new song they've written for a movie called *Main Street to Broadway*. Then we fly right back to London. We've taken a small, most attractive flat until April, and I'm going to study voice, music, and languages every day because I find I not only want to but *have* to. I seem to want it more than anything. I have *fun* learning." The couple planned to be home by the end of April, but from then on their plans were uncertain. Mary needed to think over whether she wanted to do *Kind Sir*, a straight comedy, although the thought of appearing opposite Charles Boyer in the show on Broadway appealed to her.

The year in London had been a time of real growth for Mary, not only as Nellie Forbush but also as an artist and as a person. She had become an international star, overcome some of her old hurts and fears, and stabilized an uneasy bond with her son. Mother "couldn't admit that Richard was a son of a bitch to me," Larry said, but the boy came to realize the demands his mother's eminence placed on her and how much she depended on Halliday. "If it hadn't been for Dick," she said, "I'd have worn out long ago."

Mary Martin as a child.
(Courtesy of the Mary
McCord/Edyth Renshaw
Collection on the
Performing Arts, Hamon
Arts Library, Southern
Methodist University.)

Mary Martin as a girl in
Weatherford, Texas.
(Courtesy of the Sue Austin
Collection, DeGolyer
Library, Southern Methodist
University.)

Mary Martin dancing with her husband Richard Halliday at Ciro's. (Courtesy of the Interstate Collection, Harry Ransom Humanities Research Center, The University of Texas at Austin.)

Bing Crosby and Mary Martin in Paramount's *Rhythm on the River*. (Courtesy of the Interstate Collection, Harry Ransom Humanities Research Center, The University of Texas at Austin.)

Mary Martin and Don Ameche in Paramount's *Kiss the Boys Goodbye.* (Courtesy of the Interstate Collection, Harry Ransom Humanities Research Center, The University of Texas at Austin.)

Dick Powell and Mary Martin in Paramount's *True to Life*. (Courtesy of the Interstate Collection, Harry Ransom Humanities Research Center, The University of Texas at Austin.)

Mary Martin as Venus in *One Touch of Venus*. (Courtesy of Mary McCord/Edyth Renshaw Collection on the Performing Arts, Hamon Arts Library, Southern Methodist University; photograph by Vandamm Studio, New York City.)

Mary Martin singing "That's Him" in *One Touch of Venus*. (Courtesy of Mary McCord/Edyth Renshaw Collection on the Performing Arts, Hamon Arts Library, Southern Methodist University; photograph by Vandamm Studio, New York City.)

Mary Martin and Jane Wyman in Warner Bros.' *Night and Day*. (Courtesy of the Interstate Collection, Hary Ransom Humanities Research Center, The University of Texas at Austin.)

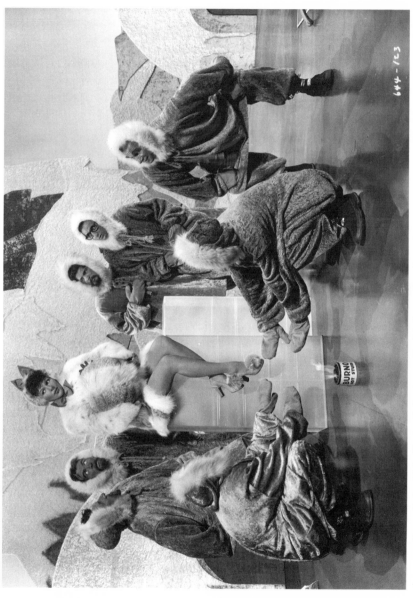

A recreation of the "My Heart Belongs to Daddy" number from Warner Bros.' *Night and Day*. (Courtesy of Mary McCord/Edyth Renshaw Collection on the Performing Arts, Hamon Arts Library, Southern Methodist University.)

Mary Martin as Annie Oakley in *Annie Get Your Gun.* (Courtesy of Mary McCord/ Edyth Renshaw Collection on the Performing Arts, Hamon Arts Library, Southern Methodist University; photograph by Vandamm Studio, New York City.)

Mary Martin in the "I'm an Indian, Too" number from *Annie Get Your Gun.* (Courtesy of Mary McCord/ Edyth Renshaw Collection on the Performing Arts, Hamon Arts Library, Southern Methodist University; photograph by Vandamm Studio, New York City.)

164

Mary Martin singing "Honey Bun" in *South Pacific*. (Courtesy of Fred Fehl Collection, Harry Ransom Humanities Research Center, University of Texas at Austin.)

Mary Martin aloft as Peter Pan in *Peter Pan.* (Author's Collection.)

Mary Martin and the children in *The Sound of Music.* (Courtesy of Fred Fehl Collection, Harry Ransom Humanities Research Center, University of Texas at Austin.)

Mary Martin as Maria in her wedding gown from *The Sound of Music*. (Courtesy of Fred Fehl Collection, Harry Ransom Humanities Research Center, University of Texas at Austin.)

A party at the Hallidays' penthouse in New York with Bessie Mae Sue Ella Austin playing violin, Mary tooting a horn, Beatrice Lillie at the piano, and Cyril Ritchard blowing a horn. (Courtesy of the Sue Austin Collection, DeGolyer Library, Southern Methodist University.)

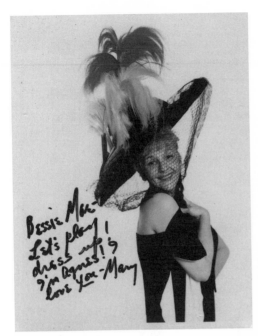

Mary Martin as "Flaming" Agnes in *I Do! I Do!* (Courtesy of the Sue Austin Collection, DeGolyer Library, Southern Methodist University).

Mary Martin with the author in San Miguel de Allende, Mexico. (Author's Collection.)

CHAPTER 8

Flying High

Mary and Richard celebrated the arrival of 1953 with Noel Coward, the Oliviers, and the Lunts in London, then left on a vacation trip through Europe and North Africa with Heller. On a visit to Spain for the opening of a new Hilton hotel in Madrid, the Hallidays attended a bullfight with Luis Miguel Dominguin, whom many considered the world's greatest torero. Dominguin explained some of the subtleties of the bullfighter's art to the American celebrities gathered for the occasion, among them Hollywood gossip columnist Hedda Hopper, radio and television personality Jinx Falkenberg, and Falkenberg's husband, Tex McCrary. A few days later, the party journeyed outside the city to the farm of a rich Spaniard who raised bulls for the arena. As they watched a succession of young bulls being fought, McCrary said, "All right, Mary, it's your turn. A Texas girl isn't afraid of cows, is she?" After a startled moment, Mary got up, walked down the aisle of the arena, and went into the ring, while Richard sputtered objections. "Mary," as Hedda Hopper remembered, "wearing a full-skirted afternoon dress and high French heels, took the cape, made several lucky passes, and escaped being gored."

In May the Hallidays landed in Houston after a three-week voyage from Genoa aboard the SS *Helen Lykes*. On the ship was a

Rolls Royce they had bought in London. Mary and eleven-year-old Heller visited family in Texas, the first time the star had been back to her home state since appearing there in *Annie Get Your Gun*. During the stay Governor Allan Shivers made Mary an honorary admiral in the Texas Navy, and a party was given for the star in the Adolphus Hotel ballroom in Dallas, with a huge ice sculpture of a Texas longhorn steer in the center of a buffet table. The actress spent a week with her sister in Fort Worth, during which they drove over to Weatherford to renew acquaintances. While in Dallas, Mary and Heller were the houseguests of Bessie Mae and Jac Austin. "We had just a few close friends of Mary's in for supper," Bessie Mae remembered. "The Hallidays and Austins had a ritual about leg of lamb. Any time they visited us, or we visited them, it was who could cook the best leg of lamb on the outside grill. But this time Richard wasn't with them." He had driven on to Connecticut.

Larry joined the Air Force soon after his year in *South Pacific* and was stationed in England for three years. While there, he produced GI shows and flew with them to Germany and Italy. He also met Swedish-born Maj Axelsson, who was working in England as a clothing designer, and the couple married in December 1955. Maj had the courage to call Mary and would help mediate the problems that the star and her rambunctious son seemed too obstinate to confront. Mary feared that she might lose contact with Larry altogether, but after his marriage his letters to his mother became warmer. "I'm beginning to understand all the anxious moments I've caused you and Richard," Larry wrote in 1955, "and all your problems and hopes."

Mary had been absent from Broadway for almost two seasons. Before leaving the New York cast of *South Pacific*, she had recommended Yul Brynner, her leading man in *Lute Song*, to Rodgers and Hammerstein for their new show, *The King and I*, which opened at the St. James Theatre in New York in March 1951. Mary thought Brynner would be perfect to play the Siamese king in the musical and urged Rodgers and Hammerstein to "kidnap him if necessary," assuring the songwriters that they'd never find anybody better for the part. Brynner, who had grown discouraged with acting, had

established himself at CBS, along with Martin Ritt and Sidney Lumet, as an important director in early television. "I really didn't want to leave my job," Brynner said. "All of my experiences on the stage had been unhappy ones, and I didn't want to risk having a flop in the theater." But Mary contacted her former costar and asked him to come to her dressing room in the Majestic Theatre. "I arrived there," Brynner remembered, "and there was no Mary, but there was the first act of *The King and I* with a request from her that I sit down and read it. I read the first act and absolutely fell in love with the character of the King. I found him absolutely irresistible, because he had things to say and problems to try to solve. I saw for the first time the possibility of playing someone and truly enjoying it." Felix Jackson, a producer at CBS at the time, recalled Brynner's coming into the studio late for a rehearsal, something he never did, putting his arms around him, and saying, "Felix, I got the part of my life."

Shortly before Larry went into the service, Mary, back from Europe, recorded two songs with him for Columbia—"You're Just in Love" from *Call Me Madam* and "Get Out Those Old Records." "We had never so much as sung 'Silent Night' together before," she said. But Mitch Miller, the artists and repertory man at Columbia, had recently scored a big hit with a single by Bing and Gary Crosby, and he talked Mary and Larry into trying to duplicate their success. Mary, under contract to Columbia at the time, had recorded the scores of *Babes in Arms, Girl Crazy, Anything Goes,* and *The Bandwagon* for the label while she was still appearing in *South Pacific* in New York. "She was a real pro," Miller said. "Goddard Lieberson produced those albums, and the whole point behind his approach was that excellence had no time limit. Quality in music from Broadway shows goes on like Faulkner and the great authors."

From their home, Mary and Richard did an interview on Edward R. Murrow's *Person to Person* show for CBS shortly after their return from Europe. On the day of the telecast, the couple entertained everyone working on the program and a few of their Connecticut neighbors with a lavish buffet supper. But the big news was that Mary was about to make her television debut as a performer. She

wasn't eager to do television, fearing it would be too much like Hollywood. But producer Leland Hayward called before she left England and asked her to star in a two-hour special celebrating the fiftieth anniversary of the founding of Ford Motor Company. Mary at first refused the offer but finally said, "All right, I'll do it if you can get Ethel Merman to do it with me." Later, Mary learned that Hayward had Merman lined up all along.

The *Ford Show* was the first time Martin and Merman worked together. The two Broadway divas, assisted by Hayward and choreographer Jerome Robbins, put together a telecast that people still talk about. Aired on the night of June 15, 1953, over CBS and NBC simultaneously with the same commercials, the live show was a spectacular event even by contemporary standards. Staged at the old Center Theatre in Rockefeller Center, the telecast opened with Mary in front of a poster from *South Pacific* and Merman in front of one from her recent hit, *Call Me Madam*. From there they walked over to two stools, set against a plain backdrop, and sang a medley of songs sitting side by side. Mary suggested that they sing some old favorites, and Merman thought of their doing some "I" songs, ending with "I Got Rhythm" and "I'm in Love with a Wonderful Guy." Mary credited the genius of Jerry Robbins for making the show the huge success it was. Robbins came up with the idea of their doing the numbers perched on high stools on an empty stage, a simple concept that has been imitated time and again on television variety shows. The choreographer also devised a comedy skit for Mary called "The Shape." Wearing a simple tube of jersey, and to the accompaniment of music and a grand voice of a narrator who delivered a fashion commentary, Mary turned the tube and a series of hats into a style show that spanned the decades from 1900 to 1950. It was a brilliant pantomime and the star was hilarious in it. "That was completely Mary," Bessie Mae Sue Ella said, "playing dress up."

"We rehearsed our heads off ten, twelve hours a day for two weeks," Mary recalled. "Ethel and I got on like gangbusters. Anything she didn't think of, I did." Yet co-producer Lawrence White didn't remember the stars' rapport being all that harmonious.

According to White, the two singers hardly spoke to one another. Both wanted top billing, so after prolonged discussion the agreement was reached that newspapers would advertise the show one day with Merman's name first and the next day with Martin's first. Mary found the cameras, the mechanical aspects of television, and all the people moving about the set difficult. "It scares me," she told reporters.

As Mary remembered, she and Merman both "looked like hell" in the Ford extravaganza, since they wore "the worst costumes I've ever seen in my life—ugly, ugly. But that was the style of that period. The dresses we wore were ghastly, and our hair wasn't becoming." Still, doing the show gave Mary insight into the basic nature of television, and she realized that it was a personality medium in which intimacy counted most.

Meanwhile, Cheryl Crawford, who had produced *One Touch of Venus* and remained a friend, was searching for a vehicle for Mary's return to Broadway. Crawford had the idea for a theater story in which the determined leading character, not unlike Mary herself, had come from the South with just enough money from giving dancing lessons to neighborhood children to get to New York, where she hoped to land a part in a Broadway show. "You're not sure whether or not she is pretty," Crawford wrote Richard. "Sometimes you think she is scrawny and a little goofy. But then suddenly she is radiant and sexually appealing in an odd way. Finally, when she really gets a part, you know she is beautiful." But the Hallidays had decided that Mary's return to the theater in New York would be in the comedy *Kind Sir*, a complete change of pace from Nellie Forbush and one that would require no singing.

Richard reasoned that the only way for his wife to top her triumph in *South Pacific* was to move in an entirely new direction. *Kind Sir* was a slick farce by Norman Krasna, who had enjoyed commercial success on Broadway in the mid-1940s with *Dear Ruth* and *John Loves Mary*. In the show Mary would play a wealthy, sophisticated stage star, wear six Mainbocher gowns and a glamorous hairdo, and appear opposite the romantic French movie actor Charles Boyer. Although she was nervous about impersonating a famous actress

in a straight play, a part originally intended for the stage debut of Joan Crawford, Mary looked upon the role as another challenge. She was eager to work again with Joshua Logan, who would be directing, excited about sharing the stage with Boyer, and thrilled by the dream wardrobe that Mainbocher had created for her. Her dialogue in the play was witty and worldly, and the set designed by Jo Mielziner glowed with elegance.

But Krasna was late finishing the script, and from the first day of rehearsal the show seemed ill-fated. Logan was ill during the production, suffering from a manic depression. "It made things awfully hard for those of us in the cast," said Dorothy Stickney, who played Mary's busybody older sister in the comedy, "because we never knew what to expect from him. We never knew what Josh was going to say next, or how he was going to ask us to play our parts. So we really ended by having very little actual direction. Josh's suggestions were so erratic at times that we just had to do the best we could on our own." At night Logan was on the phone frequently with Mary or Richard and with Boyer, all of whom were disturbed by what was happening at rehearsals. Their complaints simply made the director more agitated and excited. His explosive temper flared, and at one point he even fired Dorothy Stickney, an old friend. "I had to talk him into hiring her back," Mary said. Stickney, a seasoned actress, became so unnerved by the turmoil that she had to carry her script onstage to help her remember lines.

The company slogged on with rehearsals through August 1953 in an empty, dusty theater in the West Fifties in New York, with Logan's condition growing worse. "We all realized Josh was in bad shape," Stickney said, "but there didn't seem to be anything we could do about it. Sometimes he would yell directions from the back of the theater in a really outrageous way." The director refused to let his wife, actress Nedda Harrigan, come to the theater while the cast was rehearsing, but she slipped in incognito and conferred with the Hallidays afterward. "Josh would ask me to do the damnedest things," Mary said, "and this play wasn't very good anyway. The situation just became tragic."

Mary adored the other actors in *Kind Sir*, two of whom were Margalo Gillmore and her husband, but she was unhappy in the show from the start. "It was a nightmare," Mary remembered, "because Josh was off his rocker. We kept trying to get him to seek medical attention, but he wouldn't go. He said, 'If I go in, I'll never get out of the hospital.' The only thing that saved his life was lithium." Richard's main concern through the ordeal was that Mary be protected. He remained convinced that the role of a great lady of the American theater, who had had one hit show after another for fifteen years but no time to fall in love, was an ideal way for his wife to change pace and escape the corn-fed image of Nellie Forbush. "Mary is full of exciting contradictions," Richard said. "She has the guts of a Texas steer, and yet she's a delicate and feminine human being. I want to keep it that way."

In September the company took *Kind Sir* on a pre-Broadway tour that opened in New Orleans, near the town in Louisiana where Logan had grown up. Heller was left with her aunt and uncle, while Mary and Richard ensconced themselves in the Hotel Pontchartrain. They arrived in New Orleans to find an electric sign reading, "Welcome *Kind Sir*, starring Mary Martin and Charles Boyer, and directed by Louisiana's own Josh Logan." Most of the national magazines were geared to do a feature article on the opening, and journalists from the New York newspapers were scheduled to cover the event. But during dress rehearsals at the city's Civic Theatre, the director decided that he didn't like the way Mary made her entrance. "I don't think that looks right," he told her. "I want you to do a cartwheel when you come in." When the star refused, Logan walked out of the theater and didn't come back for hours. "Nobody left," Mary said, "because we all loved him." When the director returned, he had the ushers make bouquets with rocks in them, which he periodically threw up on the stage. "We were dodging all these rocks," Mary said. "It was murder. I could write a show on *that* show that would be hysterical."

There was a scene in the play where Boyer, cast as a wealthy diplomat, had to pass from center stage either behind or in front

of a sofa. There had been discussion about which way was better, but the actor still wasn't sure whether he was supposed to cross above the sofa or below it. On opening night he crossed below, and from the back of the house Logan yelled, "I told you *behind* the sofa!" The director raced down the aisle, screaming at the actor, and had to be placed in a sanatorium near New Orleans a few days later, having suffered a complete breakdown. He was taken from his hotel in a straitjacket.

A big party was held after the opening night performance, which was attended by a host of celebrities from out of town, as well as members of the press. A pregnant Bessie Mae Sue Ella and her husband, Jac Austin, drove down to New Orleans from Dallas for the occasion. Backstage after the play, Mary told Bessie, "Well, now that you're going to have another baby, I think you should name her after me if it's a girl. After all, I've used your name so many times in my shows." The Austins did name their youngest daughter Mary Anna; she would become an actress and later a casting director. "But *Kind Sir* was not a good show," Bessie Mae said. "Mary is capable of doing straight parts, but that play was a disappointment. I was not surprised when it didn't do well."

The *Dallas Morning News*' critic, John Rosenfield, who was also on hand for the opening in New Orleans, agreed with Bessie's assessment of the Krasna play, faulting mainly the writing. "Not even Mary Martin, who exhibits an encouraging potential as a ripened comedienne, can survive it," Rosenfield wrote in his review. "Something never suspected . . . is Miss Martin's new, deep-voiced hardness of personality. She was a woman of distinction in poise and bearing." Hedda Hopper saw the show at the Civic Theatre and smelled a fiasco, although the columnist did her best to lift Mary's spirits after the opening. "Nothing helped *Kind Sir*," Hopper said. "In the seat next to me, Mainbocher, who'd done [Mary's] costumes, slid down almost out of sight so he wouldn't be asked to take a bow."

New Orleans hospitality in part offset the gloom that hung over the show's premiere, but the cast grew increasingly apprehensive. Mary received a telegram of best wishes from three hundred residents of Weatherford, with Mayor Jim Wright, the future Speaker

of the House, heading the list of signers, and a message that read: "Your heart belongs to Daddy, Weatherford's heart belongs to you." Charles Boyer largely kept to himself during the run of the production, but the rest of the company took solace in one another. "I love Mary," Dorothy Stickney said, "she's such a wonderful person. There's no star nonsense about Mary, none at all."

Kind Sir went next to St. Louis and then to Cleveland, but without Josh Logan, who remained hospitalized. Mary never grew comfortable with farcical techniques, and there were times when she was ready to drop out of the show. But the comedy opened at the Alvin Theatre in New York on November 4, 1953, to tepid reviews. The best that could be said of the comedy was that Mary Martin and Charles Boyer were supreme examples of players capable of making something out of little. "After the first act, which is reasonably promising," Brooks Atkinson said in the *New York Times*, "it quickly becomes obvious that Miss Martin and Mr. Boyer have nothing but their own charm to work with."

Critics agreed that Mary was still adorable in this straight role, but Harold Clurman called the play, with its stunning set and costumes, "an example of conspicuous waste." Krasna's writing was judged routine, and the comedy's plot was dismissed as slight. But *Kind Sir* opened in New York with a $700,000 advance ticket sale, which assured the show of a respectable run. Audiences were eager to see Mary Martin in a non-singing part and Boyer on stage in a romantic comedy, but even diehard fans admitted that the vehicle was a letdown after all the publicity hype that had proceeded it. *Time* called Krasna's comedy "a sumptuous bore and a gilded vacuum," although the script was later turned into a movie— *Indiscreet*, starring Ingrid Bergman and Cary Grant—which proved quite successful.

Mary had agreed to do *Kind Sir* for one season while Logan, Sam Behrman, and composer Harold Rome finished writing *Fanny*, a musical the team was preparing for her that she and Richard were convinced would be a masterpiece. Mary had fallen in love with the trilogy of plays by Marcel Pagnol on which the show was to be based, and she looked forward to starring again on Broadway

with Ezio Pinza, already cast. But before *Kind Sir* closed on March 27, 1954, Mary backed out of *Fanny*. She told Logan, "You went to the hospital, I stayed on the stage. I did things that I didn't believe in, and I'm not up to doing another show with you. I just can't do it." She recommended her friend Florence Henderson for the title role in the Rome musical, which opened on Broadway in November 1954. Logan had originally wanted Rodgers and Hammerstein to write the score for *Fanny*, but they declined early in the planning. "The whole thing could have been sensational if it had been done the way it should have been done," Mary said. As it was, the show proved a modest success.

With *Fanny* no longer on Mary's agenda, the Hallidays turned to a project they had been planning for more than ten years, a musical version of *Peter Pan*. The irrepressible boy who refused to grow up had been the star's favorite character since childhood, and she longed to play the role on the stage. In Hollywood, Mary and Jean Arthur had had long talks about how Peter Pan should be done, since both actresses coveted the part. Arthur would eventually play the androgynous sprite on Broadway in 1950, with Boris Karloff as Mr. Darling and Captain Hook. But the Hallidays wanted to do a new, more fully musical version of James M. Barrie's play. They had discussed the project with Kurt Weill in 1944, and the composer had agreed to write the score, until it was discovered that Walt Disney had just bought the motion picture rights to the property. Five years later, Mary and Richard tried to talk Rodgers and Hammerstein into writing the songs for their *Peter Pan*. At that point they hoped to get Joshua Logan to direct the show and Ezio Pinza to play Captain Hook, but then they learned that a producer had optioned the stage rights and intended to star Jean Arthur in the part. Early in 1954, West Coast impresario Edwin Lester asked Mary if she would be interested in appearing in an entirely new musical version of the play with Richard as co-producer. Lester's suggestion resulted in a lifetime dream come true. "*Peter Pan* is perhaps the most important thing, to me, that I have ever done in the theater," Mary said.

Hugh Martin and Ralph Blane, who had written the score for the classic MGM musical *Meet Me in St. Louis* (1944), were approached

next to write the songs for the Hallidays' *Peter Pan*, but the couple ultimately decided on Carolyn Leigh and Mark Charlap to do the lyrics and music. "Carolyn Leigh is the one we discovered," Mary said, "and Moose Charlap was with her. He was the cutest little thing on earth, and they were wonderful together. But this was their first show, and it was difficult for them to write certain kinds of songs."

Mary and Richard had been so impressed with Jerome Robbins's creativity on the Ford anniversary show that they immediately thought of him to direct their version of *Peter Pan*. The famous choreographer had never directed a book musical before, but he took a leave of absence from ballet to collaborate on fashioning an adaptation of Barrie's play tailored to Mary's personality and talent. Robbins took no writing credit, although he envisioned which parts of the story were best suited to musical treatment. His assistant, Mary Hunter, said, "It was Jerry's idea to use children as the pirates, and I thought it was a wonderful idea, and still do think it was one of his most creative ideas, because it changed the whole show." The *Peter Pan* that Mary did was drawn from four previous versions of the play—the standard Barrie script plus the ones Maude Adams, Eva LeGallienne, and Jean Arthur had appeared in—as well as Barrie's story "Peter and Wendy." Robbins's goal was to Americanize the story, while preserving its original essence.

The celebrated Australian actor Cyril Ritchard was chosen to be Mary's Captain Hook, and the actress insisted that Heller have a part in the show. The star had simply assumed that her daughter would follow in her footsteps and opt for a career on the stage. "The theater was to me such a rewarding way of life," Mary said, "that I couldn't imagine her not embracing it." Yet Robbins objected to the casting of Heller in *Peter Pan*, claiming that the idea was inartistic and worked against the grain of what he was trying to achieve. "I don't want anybody in the theater to think of Mary's private life at all for any reason whatever," he told Mary Hunter. But his assistant said, "Jerry, if you don't want to have a rotten summer and an angry actress, you've got to do this one thing for Mary." Robbins finally gave in, and Heller was cast as Liza, the Darling family's maid.

Through the years, Mary had spent hours trying to teach her daughter things she'd learned about performing—how to whistle, dance steps she knew, how to project her voice, how to read lines, how to put on makeup. "She had me singing before I could walk," Heller said. But the busy star was less successful in teaching the girl academic fundamentals like multiplication tables and spelling. When Heller had to stay after school one day for misspelling "boat," Mary asked how she'd spelled it. "B-o-t-e," her daughter said. Mary looked at her quizzically and asked, "What's wrong with that?" But despite working long hours in the theater, the star had tried to keep a watchful eye on her daughter's upbringing and see that she was raised in a healthy atmosphere. "Whenever I needed guidance," the girl said, "Mummy was there fast."

Eventually, a ballet that featured Heller was put into *Peter Pan*. "Mummy worked right beside me, coaching, guiding, encouraging, and being my toughest critic," the girl said. Mary told her twelve-year-old daughter not to worry about being nervous onstage because everybody was, especially when doing something new. The night the show opened in San Francisco, Mary, as Peter Pan, was lying on the stage, supposedly asleep, while Heller did her dance. Without letting the audience become aware at it, the actress kept an eye open the whole time and was proud when she saw how well her daughter performed.

Mary was forty years old when she first played Peter Pan, yet she rehearsed fourteen hours a day and seemed fresh and high-spirited while everyone else in the company drooped with fatigue. She was determined to fly all over the stage in the part. The flying apparatus used was the invention of two Englishmen, Joseph Kirby and his son, who devised a harness by which Mary was suspended on a thin steel wire. The wire was wound around a revolving drum secured above the stage, and an expert propelled Peter's flights about the stage on a pulley. Mary wore a well-concealed foam-rubber saddle with hooks in the back. She wanted to sail out over the audience from the stage to the top balcony, but at the time that wasn't technically feasible without the possibility of injuring spectators. As it was, Mary suffered many painful falls during rehearsals, and on one occasion a stagehand forgot to pull a braking wire and

she slammed into a brick wall and broke a bone in her arm. The star wore a wireless mike, among the first, while singing "I'm Flying," but since she had trouble distinguishing left from right, she kept running into Wendy, played initially by Kathy Nolan, when they flew out the window of the Darling home. "I can't tell you the joy I felt in flying in that show," Mary said. "I loved it so. The freedom of spirit that was Peter Pan was suddenly there for me. I discovered I was happier in the air than on the ground."

Although many people through the years complained that Jerome Robbins was devastatingly difficult to work with, Mary found the experience thrilling. Robbins demanded discipline, and Mary had no problem with that. He would scream, get angry, and intimidate cast members, yet Mary could see the ingenuity and verve that he was lending to the production. She trusted him implicitly, and the choreographer admired her ability, her vitality, and her natural warmth. Whereas Edwin Lester remained leery of Robbins and thought he was too young and inexperienced for the job, Mary put herself totally in his hands. "We worked together until three o'clock in the morning," she said. "We rehearsed first in Los Angeles in a great big hall they had just built there. Jerry was the perfect person to direct that show, because he was really a child himself. He was absolutely fabulous. I told Ed Lester that I wouldn't do *Peter Pan* unless Jerome Robbins directed it. Robbins and Lester never got along, but Jerry and I did."

Before the show went into rehearsal, Mary had her hair dyed blonde, then went to Richard's barber and had it cut short like a little boy's haircut. "When we first saw Mummy's hair at the dinner table," Heller said, "Daddy and I laughed so hard we couldn't eat." But Mary knew that a suspension of reality would be the prime ingredient needed to turn the musical fantasy into a success, and she hoped that her gamine face and elfin figure would make her Peter wholly boyish and believable. Certainly her commitment to the part helped. Larry Hagman thought that *Peter Pan* was the show that allowed his mother to play herself. "Never Land is the way I would like real life to be," she said—"timeless, free, mischievous, filled with gaiety, tenderness, and magic."

ciation of the talent displayed," Harold Clurman said in the *Nation,* "I felt no genuine warmth or real affection for the whole event."

Despite critical carping, *Peter Pan* stands as the show in which Mary Martin made her greatest personal hit. "Miss Martin, looking trim and happy, is the liveliest Peter Pan in the record book," said Brooks Atkinson of the *New York Times.* "She has more appetite for flying and swinging than any of her more demure predecessors . . . and plays the part of Peter with affection and sincerity." The musical won Mary her second Tony Award for best actress, and the role remains the one later generations associate with her most immediately. "I don't know what all the fuss is about," Walter Kerr said in the *New York Herald Tribune.* "I always knew Mary Martin could fly. She's always bounced along as though the earth were made of inner-spring mattresses." In Mary's *Peter Pan,* reality and fantasy became one. She looked the part, lived the part, and for those who saw her in the show she *was* Peter.

Mary said that the greatest pleasure of playing *Peter Pan* before a live audience was hearing children's voices at matinees and the clapping of their hands when Peter asks them if they believe in fairies. She made a point of never getting out of costume until all of the children had left the theater, since many of them came backstage to see her. "We used to give them all fairy dust," Mary said; "we must have dispensed tons of it." Parents sometimes traveled long distances by bus bringing their kids to see *Peter Pan.* "After the performance I'd go out and thank them in the lobby," the actress said. "It did my heart good."

Noel Coward was in New York in early December 1954 and came to see Mary in the show on a Friday night. "Except for moments in the first act," Coward wrote in his diary, "it had little to do with the original. Mary was wonderful and whenever she had Barrie's lines to speak there was a 'true' quality. Her flying was miraculous, but the original music has all been banished and some honky-tonk Broadway numbers substituted. Jerome Robbins, who directed and rewrote it, is apparently opposed to sentiment."

While such fault-finding persisted, *Peter Pan* continued to delight youngsters of all ages through most of that winter. There were

times when bad colds had to be doctored in the wings, and an emergency treatment was necessary the day Mary flew head-on into a brick wall. "But thousands of children were expecting to see *Peter Pan*," the star said. "We just couldn't disappoint them." The show's initial Broadway engagement ended in February 1955 after 152 performances, but that merely marked its beginning.

Immediately after the last performance at the Winter Garden, the show went into rehearsal for a live television airing, almost intact, over NBC. The performance was done in an old film studio in Brooklyn, using the original scenery and costumes. "There were four complete sets," orchestra leader Harry Sosnik remembered. "They set up the scenery on four stages and the orchestra by itself in another room. They set up monitors on every set so the person who was going to sing a song could see the conductor on the monitor. I had an assistant conductor cue them." In those days there were no echo chambers available, so Fred Christy, the chief engineer for NBC, said, "Let's try something. We'll put a microphone in the men's room." The restroom was lined with tile, a microphone was placed in the middle of it, and a guard was stationed outside to keep people out while the sound technicians were using the facilities. Sosnik remembered that Mary's wireless mike never worked during the rehearsals, although it worked fine when the show went on the air. "While the performance was going on," the musician said, "they were moving cameras around fast from stage to stage. Also in those days commercials were live and were done right in the studio. So during one of those fast moves, the large crane camera hit one of the stagehands, broke one of his arms, and nobody stopped. They just picked him up and carried him out, and the show went on."

Peter Pan was broadcast first on March 8, 1955, to a record sixty-seven million viewers, and repeated live on NBC the following January, one of the most popular telecasts ever. "In my opinion it ranks with the best shows in TV's short history, " Walter Ames wrote in the *Los Angeles Times*. It was the first time that an entire stage play had been transformed into a two-hour color television spectacular. Because of the triumph of *Peter Pan*, children's stories became

much in demand for network programming, and its success was nearly matched in 1958 by Rodgers and Hammerstein's *Cinderella*. By then, Mary had been widely acclaimed as "the first lady of television."

The flying problem proved the stumbling block to taking *Peter Pan* on the road, so putting the show on television seemed the logical alternative to a lengthy tour. "We love the show so much that we did want as many persons as possible to see it," Mary said. A later taping and the introduction of video cassettes meant that at least two generations came to identify the star as Peter Pan. One day some years after she'd played the role for the last time, Mary was walking across Fifth Avenue when suddenly a manhole cover rose and out popped a big, brawny man with a hard hat on. He looked straight at the actress and said, "Peter, will you crow for me?" Mary said, "Certainly," and right there in the middle of the street she crowed as loud as she could. "Thank you," the workman said and disappeared back down the manhole.

Mary hoped that her *Peter Pan* would be revived often with other performers in the title role. Interestingly enough, in spite of the harsh reviews the show received when it first appeared, it has enjoyed successful Broadway revivals and lengthy tours with Sandy Duncan and still later Cathy Rigby as Peter. Mary saw Duncan in the part in Los Angeles and thought she was marvelous. "By that time she could fly out over the audience," Mary said, "which I always wanted to do and never could. Sandy, another Texan, didn't know I was coming to see her performance, and when I walked into her dressing room after the show, she went white and broke into tears." Duncan said, "You're the only Peter Pan I'll ever know." Mary told her, "But you see, *you* are *my* Peter Pan."

After the initial telecast of the show, Mary, Richard, and Heller were scheduled to take a freighter to Greece. Supposedly, their luggage was already on board the ship. Richard went to the pier in Hoboken, New Jersey, to check out their cabin, then called Mary to tell her that the departure had been postponed for several days. The tired actress was desolate. Richard said that he'd learned that there was another freighter leaving in two days for South America. "Can you get our luggage moved over?" Mary asked.

On April 8, 1955, the Hallidays arrived by sea for a ten-day vacation in Argentina. In Brazil they visited actress Janet Gaynor and her husband, Adrian, the costume designer, who were living there. Mary and Richard found their Hollywood friends ensconced in a Moorish-style home they had built in a tropical paradise fifty miles down a dusty road from the nearest telephone. The Hallidays flew in for the visit aboard a small plane and immediately fell in love with the remote ranching area. "Mary and I have never felt such strength, such health," Richard said a year later, after they'd bought property on the other side of the valley from Gaynor and Adrian. "We have never seen skies so clear, so crystal blue." The temperature there was never below fifty-eight degrees nor higher than eighty degrees. Coffee, pineapples, and sugar cane grew on the land not covered by virgin jungle full of monkeys, birds, and butterflies. The dirt in that part of Brazil was red the way it was around Weatherford, but the Brazilian landscape teemed with unbelievable beauty. Determined to return to South America one day, the Hallidays bought a place of their own near their friends.

What they purchased was a ranch with an attractive adobe house on it, surrounded by hills in every direction and rolling green valleys. Luxuries there were nonexistent—no telephone, no electricity except for about two hours' worth of power generated by a crude hydroelectric dam, food cooked over a wood fire in the kitchen, and one little refrigerator that ran on kerosene. But their ranch would become Mary and Richard's retreat, a utopia where they could unwind and enjoy a restful solitude that a major career in show business seldom permitted, made all the more complicated now that Richard was a full-fledged producer. Eventually, they hoped to retire to Brazil permanently.

Mary fully realized how blessed she was in having a fêted reputation with such extraordinary material available for her to perform. "I think we've had an awfully nice life," she said, speaking for herself and Richard. "I'm doing exactly what I love. Would anyone in his right mind be in any other business?" Yet stardom carried responsibility and performing eight times a week, month after month, was exhausting, physically and emotionally. Mary needed time to

regenerate, and that wasn't always easy, particularly since Richard's alcoholism had become chronic. In Brazil the pressures were less, the worries fewer, public scrutiny absent. Mary clung tenaciously to the belief that there was no room in her life for fear, and she taught her children not to be afraid of anything ever. Yet there were times when she came close to caving in—sensing the demons Richard must be facing, aware of the hurt she had caused and was still causing Larry, and somehow knowing that her celebrity, in different ways, had been the source of others' pain. How probing Mary was about her own nature—her fundamental immaturity, her glaring dependence on a protector and decision-maker, the pluses and minuses of an unspoiled naturalness and glee that, onstage and off, enchanted others—is difficult to assess. "If one wanted to have a deep conversation with somebody," said Richard Rodgers' daughter, Mary, "I doubt that you'd choose Mary Martin to have it with. Mary was absolutely genuine, but not a deep thinker. She had warmth and enormous instinct, but she was utterly non-intellectual."

In the face of Richard's alcohol and drug problem, Mary's concentration remained on her work. While her courage and positive attitude were beacons, she needed rest and a release. Brazil would provide that, take her back to her days as a tomboy in Weatherford, and allow Richard and her to escape the countless hassles of putting winning shows together. Mary could get up early in the morning at the ranch and enjoy the sunrise, ride horseback through the valley and over the adjoining hills, and forget for a time that Broadway existed and that Richard was destroying himself with alcohol and amphetamines.

New Challenges

While Mary was in London with *South Pacific*, Alan Jay Lerner and Frederick Loewe, at producer Cheryl Crawford's suggestion, agreed to look at Gabriel Pascal's film version of *Pygmalion*, with an eye toward turning the Shaw play into a musical. After screening the movie, the songwriters, who had been responsible for *Brigadoon* and *Paint Your Wagon* on Broadway, said they would get involved with the Shaw project if they could interest Mary Martin in playing Eliza. Neither Mary nor Alan Lerner at first was enthusiastic about the project, however. Mary didn't think she could do justice to the part of a cockney flower seller, and Lerner had doubts that he could convert the philosophical comedy into a successful musical. In November 1954, Mary and Richard agreed to listen to five songs that Lerner and Loewe had written for the show, including "Just You Wait" and "Say a Prayer for Me Tonight," which was later dropped. Neither of the Hallidays was impressed with what they heard. When they got home that night, Mary walked the floor saying over and over, "Richard, those dear boys have lost their talent." Later she told the songwriters that there was a little girl who had just come over from London named Julie Andrews and suggested that they contact her about playing Eliza in what would become *My Fair Lady*.

Meanwhile, Hedda Hopper insisted that Mary must do the screen version of *South Pacific.* "There are makeup men today who'll make Mary look like a young girl," Hopper told Josh Logan, who was slated to direct the movie that eventually had Mitzi Gaynor in the female lead. "Mitzi's a fine entertainer," the gossip columnist argued, "but she'll be only a carbon copy of Mary as Nellie Forbush." Logan wrote Hopper a twelve-page letter explaining why she was wrong. While audiences found Gaynor acceptable in the role, the motion picture proved a disappointment.

Mary was also considered for Vera, the older woman, in the film version of *Pal Joey,* but Rita Hayworth was ultimately cast in the part. Cheryl Crawford had suggested a musical treatment of *Dream Girl* as Mary's next Broadway vehicle, but after seeing the show in a television adaptation they decided that the material was not worth the effort. At one point Rodgers and Hammerstein were considering turning Edna Ferber's *Saratoga Trunk* into a musical, possibly with Mary as Clio Dulaine, but the songwriters opted instead to do *Pipe Dream,* based on a John Steinbeck story, and Mary lost interest in the offer.

After *Peter Pan,* Richard thought that Mary again needed a distinct change of pace. So the couple decided she should play Sabina in a revival of Thornton Wilder's *The Skin of Our Teeth,* a part created by Tallulah Bankhead in 1942. Wilder's Pulitzer Prize–winning allegory about mankind's constant struggle for survival and the indestructibility of the human spirit, although a comedy, thrust Mary into the realm of heavy drama. She would be playing the eternal "other woman," a timeless symbol of gaiety and abandon, opposite Helen Hayes, the acknowledged first lady of the American stage, and George Abbott, the great theater director, who was assuming his first acting assignment in twenty years. The production was put together for the State Department by the American National Theatre and Academy (ANTA) as a "Salute to France" and opened on June 28, 1955, at an International Theater Festival in the Sarah Bernhardt Theatre in Paris. Mary, with her irrepressible urge to try something new, gave her all to the straight acting job and got laughs in the comedy, none bigger than when Sabina

addressed the audience directly and admitted, "I don't understand one word of this play."

Heller was cast in the play as the Antrobuses's daughter, Gladys, and Larry came over from England to perform a rowdy drunk in one scene. With him was his wife, Maj, whom the Hallidays met for the first time. Mary decided that if she was going to Paris to star in an American classic and meet her new daughter-in-law, she should have an appropriate wardrobe designed by Mainbocher. Soon after she arrived, Mary and Helen Hayes were walking down the Champs Elysees one afternoon, with the singing star dressed to the nines, when a flock of birds flew over. One of them "took perfect aim on Mary," Hayes remembered, and dumped on her. Hayes didn't know Mary too well at the time and feared she might have an hysterical actress on her hands when she saw the mess the bird had made on her Mainbocher frock. Instead, Mary looked at the older actress with a sort of half-smile and said, "For some people they sing."

Although Hayes and Martin were at opposite poles on the acting spectrum, they became fast friends during the production. Mary had some trouble finding her way in the nonmusical and asked director Alan Schneider for extra time with him, coming to rehearsals hours ahead of everyone else to work on her scenes. Schneider's method of direction was highly personal, and he worked with each cast member differently. Hayes, an old hand at this kind of drama, told the director, "Edit me, Alan. Don't direct me." Schneider understood what she meant and simply limited his comments to telling the actress when she was doing too much or too little. With Mary he had to propose specifics, which the star would then embellish and make her own. "One day," Schneider said, "I suggested that Sabina dust everything. Not only did Mary find a dozen laughs in dusting various odd places like the floor, she even got a few out of dusting herself."

George Abbott wasn't altogether comfortable in his role, since he hadn't acted in decades. "It was one of those few times when the actual discomfort that an actor felt worked for the character," said Don Murray, who played Henry, the Antrobuses's son. "Because

the character was supposed to be a rigid man and a very moral man who was constantly getting confused by the grayness of the world, it fit Abbott's personality and he was very effective in the play." Since there was no sound system at the Sarah Bernhardt Theater, Abbott had trouble projecting his voice to the back of the house. "I always thought I had a strong, clear voice," he said, "and when they told me I couldn't be heard it shocked me beyond words."

Even with all of her laurels and great experience, Helen Hayes still got nervous before she went on stage. "I could feel it when she hugged me in the play," Don Murray said, "I could feel her trembling. That always amazed me." But when the comedy opened in Paris, Hayes got as many laughs as Mary did, even though Mary's part was funnier. Backstage, director Alan Schneider suddenly felt a hand clutching his left shoulder and heard a voice spitting into his ear. "What have you done to my wife?" the voice said. "I turned directly into the pained countenance of Richard Halliday," Schneider remembered. "At first I thought Dick must be drunk. . . . I put my finger to my lips and turned away, my heart beating loud." The director had neglected to tell Mary that Helen Hayes was an adept comedienne and might find laughs in unexpected places.

Mary ripped off a fingernail closing a faulty door in Paris, and her finger throbbed painfully throughout the opening night performance. The actress could tell from the audience's response that the French, some listening to a translation of the dialogue through earphones, were not particularly impressed with her Sabina. Mary held Schneider responsible for the lukewarm reaction. "I didn't like the director," she said. "I liked him at the beginning, but he was determined that I was going to play the part as Mary Martin. The words were written for someone like Tallulah Bankhead, so that just screwed up my entire opening in the show. I played Sabina in Paris as Mary Martin playing Mary Martin." Schneider remembered that at the celebration party in Mary's dressing room after the show on opening night, the actress hardly looked at him. "And she never spoke to me again except in passing," he said.

From Paris the production was scheduled to go to Washington, D.C., and Chicago before opening for a limited run in New York.

"I knew I wasn't good in it," Mary said, and she threatened to quit the show unless a new director was brought in. "That's when Vincent Donehue came into my life," she said. "By that time I didn't trust anybody, but I just adored Vinnie. Of all the people that directed me, next to Josh, Vinnie was the greatest I ever worked with." Although Schneider was retained as director of *The Skin of Our Teeth*, Donehue was hired to work with Mary while Schneider continued with the rest of the cast. Helen Hayes was astounded by the arrangement, and Donehue, an old friend of Schneider, seemed embarrassed to be called in. Things were so tense that Kim Stanley was standing by to take over Mary's role should that prove necessary.

In Washington the company rehearsed the scene where Sabina had to deal with scenery flying and sliding off in various directions each afternoon, hoping things would go right at that night's performance. "Every evening the scenery proved temperamental— putting poor, confused Mary into a tizzy," Schneider recalled. "We thought the stagehands were doing it on purpose. The fact was that the stagehand that worked with Mary during the day worked elsewhere at night. After rehearsal he simply wrote a note of instruction to someone else." But the company continued with dual directors through two weeks in Washington and another fortnight in Chicago, where Donehue and Schneider often had a late supper together at the Blackstone Hotel during which they tried to blend their different slants on the play. Donehue told Mary to imitate any actress she wanted to—Bankhead, Vivien Leigh, or anybody else who had performed the role, but *not* to play Mary Martin. That worked to her satisfaction. "My ten-minute soliloquy, which had fallen so flat before," Mary said, "went on for about fifteen minutes because it got such great applause, such spreading laughter, for each great Thornton Wilder line."

Through all the conflict, Mary and Helen Hayes managed to remain friends. George Abbott simply felt that Mary was too sweet for the bitchy role she was playing. Despite the tension between her and Schneider, Mary remained the darling of the company. "She was one of the real delights of my life," said Don Murray. "Mary was always so 'up,' so energetic, and just had a great sense

of humor. I remember we were doing out-of-town tryouts before we opened on Broadway. Some of the cast members and myself wrote a parody called 'No Skin Off My ——.' Mary got to laughing so hard that she got hysterical. She ended up falling on the floor, rolling around on the floor and holding her sides, laughing. She was really one of the most delightful people I've ever worked with."

On August 16, 1955, the revival of *The Skin of Our Teeth* opened a three-week engagement at the ANTA Theatre in New York. Critics responded positively, and Helen Hayes and Mary Martin both received excellent notices. Brooks Atkinson thought they not only played their parts with spirit but with religious understanding. "And what Thornton Wilder had to say about the human race in 1942," the *Times* critic said, "seems more profound and admirable today. . . . What was abstract philosophy then has become a painful part of our experience. And Mr. Wilder's celestial vaudeville has become the story of mankind." Most reviewers thought that Mary's Sabina was brilliant, although some thought she lacked Bankhead's sting and garish impudence. "Where Tallulah seemed snobbishly bored with the proceedings," Henry Hewes wrote in the *Saturday Review*, "Miss Martin is a good-hearted and folksy 'Gal Sal.'"

The production closed at the ANTA on September 3, although it could have gone on for a much longer run, to begin rehearsals for a live television performance that was aired on Sunday, September 11, over NBC. Brooks Atkinson continued to say that "it is dollars to doughnuts that . . . Miss Martin will not be more fabulous than she is as Sabina. . . . Nothing in the performance is funnier than Miss Martin's scene in the second act when she sets out to seduce Mr. Antrobus. It is a broad cartoon of all seduction scenes." Vincent Donehue directed the television version of Wilder's play, which was slightly abridged. "We performed the show as if they were photographing the stage play, " Don Murray said. "They didn't try a film technique. It was stage technique with the camera filming it."

Richard and Larry had treated one another civilly when they were together in Paris. But Heller threw her mother a wrench by announcing that she wanted to quit show business. Mary accepted the decision, hiding her disappointment. "There's a boy back home

who's been writing me," Heller told her parents. "I miss him. I want to go back home, live with my friends. I want to go back to school. I want to stop living out of a suitcase." The girl desperately wished to be with those her own age, so it was decided that she should go to boarding school. Oscar Hammerstein recommended George School, a coeducational Quaker school in Bucks County, Pennsylvania. After the performances of *The Skin of Our Teeth* were over, Mary and Richard drove their daughter down to the school and enrolled her. "I was a little nervous," Heller said, "and I guess they were, too. We had never been separated for any length of time." Although she was not an outstanding student, Heller thrived at the school, enjoyed football games there and an active social life, and in her second year was chosen to be a member of the cheering squad. A bit later she told Mary, "Mother, you haven't grown up, but I have." Mary accepted that her daughter might be right.

Before the trip to Paris, Mary had agreed to do a television special in the fall of 1955 with Noel Coward. Her relationship with Coward had become warm enough by then that the two performers were looking forward to working together again. "I trust Mary's common sense," Coward noted in his diary that May. The British playwright wrote two opening numbers for them to perform in the show—"Ninety Minutes Is a Long, Long Time" (the length of the television special) and "Together with Music" (which became the special's title), along with dialogue to bind the scenes together. In September 1955, Mary and Coward met at his home in Jamaica to plan what they were going to do and begin rehearsals. They put together a delightful potpourri that included Coward and Martin specialties, classics by Cole Porter and Rodgers and Hammerstein, Gilbert and Sullivan numbers, a jazzed-up version of "Tit Willow," and even a *Madame Butterfly* burlesque for Mary.

"Together with Music" aired live on Saturday, October 22, and marked Coward's first American television appearance. Fresh from a successful club engagement in Las Vegas, the British playwright was feeling confident, whereas Mary seemed nervous and depressed about Richard, who was in the hospital and on the critical list during most of the early rehearsals. Although Mary's relationship

with Coward had healed, the playwright's attitude toward Richard was cautious at best. Coward was relieved to have Richard off the scene while he and Mary worked out details of their show, but feared the worst when he learned that Halliday was to be released from the hospital shortly before "Together with Music" aired. "Rehearsals are going very well," the playwright noted in his diary on October 16. "Richard, wreathed in amiability, has only been to one. When he is absent, a purplish ex-drunk stands in for him, presumably to guard Mary's interests. She also has several other transient hangers-on which I find rather a bore, but I am rising above it."

Mary seemed frightened about performing the *Madame Butterfly* skit, and Coward thought she wasn't doing it very well, which made her edgier. "I have always found the whims and fancies of leading ladies fairly irritating," her impatient British costar confided to his diary, "but whereas in the old days I was prepared to fight them, now I really feel I cannot be bothered. Mary is a great performer and a very good character. She is painfully naïve and has no clue about playing comedy and never will have. She also has a strongly developed 'Rebecca of Sunnybrook Farm' quality and a desire to be perpetually sweet before the public, which is death to sharp comedy lines. She infuses our 'comedy' bickering with saccharine and shies away from any riposte that sounds as though she were being 'mean' to me. This is not a help in scenes which have been written on the assumption that we are having a light professional quarrel. The result will be that I shall play rings around her. None of this much matters, but it is certainly aggravating."

While viewers found Mary's performance on the show charming, Coward continued to have his reservations. "When the moment came to start," he wrote in his diary after the telecast, "I noticed that Mary was quivering, so I gave her a sharp, loving lecture and on we went. . . . Mary, after the first scene in which she dried up and became rather baby-talky, was absolutely superb. She infused magic into 'Kick Out of You,' 'I've Only Got Eyes for You,' and 'Daddy.' We *just* got away with 'Butterfly' and our final medley was fine and tore the place up." In spite of the playwright's misgivings, the ninety-minute special was judged a triumph. Mary's folksy charm

worked well against Coward's erudite acid wit. "Telegrams arrived like confetti from all over the country," the British playwright noted after the show aired, and the press notices were raves. "In this case," *Variety* said, "90 minutes was a sheer delight and a remarkable feat of sustained entertainment."

"Together with Music" was sponsored by Ford Motor Company and cost the manufacturer $500,000 to produce. Forty-one rehearsals, over a two-month period, had gone into preparing the show, even though its presentation looked simple. On the night of the airing, Margot Fonteyn, William Faulkner, and a host of other notables turned up at the CBS studio to watch the performance live. When the stars left to go to a party at the 21 Club afterward, a howling mob greeted them in the streets. "I adored doing that show," Mary said years later. "I have a copy of it, and it holds up like crazy. Noel was just so fabulous."

Early in 1956, the Hallidays returned to Brazil to look over the property they had bought there. Their new *fazenda*, as it was called, had twenty thousand coffee trees, plus rice, corn, huge avocado trees, lemon, lime, mango, and other fruit trees, as well as chickens, turkeys, and pigs. Three houses for workers' families stood on the land in good condition, and there was a dam that created a pool for swimming. The Hallidays' place was near the one Janet Gaynor and Adrian owned. Richard and Mary fell in love with their property immediately. Eventually, they hoped to add to their acreage and remodel and extend the main house, adding rooms of brick and tile. While they were vacationing in Brazil, Richard oversaw the digging of a well and the planting of a flower garden with magnificent ferns and orchids. Mary, who wanted the ranch to be as much like Texas as possible, insisted that they have horses and run a herd of cattle on the property.

Larry and Maj came to visit during the seven months the Hallidays were in Brazil, and almost immediately Richard got into a fight with Mary's son. "Suddenly I was the guy in the old Hollywood Western who snarls. 'This town ain't big enough for both of us,'" Larry said. "There was no changing Richard. No talking to him. He was just a pain in the ass—and that was when he was at his

best. He was worse once the booze and the speed kicked in." Later
Hagman found out that one reason Richard liked Brazil so much was
that he could buy almost any medication there over the counter.
"After eleven o'clock in the morning," Larry said, "he was impossible."

Nat Wolff, a network executive for NBC television, also tracked
down Mary and Richard in Brazil, after a succession of landings in
backcountry airports, a jeep ride with a pair of Franciscan monks,
and finally a jaunt on horseback to the Hallidays' *fazenda*. Wolff had
come to sign Mary to an exclusive television contract, at an unpre-
cedented fee of a half-million dollars, for appearances over the
next three years. They decided to launch the series in November
1956 with a Hallmark Hall of Fame presentation of *Born Yesterday*,
with Mary playing the untutored Billie Dawn, Paul Douglas recreating
the role he had done on Broadway, and the comedy's author, Garson
Kanin, directing.

"It was a disaster," Mary remembered. "I wanted to play that part
so badly, and we came back from Brazil so I could do it. Garson
Kanin wanted me to play Billie southern, and that was a mistake."
The public simply couldn't accept Mary Martin as a kept woman.
Viewers expected to hear the voice of Judy Holliday, who had
created the role on Broadway and in the movie, speaking Billie's
lines. "Mr. Hall, our sponsor, loved Mary Martin," the show's pro-
ducer, Duane Bogie said, "but when the whole significance of her
character dawned on him, he was not very pleased. I remember
his phone call from Kansas City right after we went off the air.
Born Yesterday was the only show we ever did that Mr. Hall really
didn't like. He was terribly upset and he let us know that. Mr. Hall
was a moral man and took quality very seriously." Audiences were
equally shocked that Peter Pan was now playing the dizzy mistress
of a junk dealer. Mary claimed that she received a thousand letters
protesting her accepting the role. "We had fun doing the show,"
said Arthur Hill, who played the young reporter who falls in love
with Billie, "but it was not Mary's part. Paul Douglas just walked
right over her. There was no real match going on there at all."

With Heller in boarding school and Mary and Richard wanting
to spend as much time as possible in Brazil, the Hallidays decided to

sell their home in Connecticut and buy a much bigger apartment in Manhattan. Tired of commuting, they bought a penthouse overlooking the East River, lower Manhattan, Brooklyn, and Queens, in the same building where Greta Garbo and Claire Boothe Luce lived. The apartment they selected had a view in four directions, which gave them the feeling of space. The living room also served as a dining area and had terraces on two sides that made the room look even larger than it was. A Queen Anne desk dominated Richard's study, and on one wall were pictures of Mary in her starring roles. Heller's room was in French décor, with the tablecloth that Juanita Martin had used for Sunday dinners in Weatherford lined and made into a bedspread. A gold-carpeted circular staircase led up to the second floor, which was less than half as big as the downstairs and devoted entirely to Mary and Richard's bedroom and the glass-walled sunroom that adjoined it. The master bedroom, done in pale blue, was large, sunny and bright, and had a chaise lounge in it that originally had belonged to Sarah Bernhardt. The couple slept in an emperor-size double bed, and a large tapestry from the castle of the Duke of Marlborough adorned one wall.

Richard's decorating ability was evident throughout the penthouse, which was filled with paintings and antiques, including a brass music stand with Mary's mother's violin in an open case resting against its base. A portrait of Richard's mother hung conspicuously in the apartment, even though she lived in separate quarters in the same building. Richard did some gardening on the terrace and conducted most of the Halliday business from his study, which doubled as a library and family room.

Bessie Mae Sue Ella remembered attending a party in Mary's penthouse, at which Cyril Ritchard and Beatrice Lillie were also guests. "Richard was upstairs—drunk," Bessie Mae remembered, "but Mary carried on as if nothing was wrong." There were times when Richard drank himself into oblivion, yet Mary managed to mask her devastation from the outside world. "I wonder if I ever really knew my husband," she later said. "Richard was a very private person. . . . He always wanted to be in the background." Yet at his best Halliday had the ability to make his wife's life exciting, and he

protected her with ferocity. "Nobody brought Mary bad news directly," a family friend said. "Richard absorbed all that."

In the summer and early fall of 1957 Mary starred in two of her greatest shows—*South Pacific* and *Annie Get Your Gun*—for the Los Angeles Civic Light Opera Association, to celebrate the organization's twentieth anniversary season. She and Richard arrived on the West Coast on May 1 aboard the Santa Fe Super Chief and spent six months there. Mary, wearing her hair light and in a short boyish cut, recreated Nellie Forbush first, opposite opera basso Giorgio Tozzi. Albert Marre staged the revival, and Myron McCormick again played Luther Billis. The company opened at the Curran Theatre in San Francisco and then played the show at the Philharmonic Auditorium in Los Angeles, beginning there on July 8.

Annie Get Your Gun, directed by Vincent Donehue, opened in San Francisco in August for five weeks, with John Raitt as Frank Butler and Reta Shaw as Dolly Tate, and moved to Los Angeles in October for five more weeks. "One of the great experiences of my life was playing opposite Mary Martin in *Annie Get Your Gun,*" Raitt said. "We developed a lasting affection for one another. Mary had the ability to make an audience feel that they could never possibly love her as much as she loved them. Richard Halliday just did everything for her, all the menial tasks, so she was a free bird. She didn't have to worry about anything else but performing."

Mary rode a horse on a treadmill in this production of *Annie* as she fired at targets, and she and Raitt rode together on the same horse before the curtain fell. A young girl from Texas had been hired for the chorus, and the neophyte was so thrilled at getting a spot in her first show that she called home to tell her best friend the news. "I'm in a show at last," she announced in a giddy voice. "It's *Annie Get Your Gun* with Mary Martin." When the friend didn't respond with the proper degree of enthusiasm, the girl repeated, "Did you hear what I said? I'm in a show with Mary Martin!" There was silence on the other end of the phone, then the friend asked in disbelief, "You mean *the original* Mary Martin!" Mary told the story with glee.

Toward the end of the engagement in Los Angeles, Mary was bedridden with the flu. She got out of a sickbed to do the show on November 7, since a group of television people were to be in the audience to preview *Annie* for a fall telecast that was scheduled, but she had to give up shortly after reaching the theater. "I just can't do it," she said. Twenty-one-year-old Renee Guerin from Juneau, Alaska, Mary's understudy, played Annie Oakley for four times before the star was well enough to resume work.

Part of the plan for *Annie Get Your Gun* was that the revival would move directly from the theater in Los Angeles to the NBC studio in Burbank for a live airing in late November. Pepsi Cola sponsored the two-hour special, which was advertised as a major event. One of John Raitt's guns didn't fire during the telecast, and at a final rehearsal Mary almost disabled herself by skinning her shin in the Indian dance. The stages at the television studio were so widely separated that the star had to be carried piggyback from one set to the next, so that she wouldn't arrive too out of breath to sing. The show's songs were also recorded for Capitol, an album that Mary considered among her best.

Particularly as Mary got older, it became difficult to find good plays that were right for her. Vincent Donehue had seen a German film called *The Trapp Family Singers* and urged the Hallidays to see it. When they did, they became excited over the story's potential for the stage, envisioning it as an essentially straight play, using a selection or two from the actual music the Trapp family sang with maybe one new song for Mary. They got producer Leland Hayward involved in the project and eventually asked Rodgers and Hammerstein to write the number for Mary. "Oscar and I saw the picture," Rodgers remembered, "and agreed that it had the makings of an impressive stage production, but we disagreed with their concept." The songwriters thought that mixing a new song with the Trapp family's songs would be a clash of styles. When they suggested a fresh score for a full-blown musical, Hayward and the Hallidays immediately asked them to write the music. Rodgers and Hammerstein appeared interested but explained that they would be tied up for a year with another show, *Flower Drum Song.* The Hallidays said they would wait.

With a commitment from Rodgers and Hammerstein to write songs for a new musical tailored especially to Mary's talent, the question was what could the star do for a year while she waited. Since Mary loved the road and had always wanted to do a tour of one-night stands, she and Richard decided to put together an essentially one-woman show and take it all over the country. Mary appeared in the show, accompanied by a seventeen-piece orchestra conducted by John Lesko, in sixty-four cities. *Music with Mary Martin* was the singer's first venture into the concert field, and the tour was arranged through Columbia Artists Management. The star did a selection of old favorites like "By the Light of the Silvery Moon" and "Wait Till the Sun Shines, Nellie," decked out in a black cocktail dress designed by Mainbocher, and sang "Alice Blue Gown" atop a piano. She did some jazz numbers with a combo and included "I Enjoy Being a Girl" from Rodgers and Hammerstein's current show, *Flower Drum Song.* Then the star donned replicas of the costumes for her various roles and sang "My Heart Belongs to Daddy," "Mountain High, Valley Low," "You Can't Get a Man with a Gun," "A Wonderful Guy," "I've Gotta Crow," and ended with "I'm Flying," actually taking to the air via wires, as she had in *Peter Pan.*

Dancer Dirk Sanders and Brazilian guitarist Luiz Bonfa were the only other performers in *Music with Mary Martin* aside from the orchestra members. In September 1958, they broke in the show in Alaska for the Defense Department, giving thirteen performances in nine days at eleven army, air force, and naval installations. "No matter how tired she might be, Miss Martin was always ready to take time out to chat with her fans and to sign autographs for them," said Lieutenant Colonel Robert Knox, Mary's escort officer during the Alaskan trip. "She's a most gracious lady and a real trouper." Fog forced the musicians to detour into Nome, where it was arranged to have the show beamed by short wave to servicemen in Kotzebue, above the Arctic Circle. The only place in Nome that had a piano in tune was a waterfront saloon. Mary, wearing her lavish Mainbocher creations, put on her show there with an audience of Eskimos who'd never heard of her looking on. She loved it!

After returning to New York, Mary and her troupe resumed rehearsals in Poughkeepsie on September 20 and opened there a week later. At one performance the musical comedy star sailed into the wings as Peter Pan and failed to reemerge. Out front, everyone gasped. Then she reappeared, giving the audience an impish laugh. Mary had held onto a guy rope just to give fans a scare.

At Constitution Hall in Washington, D.C., the dressing room was so far from the stage, and Mary had so many costume changes to make with only a few seconds for each one, that she had to dress in the men's room. "You should have seen me hanging my Mainbocher clothes over whatever I could find in there," she said. They played cities like Minneapolis, Omaha, Oklahoma City, Dallas, and Austin, but also such places as Beaumont, Texas, Youngstown, Ohio, and Binghamton, New York. Some of the theaters were real rats' nests, and others were gymnasiums and civic halls, but Mary had a ball. "I wasn't sick one day," she said. "Ernest, our black chauffeur, drove us from town to town in our 1947 Rolls Royce, and Nena Smith, my gal who was with me for years in the theater, was with us. I'd visit with all the people backstage, and then we'd get on the road and drive to the next city. We had cocktails and dinner in the car. The Rolls had these beautiful inlaid shelves that came out, where we could have drinks and eat the meal Ernest had prepared for us." The orchestra followed them in a bus, and they spent most nights in motels.

At matinee performances Mary did a charming mini-musical for children called *Three to Make Music*. Included was a condensation of Rodgers and Hammerstein's *Cinderella* and a miniature revue by Richard Rodgers' two daughters. "Mary took a chance with us," Mary Rodgers said. "I wasn't very old and hadn't done anything like that before. Mary was utterly professional. The more difficult person in that pair was her husband, who could have a really mean tongue and a really mean temper when he got frustrated and angry. Richard had the typical alcoholic's personality—the sudden irascibility and the awful thing of one's never knowing what was coming at you or why. But Mary was absolutely fabulous. She didn't get emotional if something didn't work, or if something was too long and needed to be shorter."

Mary's goal with her one-woman show was to reach as many people as possible. "We've played so many places it's hard to keep up with where we are," she said when they reached Dallas. But Mary turned the tour into an adventure. Friends said she seemed more relaxed than she had been in years. "This is the first time I observed not a single moment of tension or self-awareness," Cheryl Crawford wrote the Hallidays in Phoenix after a recent visit. The singing star stayed trim, with no need to diet, was full of energy, and bubbled with enthusiasm over the next challenge. "I guess Mary's perpetual joy stems from her passion for the stage," Richard said. "I think she's the happiest star in show business."

The tour ended in New Haven, Connecticut, where most New York–bound shows tried out in that era. A few days later, on Easter Sunday, 1959, Mary performed not once but twice on live television. In the late afternoon she did a condensed version of the children's show she had played on the road. That evening she did *Music with Mary Martin*, also on NBC. "They wanted me to tape one or the other of the shows," Mary said. "But I've always been live and I always want to be." In the studio to watch the children's performance were 250 youngsters, aged six to twelve. For the evening show 250 grownups were invited to be a studio audience. "I try to make people who are watching TV at home feel as though they are in the theater," Mary said.

Exhausted by the end of a long tour, Mary came down with pneumonia right before the Easter marathon, but she insisted on going ahead with both shows. "Nobody in her right mind would do that," she said, "but I did it." A stand-in, a girl called Beryl Towbin, was in the studio for all the camera blocking, because Mary was too ill to be there. "The whole cast was sick and in and out of the hospital," Mary Rodgers remembered. "There was a flu epidemic. I don't know how Mary got through those two performances." But her misery did little to spoil the enchantment of the shows for audiences. "Some silver has gone out of her soprano and some notes out of her throat," Mary's friend, critic John Rosenfield, wrote. "But she was too artful a show woman to let this impair her effectiveness. . . . If not a beauty, Mary looks like one."

With Mary's busy Easter Sunday behind her, she and Richard were quick to hop a freighter bound for Brazil. She needed a long rest before starting rehearsals in August for what would become *The Sound of Music*. Richard Rodgers and Oscar Hammerstein were in Jamaica writing the score for Mary's next musical, while veteran playwrights Howard Lindsay and Russel Crouse were busy working on the book. The star was delighted that Larry had opened in a play, *God and Kate Murphy*, on Broadway, and pleased that Heller had decided she wanted to be a nurse. All seemed bliss in Mary's world except for Richard's drinking problem. That darker side of their lives she kept hidden from the public, who saw the star as eternally joyful. "One trick I have is to make myself not think of ugly and disagreeable things," Mary said. "I believe people dwell too much on the unpleasant. I seem to have an instinct for accepting my problems, dealing with them, and then discarding them."

CHAPTER 10

Austrian Maria

Mary hadn't done anything new on Broadway since *Peter Pan* opened in 1954. Believing that a stage career is like a love affair—it can only go forward or languish, but must never stand still—she and Richard were constantly on the lookout for fresh material. They were convinced that the Trapp family story had audience appeal and contained an ideal role for Mary. With Rodgers and Hammerstein set to write the score for the musical, and with the illustrious Howard Lindsay and Russel Crouse signed to write the book, the Hallidays were certain they had the makings of a major Broadway hit. Six trips to Germany were necessary before legal clearances from the seven von Trapp children had been secured, and Baroness von Trapp gave her permission from her sickbed in a hospital in Innsbruck, where she was recuperating from a case of malaria contracted in New Guinea.

When the Baroness learned that Mary Martin was to play her onstage, she made a trip to San Francisco as soon as she was able to see the musical comedy star in *Annie Get Your Gun.* In their meeting backstage, Mary was hesitant about whether a middle-aged Texan could play a young Austrian girl and make her believable. "But my dear, you *are* me," the Baroness assured her. The two women became friends, and Mary visited the von Trapps at their farm in Vermont

to soak up family atmosphere and study the mannerisms of the baroness before the show went into rehearsal.

Originally called *The Singing Heart, The Sound of Music* would be based on the thirty-minute German film, *The Trapp Family Singers* (1955), that Vincent Donehue had recommended to the Hallidays, and on Baroness Maria Augusta Trapp's autobiography. Maria, a would-be postulant at Nonnberg Abbey in Austria, became governess and eventually stepmother to the seven children of a widowed sea captain, Baron Georg von Trapp. Later, after their escape from the Nazi occupation of Austria in 1938, the family pastime of madrigal singing grew into a profitable profession for the von Trapps. The Broadway musical would have a plethora of children—a Martin specialty—and the story lent itself readily to music. Mary brushed up on her guitar playing, learned to yodel, and Lindsay and Crouse, working in conjunction with Rodgers and Hammerstein, idealized and romanticized the character of Maria until the spunky postulant showed off Mary's talent to full advantage. At forty-five years of age, Mary was long past the point of impersonating a spirited young tomboy onstage, but audiences didn't seem to care. To all but her sharpest critics, she was still the image of eternal youth.

Mary and Richard felt that Vincent Donehue had the exact sensitive touch needed to direct *The Sound of Music,* although Richard Rodgers and Oscar Hammerstein had reservations about his ability. "Vincent Donehue really wasn't very bright," the show's costume designer, Lucinda Ballard, said. "In the first place he was putty in the Hallidays' hands. He worshipped both Mary and Dick, and they insisted on his directing *The Sound of Music.* I know that Dick and Oscar weren't that crazy about him. Mary had changed a great deal by that time, and Dick Halliday was drunk all the time and not making too much sense."

Oscar Hammerstein was ill during most of the preparations for *The Sound of Music* and unable to attend rehearsals, so much of the burden the team normally shouldered fell on Richard Rodgers. Since Rodgers and Hammerstein, Leland Hayward, and Richard Halliday co-produced the show, Rodgers became the songwriters' principal spokesperson in production disputes. Mary was never

comfortable in the opening scene, in which Maria is discovered in a tree pushed toward the middle of the stage. "I just loathed that bloody tree," she said. "The show opened with that marvelous music of the nuns, and then suddenly, from way in the back coming forward, came this tree. I was sitting on it, and it would jerk a lot. I tried anything and everything to make that entrance more amusing— even hanging by my heels. I liked the song I sang, but for the entire two years I was in the show I was embarrassed to be in that tree. It never seemed right, and I didn't think the scene was very funny."

In desperation, Mary decided that she should catch her postulant's uniform on a branch and reveal that she was wearing white lace drawers with blue ribbons underneath. Lucinda Ballard told her, "Mary, Dick Rodgers is never going to stand for that, and I really think it's wrong for this character. Nuns wear underwear made out of thick white cloth that scratches. Come on, you know you can't have lace and blue ribbons on a nun's drawers!" But Mary made a big fuss over the incident and kept on until Richard Rodgers couldn't cope with her anymore and sent for Leland Hayward. "I wasn't there at the time this happened, but they had a big fight over the drawers," Ballard said, "and Leland and Dick Rodgers walked down the corridor with Dick Halliday shouting at them, 'All you think about is the show! You don't care about Mary.'" Ballard thought those statements were terribly revealing.

Having become enamored with Mainbocher's designs—to the point that he created much of the star's personal wardrobe—Mary wanted Mainbocher to design her wedding gown and party dress for *The Sound of Music*, leaving the rest of the costumes to Lucinda Ballard. "I didn't care," Ballard said, "but Mainbocher was really a terrible designer for the stage, unless the clothes were modern. Dick Rodgers and Oscar Hammerstein hated his designs so much. I'll never forget when Dick saw the first headdress Mary wore in the wedding scene, he stood up and shouted, 'She looks like she just had a lobotomy, not like she's going to be married!' So I had to make some changes on the veil and the dress. The party dress I didn't make any changes on, and it was really so wrong."

Rodgers tried valiantly to ease the quarrels and keep an artistic perspective, but his fights with Dick Halliday became brutal, while Mary remained in the background, claiming innocence. "Richard Rodgers knew more about the theater than [Halliday] did," said Anna Crouse, writer Russel Crouse's wife, "but Halliday was always out there protecting Mary. . . . I saw Dick [Rodgers] lose his temper with Halliday and speak his mind. . . . Dick just took off after Halliday. Mary and Dick [Rodgers] didn't speak for quite a while after that."

Lindsay and Crouse, the book writers, were perfect gentlemen, men of great dignity, and they essentially stayed out of the turmoil. The writers had been signed to supply the libretto before Rodgers and Hammerstein became involved with the project, so *The Sound of Music* would be one of the few shows for which Oscar Hammerstein's writing was limited to lyrics. Craftsmen though Lindsay and Crouse were, their work on the musical came in for sharp criticism, mainly to the effect that the story was too sweet and sentimental. "I must say that I agreed with some of what the critics had to say," said Theodore Bikel, the production's original Captain von Trapp. "At times you had a feeling that if you were a diabetic, you'd go into some kind of shock if you saw the show."

Bikel remembered that during the first dress rehearsal the Nazis in *The Sound of Music* wore swastika armbands and said, "Heil, Hitler," but that was soon changed. "In those days musicals weren't supposed to be incisive and politically astute or biting," Bikel said. "The powers that be decided that the Nazi menace had to be toned down, because it worked against the sweet atmosphere of the musical. So the armbands went off to keep the show within the realm of rose-tinted glasses. Our Nazis wore brown shirts all right, but of a paler shade of brown than the real ones, and they didn't give the full 'Heil Hitler!' Nazi salute, but merely a meek 'Heil.'"

Richard Rodgers didn't find *The Sound of Music* sweet so much as he found it optimistic. Once the composer had made up his mind that the nuns in the show could sing, it was fairly easy to find places where music with a religious atmosphere could be devised.

The Sound of Music broke with a Broadway convention by having no overture. A group of nuns are simply heard chanting a prayer offstage as others go about their duties. Magically, the chorus of nuns singing sacred music blends into a group of nuns singing a song of comic bafflement about the novice Maria. Rodgers didn't try to imitate the music the Trapp family had sung in their concerts. The songs he wrote for Mary—the title song, "My Favorite Things," "Do-Re-Mi," "The Lonely Goatherd," and "An Ordinary Couple"— were ideally suited to her voice. "They should be," the composer told the star. "Remember I'm an old professional plumber and I do know your pipes!" The songs were simple, spirited, and disarming when fueled by Mary's special brand of wonder.

By the time the production was ready for out-of-town tryouts, the company was aware that Oscar Hammerstein had cancer and was dying. "The religious feeling of 'Climb Every Mountain' just broke our hearts," said agent Lucy Kroll, who followed the show on the road. "Hammerstein couldn't travel with us, but his lyrics were with us all the time." Mary remembered Oscar meeting her at the stage door one evening during rehearsals, handing her a slip of paper, and telling her, "Mary, I wrote this last night. I don't know where we're going to put it in the show, but it's for you." Inside her dressing room she opened the paper and saw that Hammerstein had written on it, "Love isn't love till you give it away."

Richard Rodgers approached Mary during a rehearsal in Boston and asked, "What are we going to do about our good luck token?" Rodgers remembered that Mary had used Bessie Mae Sue Ella's name in *South Pacific* and in most of her other hit shows. In a musical taking place in Austria, the name clearly didn't fit. So they decided to add a fictitious line in the listing of the cast in the program: "A Postulant—Sue Yaeger." That worked fine until Bessie Mae got a summons from the Internal Revenue Service demanding to know why she hadn't reported the income she'd received from playing a role in *The Sound of Music*. It took two years to straighten out the confusion.

"Dick Rodgers was such a cut-up and so impish," Theodore Bikel said. While the show was trying out in Boston, Rodgers took the

actor to dinner one evening at a Chinese restaurant, where Muzak was playing. "Every time they played one of his tunes, which was about every ten minutes," Bikel remembered, "Dick stood up and took a bow." Rodgers also had quite an array of raunchy jokes, handled his liquor well, and did his share of womanizing through the years. "Dick loved money more than anybody I've ever known except Oscar," Lucinda Ballard said. "But it was different with Oscar. Part of Oscar's nature was that he couldn't bear to spend money. He was very stingy. And yet Oscar was the most lovable person, and Dick really was not. I think Dick was a genius, much more so than Oscar. But Dick gave the impression of not being at ease a lot of the time. I'm not altogether sure why."

As ill as he was, Hammerstein was unable to go to New Haven with the show and did not see *The Sound of Music* in its entirety until the musical played in Boston. Eleven days before the production was to open in New York, Rodgers and Hammerstein determined that something was missing in the score and that the void centered in the character Theodore Bikel portrayed. The actor had never done a musical before, although he had had a long career as a folk singer. Wanting to come up with something that would utilize Bikel's special talent, the songwriters retired to a suite in the Ritz Carlton Hotel with a piano and wrote "Edelweiss," Captain von Trapp's expression of love for his homeland, which had the sound of an authentic folk song. It was the last lyric that Oscar Hammerstein wrote before his death in August 1960.

Bikel lost weight before the show went on the road and had a gray streak dyed in his hair to make him look more distinguished. Mary went into Spartan training—vocalizing for hours every day and exercising and taking ballet classes to limber up. Her singing teacher, William Herman, even had her singing scales while working out with a punching bag. The star appeared in eighteen of the show's nineteen scenes, had fourteen costume changes, sang ten times, and had to climb stairs six times. "Nothing we ever suggested for her was considered too demanding," Richard Rodgers said. "In all the years I've known Mary, I have never seen her give a performance that was anything less than the best that was in her."

The actress's hair was cut short and dyed champagne blonde for her role as a mountain-climbing governess. Bikel enjoyed working with Mary, found her a great performer, but was amazed at how completely protected she was. "She was kept in a glass bowl, wrapped up in cotton, and so guarded and taken care of," the actor recalled. "She was brought to the theater in a limousine and taken away after the performance. She got there very early and spent two hours in the theater before the show even started. Then she was driven back home to the penthouse. Mary had little contact with ordinary people, yet she always played little people. She hadn't met any recently, but she played what she remembered from her youth."

Some three hundred youngsters were interviewed for the roles of the seven Trapp children, and Margaret Truman, the former president's daughter, was offered, but declined, one of the nun's parts. Director Vincent Donehue, working with choreographer Joe Layton, tried to mesh acting with dance in the show. "Vincent was extremely sensitive to the performer," his agent, Lucy Kroll, said. "He had a wonderful sense of space and color. He was totally embroiled in every aspect of the theater and highly disciplined. Vincent would not tolerate a lack of discipline from anybody."

The Sound of Music opened at the Lunt-Fontanne Theatre in New York on November 16, 1959, to an advance ticket sale of $2,325,000, a new record. The reunion of Mary Martin with Rodgers and Hammerstein was considered one of the big events of the theater season. The show's notices were decidedly mixed, with composer Richard Rodgers faring best. Critics even thought Mary came off a little too lovable. "It is disappointing to see the American musical stage succumbing to the clichés of operetta," Brooks Atkinson wrote in the *New York Times.* "The revolution of the 1940s and 1950s has lost its fire. But *The Sound of Music* retains some of the treasures of those golden days—melodies, rapturous singing, and Mary Martin." Some reviewers complained that the direction was weak, while others said that *The Sound of Music* had the trite look of the very kind of musical theater that Rodgers and Hammerstein had replaced with *Oklahoma!* in 1943. "Rodgers and Hammerstein have by now . . . developed so pat a routine, and are so sure of their audience

they are writing for, that even such strong stuff as the cultural background of Austria crumbled under their assault," Charles Woodruff wrote in the *New Republic.* "With deadly accuracy they reduced the whole thing to another typical Broadway show."

Yet audiences loved *The Sound of Music.* The production remained on Broadway for over three and a half years and had a London run of almost twice that long. Mary knew from the opening night response that the schmaltzy musical, despite continued carping from professional critics, would be a winner at the box office. Outside the Lunt-Fontanne Theatre, a mob stood cheering before and after the opening night performance, totally blocking the sidewalk, waiting for Mary's autograph. In the first-night audience were Gypsy Rose Lee, Katharine Cornell, Gilbert Miller, Helen Hayes, Jack Benny, Phil Silvers, Vera Zorina, Kitty Carlisle, Moss Hart, Gladys Swarthout, Eva Gabor, and Maria von Trapp herself. Mary admitted later that she had been nervous before the curtain went up, knowing that people expected so much from the show. "We were *all* nervous," she said, "and I was the worst of all. My mouth was sticking to my teeth!" After the opening night show, she and Richard were driven to the St. Regis roof for the company's celebration, a private gathering highlighted by a lavish buffet and a dance band. At 1 AM Mary was still dancing with every partner that came along, paying little mind to the qualified reviews that kept coming in.

Richard advised his wife not to be disoriented by the criticism. "It's your judgment that counts now," he told Mary. She heeded his advice and remained the consummate professional, getting plenty of rest so that she could give her best at every show. Mary was in *The Sound of Music* for two years and missed only one performance. "This is the hardest show I've ever done," she said. "I had to remember the character always, keep a tight rein on my emotions and my performance. . . . The treatment had to be very skillful, totally controlled." But she adored the musical, believed in its message of love, and she and Richard remained the principal investors in the original production. People left their seats in a glow after seeing the show, and for Mary that was more important than anything the critics chose to write.

When it came time to pass out the Tonys in 1960, Mary won the award for best actress in a musical—her third—beating out Ethel Merman in *Gypsy*, even though *Gypsy*'s Mama Rose is considered almost the Hamlet of musical comedy. When Cheryl Crawford attempted to offer Merman condolence after she'd lost the prize, Merman shrugged off the defeat by saying, "How are you going to buck a nun?" *The Sound of Music* tied with *Fiorello!* for best musical of the year. Gradually, even tough critics admitted that there was a core of honest sentiment that shone through *The Sound of Music* and that the show had moments that were genuinely moving.

Cabaret singer Andrea Marcovici saw the show as a child, in part because her father was Mary Martin's physician at the time, and the girl was taken backstage to meet the star afterward. "I was surprised that she looked like a work horse after doing the show I'd just seen," Marcovici said. "I hadn't realized how hard it is to give a performance like that. There was Mary Martin in her bathrobe, and there was sweat running down the massive eyelashes that were still on. She seemed to have been running. But Mary Martin is an ideal example of what I think a voice on the Broadway stage should be. Her singing was so human, emotional, and touching. I miss that kind of warm, female mid-range voice that was full of heart and spirit. I don't think we have too much of that today. Instead we have ear-splitting sounds."

Sure enough, Mary did do a lot of running in *The Sound of Music*, making costume changes and getting from one place to another. Richard said at one point that he'd like to know just how much his wife traveled during a performance, so he put a pedometer on her belt. They discovered that Mary walked two and a half miles a night and five miles on matinee days. "No wonder I've been losing weight," the star said. "When I come home at the end of the week, I'm all in. . . . I find that if I do anything besides the show, I pay for it the next two days."

Theodore Bikel remembered playing a matinee with Mary and noticing that her performance was quite different from what it had been. "She came in as this little postulant nun and very bravely stood up to this martinet that I played. But there was something

different in her attitude. She was smiling." They went through the entire scene, and Mary kept smiling at her leading man the whole time. Bikel went to her dressing room at intermission to find out why. It turned out that Mary had gotten contact lenses and could *see* Captain von Trapp, whereas before he had been a blur.

During the summer of 1960, all the lights went out in Manhattan just before curtain time on Broadway. Richard rushed out and bought candles, and *The Sound of Music* cast began the show holding candles under their faces. "That was a special night," Mary remembered. "The audience wouldn't go home. I went up on a ladder in my role, and we just played the show like that until suddenly the lights all came on—almost at the beginning of the second act. We said, 'Well, if you'll wait, we'll go put on the costumes.' I don't think anybody went home until two o'clock in the morning."

Oscar Hammerstein died on August 23, 1960, and Mary was so distraught by his death that she had to take a sedative before going onstage for the next performance. At the final curtain call that evening, she blew a heartfelt kiss up past the upper balcony before collapsing backstage. Mary dearly loved and respected Hammerstein. "I had just returned from a tour of Europe, which my parents had given me as a graduation present," Heller recalled. "I found Mummy almost completely drained of her amazing energy."

In the election that fall Mary and Richard were Nixon supporters, whereas Theodore Bikel was an active campaigner for John Kennedy. "I would go out sometimes between matinee and evening performances, go to a rally and speak from a flat-bed truck, and then come back to the theater," Bikel remembered. "The management—meaning Leland Hayward and Richard Halliday—thought that was most unbecoming for me to do that, and they called me on the carpet." Later, between shows, a limousine stood waiting at the stage door for Bikel, and the actor told Hayward and Halliday that there was someone outside he wanted them to meet. He walked the producers to the curb, opened the door of the limousine, inside of which, waiting to ride with Bikel to a Democratic rally, was Eleanor Roosevelt! That ended the producers' complaints about the actor's unbecoming political activism.

Not only did Mary have Oscar Hammerstein's death to absorb, she also had to confront Richard's acute alcoholism. In 1960, Halliday committed himself to a hospital and spent several months drying out. During part of that time, Mary was forbidden to see her husband. Heller was then in nursing school in Boston and would soon marry advertising man Anthony Weir, so Mary felt the pain of loneliness perhaps more than she ever had in her life. Ben Washer, who had known Richard since they were young journalists in New York thirty years before, was hired as Mary's press representative and caretaker. Washer's favorite response when asked about his duties with Mary Martin was "Babysitter for the oldest baby in captivity."

In October 1960, after a performance of *The Sound of Music*, Mary sat smiling in front of the mirror in her dressing room while a barber tucked a white sheet under her chin and began snipping away at her champagne-colored hair. Within minutes, the star again had been transformed into the boyish Peter Pan. She spent almost two full months preparing for another television appearance as Peter, this one taped in color, with most of the original cast, and aired on December 8 over NBC. Since Mary would not leave *The Sound of Music*, she rehearsed *Peter Pan* four days a week at the Helen Hayes Theatre and played Maria von Trapp across the street six nights a week and twice on matinee days. "It is hard work but it is sheer joy," the vivacious actress said. "People love *Peter Pan*, so it is worth any effort. Why, since we last did the show on television in 1956, the mail has never stopped coming in—mail from people all over, from adults and from children, asking that we do it again. Now that the show is being put on tape, it will be a permanent treasure."

In the third week of rehearsal for the telecast, Mary slammed up against a wall of the theater while flying and injured her left arm. She handled the pain like a trouper and didn't miss a single performance. "The old bones aren't what they used to be," the star said stoically. Vincent Donehue directed the revival of *Peter Pan*, although he adhered closely to Jerome Robbins's original staging. NBC had been astute enough to store the sets from the earlier stage production, and all the designers needed to do was

just a little repainting. The taping was done over a weekend at the network's studios in Brooklyn. "We worked straight through until Monday night when I returned to the theater," Mary said. "Every member of the cast just loved doing it, and we were a little sad when the taping was finished."

When *Peter Pan* was broadcast in 1960, critic Aleene Barnes of the *Los Angeles Times* said, "There is no doubt that the show belongs to Mary Martin. She *is* Peter Pan. It has been said that her Peter Pan is Nellie Forbush's brother, and I am inclined to agree. Certainly this ranks as one of Miss Martin's most enchanted evenings."

Mary finished her run in *The Sound of Music* wearing wigs. (Martha Wright eventually replaced her in the musical.) Theodore Bikel's contract with the producers was tied to the length of Mary's commitment to the show. "She didn't like changes," the actor said. So Bikel was in the musical for slightly more than two years. "That's too long," he maintained. "What happens is that if you have any kind of sense of artistic responsibility, you exhaust your creative juices after a number of months, probably nine. After that you take your performance from your nervous system. You concentrate triply hard, and it involves an extraordinary effort."

Even Mary was exhausted after her long run in *The Sound of Music* and needed a complete rest. Richard suggested that they lease a cottage in Bermuda and ask Bessie Mae Sue Ella to meet Mary there and stay with her friend during her vacation. Richard's therapist had suggested that he do something professionally on his own—something without Mary—which he hadn't done in years. Halliday decided to produce *Daughter of Silence*, a play by Australian novelist Morris West, and would be taken up with that while his wife rested.

Mary and Bessie Mae Sue Ella spent the last three weeks of October 1961 together in Bermuda. "It was the first time Mary and I had been alone together since that time when she came and stayed with my family in Mineral Wells after Larry was born," Bessie Mae said. "We laughed, we cried, we remembered, we ate, we sunned, and she dyed my hair, turned me into a blonde. We shopped for clothes and did the things that college-age girls do together." One

night as they sat visiting, Mary wanted Bessie to tell her some of the things she had missed by leaving Weatherford. "So I told her about her father's funeral," Bessie Mae said. "Mary hadn't been to either her father's or her mother's funerals, whereas I had been to both of them, and I tried to tell her about the flowers and the people who were there." Mary confessed to Bessie Mae that Richard was an alcoholic and had emotional problems. "I hadn't known anything about that," Bessie said, "although I saw evidence of it later." But Mary told her friend, "He *has* to prove himself. I don't know why he has to do it now, because he's done it always and forever. But for some reason he feels that he has to do something now without me."

When reporters in Bermuda discovered a star in their midst, Mary and Bessie Mae sang a duet for them, a strange combination they had discovered a few evenings before. While Bessie sang "Rock of Ages," Mary sang the words to "On the Sunny Side of the Street," surprising everyone that the two actually went together. A few nights later, while a tropical storm raged outside, Bessie Mae tried to show Mary a card game that she enjoyed. Mary made a half-hearted effort to learn, but finally threw the cards down on the table. "Bessie, the only reason I went on the stage was so I wouldn't have to play bridge!" she said. Bessie knew that nothing else would have been as fulfilling to her friend. "She wouldn't have had it any other way," Bessie Mae said. "I think Mary was born for show business."

The two women flew from Bermuda back to New York together and were met at the airport by Heller, Tony Weir, Larry, and Maj. The children took Bessie Mae and their mother to dinner that night, but Mary was nervous, concerned about Richard and his play, which was trying out in Philadelphia. When she and Bessie Mae got into bed that night, after the young people had left the penthouse, Mary said, "Bessie, I don't know what to do. I don't know whether to call Richard. I don't want to impose myself on him, but I want him to know that I care so deeply about what he is doing." Bessie told her friend, "Mary, there is a prayer in the prayer book, it's for guidance." So Mary reached to her side of the bed and got

a prayer book out of the drawer, found the prayer, and read it. Then she said, "I think I know what to do." She got out of bed, called her driver, Ernest, told him to get the car and pick her up at the front door, and said, "I'm going to Philadelphia right now."

As troubled as Mary and Richard's relationship was, they genuinely loved and needed one another. "All of Richard's work had been for me," Mary said. "He would do wonderful little things. For instance, we lost a little dog, and he brought me a white mink muff and had flowers sticking out of it. I heard this little sound, and there inside the muff was another little dog. He just did thoughtful things constantly, daily, and believed in me. He made my career possible."

After Bessie Mae returned to Texas, she received a letter from one of Mary's friends whom she had met in Bermuda: "It was the first occasion I have ever had to know Mary as 'Mary' and not as the world famous actress," the friend wrote. "I have a feeling there are very few people who do know her as you do, and now as we do—as a warm, simple, thoughtful, and completely guileless person, with a heart that simply bursts out all over! I hate to say it cause I love Richard, too, but I know if he had been here, it would have been quite different. I feel . . . that Mary needed to be 'Mary' again very badly and that she got completely 'aired out' in the past three weeks. I have a theory that Richard identifies her as Mary Martin *far* more than Mary does, and that she needed badly to be herself again for a while."

Halliday did view his wife first and foremost as Mary Martin, the celebrated Broadway superstar, and to a consuming degree that image was also his. *He* was as much Mary Martin as Mary was. He picked the wardrobe for his wife that *he* might have enjoyed wearing and crafted her image as carefully as a drag queen putting on makeup. Insecure and full of complexes, Richard buttressed his own ego with Mary's celebrity and expressed his bisexual urges by turning her into the most feminine clotheshorse in the business. Yet part of him no doubt resented that *she* was the one who got all the attention, that *she* was the star and not he.

Richard saw to it that *Daughter of Silence*, a courtroom drama, had an expensive production, with the best of everything. Emlyn

Williams, Rip Torn, and Vincent Gardenia starred in the play, which opened at the Music Box in New York on November 30, 1961. The *Daily News* critic, John Chapman, called it "a distinguished play," and Robert Coleman of the *New York Mirror* described the drama as "a literate and exciting excursion into the world of illusion." But the show, despite many rewrites, an elaborate production, and some cast changes in Philadelphia, closed after a short run on Broadway, leaving Richard distraught. "As you can guess, life is mighty hectic right now, " Mary wrote Bessie Mae Sue Ella on December 4.

A bit later, Mary wrote her friend, "Bessie, you will never know what you have done for me. I feel, if it would not be sacrilegious to say it, that I am 'resurrected.' I *live* again. I adore you with *all* my heart." In many ways Bessie Mae was Mary's touchstone with reality, representing all the good things she had known and internalized in Weatherford. She needed Bessie as a reminder of what she had been, who she really was, the loving person she wanted to be.

After *The Sound of Music*, Mary had no immediate professional plans, although a new musical tentatively called *Blood and Thunder* was being written for her. "I'm going to keep coming back to the stage," she said, "as long as there's anyone left to clap for me. . . . I can't imagine a time in the future when I won't be doing a play." Mary appreciated how lucky she had been in having songs composed for her by Cole Porter, Kurt Weill, Irving Berlin, and Richard Rodgers. "I've had a blessed life," she often said, and "haven't had a dull moment since as far back as I can remember. . . . I have so many plans, so many ambitions to keep growing. I guess it is part of my nature to be a positive thinker." Mary was thankful for the doctors who had helped Richard find his way back from what she described as "utter despair," but she knew that his balance was delicate. She had been terrified when he had been hospitalized, fearing that perhaps her own energy and need to work had pushed Richard toward a crisis. His troubled side would always be a mystery to her, for her positive nature was diametrically at odds with Richard's darker disposition.

Before the national company of *The Sound of Music* went on the road, with Mary's friend Florence Henderson as Maria, that cast

gave a performance at the Lunt-Fontanne Theatre in Manhattan. Most of the New York theater world turned out for the event, including Mary. "Talk about being scared!" Henderson said. After the show, Mary came up to the second floor to see Florence in her old dressing room. "You know, finally being able to see this show, I learned so much. There were things I was embarrassed about—especially that tree where Maria sings 'The Sound of Music.' But now I see how effective it is." Mary claimed that she cried so hard at one point in the performance that she washed a contact lens out. "During the intermission we were all on the floor trying to find the damned thing," she said.

Heller and Tony Weir married on January 20,1962, at the First Methodist Church in Leesburg, Virginia. Mary and Heller had initially planned a big wedding in a large Fifth Avenue church in New York, followed by a reception for at least six hundred people at a posh East Side club. But Tony preferred a small, quiet wedding, and his wishes eventually prevailed. Mary and Richard were present for the nuptials, along with about twenty others. "It was the longest, merriest, fun wedding anyone could ever have—and so unplanned," Mary wrote Bessie Mae Sue Ella after she returned to Manhattan. "Our darling daughter and Tony are blissfully happy, and we are mad about him and his family."

To allow Mary to continue her rest after finishing *The Sound of Music*, the Hallidays leased a small house in rural Connecticut. "Richard can't leave New York for long," Mary wrote Bessie Mae, "so he'll come up on weekends." Since Mary couldn't stand to be totally idle, she decided to begin writing her memoirs, while Richard was deeply involved with getting the production team for *Blood and Thunder* assembled. "So far we have heard three songs we like," Mary wrote Bessie Mae. "Max Shulman, who wrote *Rally Round the Flag Boys*, is doing a treatment of Dwight Taylor's book—actually a new plot. The way it is now I am a young woman (not a girl) who has a young ladies seminary in Seattle, Washington. My mother, we hope played by Jean Dixon, owns the school, and guess what I am? Head of the gym department! (Max Shulman didn't even know about my athletic prowess!!)" Later the plot was completely changed,

and based on the early life of actress Laurette Taylor, and the show became *Jennie*.

Heller took a job modeling at Elizabeth Arden's soon after her marriage ceremony, and she and Tony sometimes "double-dated" with Mary and Richard. "We all love to stay up late talking," Heller said. "We get together in our apartment [in New York] for dinner— and Mummy always wants to do the dishes." Heller considered Mary her best friend. "One of the things I admire Mummy most for is her amazing spirit," Heller said. "She has an incredible enthusiasm for life that has carried her through tragedy many times."

When not working on her memoirs, Mary did needlepoint and painted, although she always painted people from the back, showing nothing of their faces, claiming she didn't know how to paint faces. (For three successive Christmases, she and Bessie Mae exchanged humorous self-portraits.) But above all, Mary was "the first lady of the American musical theater," a title she still shared with Ethel Merman, and it would be only a matter of time before she needed to get back to work. Her happiness demanded that. She needed the footlights, the applause, and the love she gave and received from audiences. Mary knew almost every policeman in Manhattan's theater district, at least well enough that they waved, blew her kisses, and shouted holiday greetings her way, and she missed the excitement of getting "up" for a performance. Those were the essentials that ultimately made her world go around. As much as she loved Richard and her family, Mary's first love was always the theater. And she was probably happiest when she was onstage, doing what she did best, secure in her craft, showering her audiences with radiance, and savoring the vibes she got back in return.

CHAPTER 11

Hits and a Miss

By the summer of 1962, it was clear that the opening of *Blood and Thunder* would have to be postponed a year. What started out as a musical about a small-town gymnastics teacher, based on some funny stories by Dwight Taylor, got shifted to a story about an old-time melodrama queen. By then called *Jennie*, the plot had been suggested by the early career of the writer's mother, Laurette Taylor, the distinguished actress who later won plaudits as Amanda in the original production of Tennessee Williams's *The Glass Menagerie*. But in her salad days Laurette Taylor had traveled from stock company to stock company playing battered heroines who managed to escape doom just in the nick of time.

S. N. Behrman had originally been signed to write the book for Mary's show, only to be replaced by Max Shulman and still later by Arnold Schulman. Howard Dietz and Arthur Schwartz, who had written the songs for *Three's a Crowd* (1930) and *The Bandwagon* (1931) on Broadway, did the score. Initially, Mary's first song, delivered by the bloomer-clad gymnastics teacher, was to be an inventory of instruction and advice to her class of demure young ladies. "Can't wait to make my entrance, blowing a whistle in those bloomers!" Mary wrote Bessie Mae Sue Ella in February 1962. "I finally get involved with Charlie Taylor's traveling show as a stunt girl. And,

ye Gods! the stunts they have thought of. *Peter Pan* and *Annie* were child's play! I'll have to go into training six months ahead of time. Ah well, I guess I just was not meant to play *The Barretts of Wimpole* type."

But *Jennie* evolved into the story of a brave young actress who roamed the tank-towns of the West at the turn of the century, emoting in claptrap cliffhangers. The opening scene had Mary, chased by a bear, reaching out to save her baby from a plunge over a gigantic, stage-filling waterfall, as the pit orchestra throbbed silent-movie music. But the author claimed that he was writing a serious play, whereas the composer and lyricist insisted they were writing a light, entertaining score. The clash that followed, in Mary's words, "got very tacky." As Howard Dietz remembered the problem: "We had not foreseen that with Mary and her husband, Dick Halliday, as producers, we would have little to say. We were not protected contractually, and I was ill and couldn't take a firm position."

Co-producer Cheryl Crawford had suggested the switch in plot from gym teacher to the early stage perils of Laurette Taylor, and Mary liked the notion. The venerable actress, dead since 1946, had been a friend, and Mary had once even asked to study acting with Taylor. The veteran thespian had shaken her head at the suggestion and told Mary, "You have nothing more to learn. You have the same teacher as I—your heart." When Marguerite Courtney, Laurette Taylor's daughter, was writing her biography of her mother, she sent chapters as they were written to the Hallidays for criticism. So when Cheryl Crawford suggested turning *Blood and Thunder* into *Jennie*, Mary and Richard readily agreed, even though a nonmusical stage biography of the old actress had closed on the road two years earlier with Judy Holliday in the lead. "I wanted *Jennie* to be a big success," Mary said, "because I loved Laurette Taylor. She was so close to me and really was very precious."

While the Hallidays waited for this mismatch to reach fruition, they talked about another television spectacular with Abe Burrows writing and directing, and Mary did a Christmas show with Bing Crosby on ABC. She and Richard spent some time at their ranch in Brazil, and in May 1963, Mary visited her sister Jerry and Bessie Mae and Jac Austin in Texas. The Austins also came to New York

several times while Mary was between shows, and on one of those occasions Jac helped Richard rearrange the pictures in the Halliday's penthouse while Mary and Bessie Mae went upstairs and stayed out of their way. "We were in New York when Heller's son Timmy was born," Bessie remembered, "and we were there when Heller's Matthew was born. I stayed in Heller's apartment and took care of Timmy while Jac went to the hospital to get Heller and Matthew out. Richard was having a hernia operation, and Heller's husband was out of town. Jac and Richard had jokes together just like Mary and I did."

The Austins were visiting the Hallidays when Mary went to her first costume fittings for *Jennie* with designer Irene Sharaff. (Lucinda Ballard, Dietz's wife, was initially scheduled to do the costumes for the show, but she was unceremoniously replaced and informed by letter that the producers had discovered a prior commitment with Sharaff.) "Watching Mary stand for at least six hours for fittings exhausted me," Bessie said. "She not only had to look beautiful, she had to feel just right in each costume." The star would wear seventeen outfits as Jennie, each an exquisite period creation dating back to around 1903. "I'm *mad* about Irene Sharaff's designs," Mary told Bessie Mae. "I look feminine at last—also my hair will be long in this show!"

Rehearsals for *Jennie* started on June 17, 1963. By then, the tension between factions within the production team was such that all involved knew that they were in for a bumpy ride. The name of the title character had been changed, since *Laurette* with Judy Holliday had failed before coming into New York. Mary and Richard had insisted on Vincent Donehue as the show's director, and, like others, Dietz and Schwartz felt that he was totally under their thumb and not the best choice. The songwriters had thought they knew the kind of musical they were writing, until the Hallidays and Donehue decided that there should be no funny songs. "Mary Martin was a great performer and fun," Dietz said. But she "was victimized by her lack of trust in anyone but herself."

Actually, it was her loyalty to Richard and the coterie that surrounded the couple that victimized her. More and more, Richard

answered any question directed to his wife, while Mary merely added agreement. In production meetings it was always, "we thought," or "we feel," or "we decided." One of the best songs in the score of *Jennie* was "Before I Kiss the World Goodbye," which the star refused to sing as written. One of its couplets, she said, was filthy. When asked which one, she told the lyricist: "Before I go to meet my maker, I want to use the salt left in the shaker." Somehow that line was construed as dirty. "There was always a nun or two or a priest watching rehearsals," Dietz said, "and Mary fell under the spell of one of the nuns," whom she had met years before.

Lucinda Ballard maintained that Dick Halliday was drunk all the time *Jennie* was going through its metamorphosis. Dietz and Schwartz wanted Oliver Smith to design the show's sets, but he was passed over for George Jenkins, who had been Jo Mielziner's assistant. Carol Haney, the initial choreographer, was fired in Detroit, and Matt Mattox took over. The rest of the production team consisted mainly of Halliday regulars: John Lesko as musical director, Robert Russell Bennett and Trude Rittman, both from the Rodgers and Hammerstein shows, as orchestrator and arranger, and also the Hallidays' choice of electricians, carpenters, sound men, prop men, and lighting crew. Mary had wanted Dan Dailey, best remembered for his movie musicals with Betty Grable, as her leading man, but she got film star Dennis O'Keefe instead, only to have him replaced during out-of-town tryouts by George Wallace, whom she considered weak in the part. Howard Dietz, who was in and out of the hospital during this period, said, "*Jennie* had more operations than I did, but despite the surgery it had trouble talking, walking, and being entertaining. To flatter it, one would call it a flop."

In Boston, where the show played first, a young man with a glorious voice sang "When You're Far Away from New York Town," and the song stopped the show. "I remember I was in the sitting room of the Ritz Carleton Hotel," Lucinda Ballard said, "and I saw those miserable pages slipped under the door. I knew they were going to take that song away from that boy, and they did and gave it to Mary. It was put into a different place in the show and just

didn't work at all there. . . . But that book was so dreadful. It was literally unbelievable it was so terrible."

Cheryl Crawford admitted that *Jennie* turned into "the toughest production" she had ever tackled, and Mary called it "just dreadful." One of the better things in the show was veteran singer Ethel Shutta's performance as Jennie's mother. "I adored her," Mary said. "They finally wrote a hymn for us to sing together. But everybody connected with *Jennie* got furious at everybody else." The Hallidays were ready to close the show on the road, but by that time the advance ticket sale in New York had reached $2 million, and the producers were threatened with a $900,000 lawsuit if they reneged on their agreement to open. So Richard said, "Well, I guess we'd better go in."

Mary finally decided she needed a funny song, even though there was no place in the plot that supported one. So it was decided that she would sing "Lonely Nights" as Shalamar the Slave Girl in a show within the show. In the number a none-too-affectionate sultan is tormenting her. Mary had an apparatus in her bedroom that she worked out on, a contraption that spun around. The device was painted gold, turned into a torture rack, and after singing "Lonely Nights," she spun end over end, sometimes standing on her head. "The song stopped the show," Mary remembered. "That's the only thing that ever did. But it meant my going around real fast like forty or fifty times. We put the number in because I had nothing else to do. The show was just a disaster." Richard received letters from doctors cautioning that spinning around like that was dangerous for his wife's heart. When he showed Mary the warnings, she said, "To heck with them. I'm going to do it anyway. It's the only thing that's funny in the show."

The Boston critics were unanimous in voicing delight with Mary Martin, but they found *Jennie* a sad disappointment. The august Elliot Norton of the *Record American* thought the musical was "fine for one act" but "too long, too cultured, and sometimes even too solemn for its own good." The second act, Norton said, was a mess that needed to be rewritten. Mary herself felt that the show was "too complicated in plot and script. . . . It became more and more

a patchwork quilt." The problem of the leading man never got solved. "We had one and he was very good," Mary said. "But he drank like crazy, and he'd miss shows, rehearsals, and everything else. The man who came over from England to play the second lead [Robin Bailey] was marvelous."

The altercations between the playwright and the songwriters continued, even though Howard Dietz was in the hospital part of the time the show was in Boston. Despite the changes and new material, *Jennie* refused to jell. Lucinda Ballard remembered writing actress Vivien Leigh and telling her, "The scenery of this show looks like a lonesome freight yard in the middle of the night with freight trains knocking into each other." By the time the company left Boston, Mary was tired from rehearsing most of the day and playing the show at night. Her nerves were on edge, and her vocal cords were strained. "I needed a doctor daily and soon required a throat specialist," she said.

With tempers short and hopes for success dashed, the show limped into Detroit in late August. Rehearsals continued with Mary suffering fatigue. The star's net salary per week at the Fisher Theatre was $5,205.62, but the show had become a "torturous and frightening experience" for her. In the beginning she had had faith that she could bring the opposing viewpoints together into a successful whole, but she was forced to accept that such confidence had been pure conceit. The friction and fractures simply grew worse. "Things were so strained," Mary said, "that no one spoke to anyone else for years." Cheryl Crawford remained the only contact among the various parties, and the producer spent nights until 3 AM going up and down in elevators to assorted rooms trying to effect compromises. There was a big fight over how to end the show. Finally, Crawford suggested that they bring in Elliot Norton from Boston, since everyone trusted his judgment, to help decide which ending to use. Norton voted for the one that Mary preferred, which distressed some others. "It was a dreary, exhausting time for me," Crawford recalled. "Things deteriorated until everyone was in an unbearable state of tension."

Jennie opened at the Majestic Theatre in New York on October 17, 1963, to mostly unfavorable reviews. Walter Kerr of the *New York Herald Tribune* called it "a woeful tale of some woeful people told in a woeful way." Critics agreed that Mary's luster and ability to communicate good feelings was still enchanting, but she was not shown to good advantage in this weak variant of *East Lynne.* "Miss Martin can't do it alone," Howard Taubman wrote in the *New York Times.* "For more years than a gentleman should mention my heart has belonged to Mary Martin. But *Jennie* does not make it easy to remain faithful."

Noel Coward saw the show five nights after it opened and described the experience as "ghastly." Everyone was relieved when *Jennie* closed after eighty-two performances. Anything Mary did in the theater was considered special, but in this case even her ardent fans judged the outing substandard. "I doubted at the time that I would ever want, or be able, to appear on the stage again," Mary said in 1969. *Jennie* lost $450,000. With most of her shows Mary had found the real fun lay in its preparation, but this time everything about the experience had been a nightmare.

She was offered the lead in *Funny Girl,* a new musical based on the life of comedienne Fanny Brice, with songs composed by Jule Styne, but she turned the show down, claiming she disliked the book. A musical version of *Hobson's Choice* was written for her, but Mary decided not to do that either. Instead, she and Richard retreated to Brazil. "We do love our place there," Mary wrote Blanche Knopf, wife of publisher Alfred A. Knopf. "Now Brazil's three main highways meet within eleven miles of our place." Mary had no clue as to the size of the Halliday bank account, but she knew there was no pressing need to work. She was exhausted and spent her first weeks in Brazil sleeping twelve, sometimes thirteen, hours a night. "I saw the sunny days through a haze," she said. Slowly, she became aware of the spectacular sunsets Brazil offered and noticed that the sky at night was full of stars. One day she finally uncovered her oil paints and started painting again. "Gradually I became aware of the world about me," she said. Mary didn't like the word "fear,"

yet for one of the few times in her life she had felt fear, aware that *Jennie* was a failure and having to open in New York with a show that she knew was a jumble. For a while, her self-confidence was shattered.

In the summer of 1964, Marge and Gower Champion flew to Brazil with the intent of talking Mary into appearing in a touring production of *Hello, Dolly!*, which would travel across the United States and eventually go to Asia and London. Gower Champion had choreographed and directed the show for Broadway, and it was already a huge success in New York with Carol Channing in the title role. "Richard and I were blissful at the farm," Mary said. "But then along came an invitation we couldn't resist." She loved the road, and Dolly Levi was a part with plenty of dynamics and heart. Mary had no objection to playing a role that another reigning star had created, so long as the part was as good as this one. She was fully aware that such opportunities didn't fall into an entertainer's lap, especially at her age, with any frequency. "It's a role that can be adapted to almost any style," Mary said of Dolly. "When I saw Carol on that staircase [in the show], I was willing to die to play the same part."

Upon returning to New York, she dyed her hair red and began rehearsals with Gower Champion in February 1965, first for a television show they did together, then on a new production of *Hello, Dolly!* "I've never seen Mary so peaceful during a rehearsal period," Richard wrote Bessie Mae and Jac Austin. "She and Champion are sweating happily away." Mary based her characterization of Dolly Levi on her sister, Jerry, who loved everybody but, according to Mary, was "the con woman of all time." The Hallidays recognized the genius of Gower Champion, admired the verve and movement he put into shows, and liked his concepts for staging numbers. Fully aware that *Hello, Dolly!* was a strong personal vehicle, superbly constructed, Mary set about making the show her own.

In April, the production opened in Minneapolis with Carleton Carpenter as Cornelius Hackl and Loring Smith as Horace Vandergelder. Then the show traveled to Kansas City, where Mary played *Hello, Dolly!* while former President Harry Truman watched from the audience. "I've never felt so much love from audiences in my

life," the star told Hedda Hopper by telephone. "It's like a revival meeting." In New Orleans the *Times-Picayune* said, "Miss Martin comes on in character and builds the character of the matchmaking Dolly Gallagher Levi into one of the most lovable figures of contemporary musical comedy. . . . She is sly, subtle, and completely captivating." More than a hundred people came from Weatherford to Dallas by bus to see Mary in *Hello, Dolly!* Her sister, Jerry, attended all sixteen performances in Dallas and sat down front. With her at one show was sixty-eight-year-old Billie Jones, the kindly black woman who had taken care of Mary as a child, decked out in a black dress, matching hat, and pearls. John Rosenfield of the *Dallas Morning News* said that Mary played Thornton Wilder's matchmaker "with a fine sense of tasteful but outrageous travesty." The musical broke house records everywhere it played.

In Toronto the actress received word that Ben Hagman, Larry's father, had died of a stroke. Larry, who had seen his mother's show in Dallas, had by then enjoyed success on Broadway, played a part in Joshua Logan's film *Ensign Pulver*, appeared two years in the daytime soap opera *The Edge of Night*, and fathered two children. In the fall of 1965 he would score a big success, opposite Barbara Eden, in *I Dream of Jeannie*, a television sitcom that lasted for five seasons.

That October, Mary's *Hello, Dolly!* company flew from San Francisco to Japan. Sponsored by the State Department's Cultural Exchange Program, the tour was intended to include Russia. In Tokyo they played at the Takarazuka Theatre, and Mary brought down the house when she sang a Japanese version of the title song as an encore after the final curtain. When Russia unexpectedly canceled *Dolly*'s engagement in Moscow, President Lyndon Johnson asked the musical's producer, David Merrick, to take the show to Vietnam. Richard quickly made arrangements with the military to fly him in advance to Saigon, along with an electrician, a carpenter, and a sound man to check out whether or not the production could be done there, while the cast continued its performances in Tokyo. After Halliday made two more trips to Vietnam to supervise preparations, the company of seventy-three members left Tokyo in a drab, windowless troop transport plane bound for Saigon.

Upon arriving, Mary left the plane during a cloudburst with a major general holding a leaky Japanese parasol over her head. The effervescent star bounced down the ramp, her arms spread wide, and shouted, "I'm thrilled to be here, and I couldn't care less about the rain!" The company's goal in Vietnam was to bring color and gaiety to the combat troops, but the risks were many and the criticism from war opponents sharp. In Saigon a Vietcong guerrilla in the uniform of a South Vietnamese police officer was discovered trying to plant a bomb under the stage where the company was to play. The principals had been invited to a reception given by U.S. Ambassador Henry Cabot Lodge, but they arrived to find that the front part of the house had been blow away by explosives the night before. The reception was held despite the damage in the back portions of the house, and Mary entertained guests there by singing songs from *South Pacific*. A few days later the *Dolly* company flew into the steaming jungle of South Vietnam with the war raging all around them.

The problems for the show folks and the military were endless. Packing and unpacking crates of costumes and pieces of scenery was tedious work under the best of conditions, but in Vietnam the rice paddies around the workers rumbled with artillery, and armed helicopters hovered over them. "At each stop we've had bright young soldiers helping put the show up backstage, taking the show down, and loading it on trucks and planes," Mary told reporters. More than once as Dolly Levi sashayed in her feathers and plumes around the make-believe interior of the Harmonica Gardens restaurant, the star could see helicopters land their wounded and swiftly take off again right behind her audience. Jay Blackton, the show's musical director, did a skillful job of blending the five musicians the troupe took with them—a pianist, a banjo player, a trumpeter, a violinist, and a drummer—into the full background of orchestral music that had been taped in Tokyo.

When traveling to the outlying bases, the company was furnished with the open helicopters used by the military. As Mary remembered her first flight, "I was lying on a stretcher with my head resting on grenades, while alongside me were a couple of soldiers

with tommy-guns ready." In Bien Hoa they played in an airplane hangar, while four thousand servicemen sat on sandbags in ninety-degree heat and watched the show. The stage there consisted of three forty-foot ammunition trailers, and military policemen with loaded rifles stood on either side of the stage and at every door. For most of the soldiers, *Hello, Dolly!* was the first live Broadway show they had ever seen.

At the air base in Nha Trang, the company watched teary-eyed as a recently wounded rifleman was surprisingly reunited with his girlfriend, a dancer in the troupe. Mary, who had never been anywhere near a battlefront before, left the war zone convinced of "the futility of war." Members of the company who opposed the war were vocal, and some felt bringing servicemen such frivolous entertainment was inappropriate. "Our happy company was at odds," Mary said, and "I questioned my own presence there." But she kept up such a brave front that fellow players nicknamed her "Foxhole Mary." Members of the company couldn't go out at night, always had to be in before dark, and were never permitted to go anywhere alone. But Mary said the sound of the soldiers' applause was unlike anything she had ever heard. "Maybe if you put the Yankee Stadium, Madison Square Garden, and the Hollywood Bowl together you could get the picture," she wrote her family.

In Vietnam the star suffered a severe allergic reaction to penicillin and required massive doses of cortisone. Nonetheless, she continued on to Okinawa and Korea, where the *Dolly* company entertained more troops. When not performing, the actors talked with soldiers and visited the wounded in hospitals. "I would answer their questions," Mary said, "and sometimes return to the hospital the next day and find that there on a stretcher dead was a boy I had talked to the day before. It was devastating."

Badly in need of rest before opening the show in London, Mary and Richard took a vacation trip to Hong Kong, Bombay, Beirut, and Rome. Then Mary joined the other principals in London to start rehearsals with Gower Champion and a predominantly English cast. Mary opened in *Hello, Dolly!* at the Theatre Royal in Drury Lane on December 2, 1965, and played there for six months.

The show was sold out for every performance. The London critics liked Mary, but thought the musical was "poor material" and "a great big disappointment." Nevertheless, Mary drew twenty-five curtain calls from an opening night audience that included the Queen Mother. A resplendent audience clapped, cheered, and yelled, "Come on, Dolly, one more." Finally, Mary pleaded for silence and meekly said, "This would have made even Dolly Levi speechless. It certainly has made Mary Martin speechless." Then she sang, "Hello, London! Well hello, London! It's so nice to be back home in Drury Lane."

The next day Peter Lewis of the *Daily Mail* wrote, "By our current dud standards *Dolly!* is the best musical of a bad year. But by the standards of *South Pacific, Kiss Me, Kate,* or *My Fair Lady* it is sadly non-vintage, indeed mediocre stuff." Whatever reservations the press may have had about the show, critics unanimously gave Mary a hearty personal welcome. When Noel Coward saw the musical, he wrote in his diary: "Mary Martin, who was, I thought, brilliant. Gower's production is wonderful, and although I didn't really like the show, I enjoyed it thoroughly."

Mary celebrated her fifty-second birthday in London and in May returned to the United States. She almost immediately began preparations for *I Do! I Do!,* a new musical that David Merrick would produce and Gower Champion would direct. But the exhausted star needed rest before starting another demanding show and, before accepting the offer to star in *I Do! I Do!,* she insisted that Merrick fly composer Harvey Schmidt to Brazil, where she and Richard would be spending the summer, to teach her the show's songs. "That was no hardship for me," Schmidt said. "Going to their ranch in Brazil was a lovely experience. We worked on learning music each morning, and in the afternoons we'd go horseback riding or exploring. It was great. I loved having a chance to get to know Mary before we started rehearsals."

The Hallidays came back to New York in August, and Mary went into training for her new assignment. Based on Jan de Hartog's *The Fourposter, I Do! I Do!* teamed Mary with Robert Preston, a colleague from her Paramount days. The two veterans would share the songs

and make up the complete cast. Mary already had full confidence in Gower Champion, who thought in terms of movement in staging as she did. "Gower was fabulous," Mary said, "such a perfectionist." Champion announced at the outset of the show that he was a benevolent dictator, and indeed he remained the absolute, unquestioned center of any production he directed. "He couldn't stand Merrick," Mary said, "because Merrick wanted to be in on everything. Gower said, 'No, I don't want you in the theater. I only have two people in this cast, and I want to work with them. I don't want to know you're anywhere around.'" Anytime Merrick violated that dictate, the director would snap his fingers, and the rehearsal would stop until the producer had left the theater.

Champion had a keen sense of how slow or how fast a scene should move. He had warmth, charm, and stunning good looks, yet at the same time he maintained an air of aloofness. "Gower was strong," lyricist–book writer Tom Jones said. "He was able to handle power gracefully and unquestioningly." Consequently, the director's stamp was evident on *I Do! I Do!* in every aspect. He called his cast back to work with a horn off an old car, but since he and his two stars got along so well, rehearsals remained pretty much a lovefest.

The company continued to view David Merrick, who boasted of having a heart of stone, as something of the villain. "Merrick was a fascinating, brilliant man," Harvey Schmidt said, "but everybody in the business knew horror stories about him." Tumultuous and unpredictable, Merrick was one of the top producers of his day, responsible for ten or twelve shows a season, among them *Gypsy, Hello Dolly!* and *Carnival.* Yet he could be an unmitigated bully. "When *I Do! I Do!* was out of town for tryouts," Tom Jones said, "I happened to be reading *The Rise and Fall of the Third Reich.* Perhaps because of that I couldn't help seeing many similarities. I saw Harvey and me as Czechoslovakia and David Merrick as Hitler."

Initially, the show started out just using two pianos as accompaniment, one for each cast member. "They both played all during the rehearsal period," Schmidt recalled, "and the effect was engaging and scintillating. I had hoped that quality of dialogue between two pianos would be retained in the score as it was orchestrated, but

Phil Lang never quite captured that the way I would have liked."
To make the musical more intimate, Champion came up with the
idea of concealing the orchestra onstage behind the scenery.

Since *I Do! I Do!* is the story of a fifty-year marriage, the songs
needed to depict the problems that the couple faced through the
years. Harvey Schmidt and Tom Jones had had great success off-
Broadway with *The Fantasticks* and preferred a presentational approach
in their shows, directly addressing the audience. The songwriters
had learned early in rehearsal that Bob Preston had once studied
the saxophone and that Mary played the violin, so they incor-
porated those skills into "When the Kids Get Married." They even
worked Bessie Mae Sue Ella's name into that number. "Flaming
Agnes," which Mary sang when her character was planning to
leave her errant husband, proved a showstopper. Wearing a huge
hat topped with egret and bird of paradise feathers, Mary devised
her own staging for the song and really belted it out, turning the
number into a Martin forte. "What Is a Woman?," which she sang
a step down off the stage, almost in the audience, was particularly
right for her age. "Somehow those 1920s clothes that she was
wearing, standing right on the lip of the stage, made the song so
intimate," Schmidt said. "Mary did it so beautifully and made that
a lovely, private moment."

"My Cup Runneth Over," which made the popular charts after
I Do! I Do! opened, was almost cut during rehearsals. As written,
the song had been a much bigger number than what it became in
the show, with the two characters supposed to hold long notes at
the end of segments, which neither star was comfortable doing.
Champion felt the song didn't work without that. Eventually, Mary
said, "It's such a sweet little song, let's put it in, and we just won't
hold those phrases." Champion agreed if the stars would be willing
not to go for applause. So he restaged the number, and it was
decided that Mary's character would have her first labor pains at
the end of it.

In professional discussions Tom Jones found Mary "a marvelous
mixture of simple and high-class, warm and soft, and tough-as-nails."
With two titans like Gower Champion and David Merrick at the

helm, Richard remained somewhat in the background, although, as Jones said, "he was very much a part of Mary Martin." Since the songwriters were relative newcomers to Broadway, they felt a tad insecure. "It was a very nervous feeling when we were out of town," Jones said, "to get in an elevator and there was Jerry Herman or Comden and Green or Jule Styne. There were threats of bringing in other people, but Harvey and I actually wrote the entire score."

Some of the songs were written under pressure, and many of the rewrites were done while the musical was on the road trying out. "Gower was so great out of town about not rabidly ripping the show apart," Schmidt said. But fundamental changes were made, particularly in the second act. One song called "Thousands of Flowers," which had been everybody's favorite until the company got to Boston, was dropped. Harvey Schmidt was working on a new number late one night when the tape recorder he was using began picking up the radio system in the Ritz-Carlton Hotel. "Here on this very crucial night when I had to write this very important song," the composer remembered, "they were playing the entire score of *South Pacific*. Whenever I'd play back my music, *South Pacific* would also be on the recorder, only louder. So there was Mary singing these landmark songs from her all-time, legendary, landmark show, and in the background I'd hear my dim little paltry melodies."

The last song written for *I Do! I Do!* was "This Has Been a Very Good Bed," which was put into the show in Cincinnati, a stop added to the tryout schedule when Champion decided that the production wasn't ready to go into New York. "I'm very fond of that little number," Jones said. "It's simple but touching, and it serves its function well." Although Act I of the musical had strong songs such as "Together Forever," "I Love My Wife," and "Nobody's Perfect," Act II became a beautiful piece of work after all the rewrites on the road. "All of our work was worth it," Jones maintained.

Stage lighting for *I Do! I Do!* was done by Jean Rosenthal, one of Broadway's pioneer lighting designers. Rosenthal's work was sensitive and creative and full of romantic moments where the lighting came up on a certain note. The designer approached her work

with the meticulous care that a painter gives a nearly completed canvas. "Jean had patience and took time with things that hadn't been done before," Rosenthal's colleague, Tharon Musser, said. "In her hands lighting design became an art."

Originally, Martin and Preston played eight performances a week out of town, but that proved too much for them during the run in New York. "*I Do! I Do!* is a killer show," Tom Jones said. "Mary was not a fast study; in fact she was very slow. And she and Preston had to conserve their energy." So it was decided that the stars would only do evening performances. With a two-person show, even when the actors were off-stage, they were talking into a microphone as they changed costumes.

The show went into New York two weeks later than planned and opened at the 46th Street Theatre on December 5, 1966. Most critics thought that the music and book were thin, but said the production was highly polished and that Mary Martin and Robert Preston comported themselves appealingly. "Miss Martin is a delight to have around, even when her material is something less than electrifying," John McCarten said in *The New Yorker*. Walter Kerr, writing for the *New York Times*, agreed that the stars were delightful and noted that Mary, as always, had "that mellow sound that comes from her throat like red wine at room temperature." But he judged the show "barely passable" and most of its songs too folksy. "A Santa Claus who shall here be known as David Merrick has hitched a very high-powered Donner and a very high-powered Blitzen to a very low-powered One Horse Shay," Kerr said.

Although the stars were happy with their reviews and sensed that *I Do! I Do!* was in for a long run, the opening was a disappointment for the songwriters. "I have never had a show where I felt after the cast party I could tip the cab driver five dollars with a clear conscience," Tom Jones said. "I've never known what tomorrow was going to bring. Even with Mary Martin and Robert Preston and Gower Champion and David Merrick doing *I Do! I Do!*, when the notices came in, we didn't know." Looking back, both Jones and Schmidt realized that they had gotten in on the tail end of old Broadway, before shows had grown too expensive to try out on

the road. "In Boston and New Haven we probably stayed in some of the same hotel rooms where so many other shows from the past had been worked on," Harvey Schmidt said. "To me that was thrilling."

Both roles in *I Do! I Do!* required the stamina of boxers. Mary had to make fifteen costumes changes in the show and five wig changes. For the last number the stars even applied their aging makeup right onstage. "My life was rest, dinner, the show, and back home again to bed," Mary said. "Each performance was the premiere for that particular audience, so I had to give a premiere performance." During the weekend she conserved her voice by not speaking. Mary and Preston played the show in New York for a year without understudies. Worn-out, Mary collapsed during a performance in October 1967 and was unable to finish the show. The next day's matinee had to be cancelled. From then on, she and Preston did only evening performances in New York, since Preston was also showing signs of exhaustion.

In December, Carol Lawrence and Gordon MacRae took over the roles, and Mary and Richard went to Brazil for three months. She had agreed to take *I Do! I Do!* on a national tour with Preston for a year, beginning in March 1968, but needed rest before undertaking the ordeal. "The second year of a New York show is miserable," Mary said. "No matter how much you like the play, you are faced with going down the same street, entering the same stage door, and using the same dressing room until you almost go out of your mind." That's the reason she preferred to take a show on the road. "The traveling is rough," Mary said, "but you're looking at the show through a different frame every week. And the audiences can be a revelation."

By March, after recovering from a hysterectomy, Mary was eager to get back to work but wasn't sure of her voice. "For the first time in my life," she said, "I had heard no music for three months. I had not whistled or hummed or sung a note. I think I was frightened to hear the sound that would come out of my abused voice. What was more terrifying was that I felt no music within me. I could not even recall the joy of singing." But once she got into the show again, the old spark returned and she came alive in the part. *I Do!*

I Do! was scheduled to play twenty-seven cities from coast to coast, opening in Rochester. Then came engagements in Indianapolis, Minneapolis, Los Angeles, San Francisco, Vancouver, Seattle, Portland, St Louis, Phoenix, Omaha, St. Paul, Milwaukee, Kansas City, and Dallas.

By the time Mary reached Dallas in November, it was clear to Bessie Mae Sue Ella that her friend was not at all well. Mary had injured her foot and had to cancel a performance in October, and she was still taking cortisone from the bad reaction she had had to penicillin in Vietnam. As soon as the Hallidays arrived in Dallas, the Austins got a call from Richard. "I don't have time to be polite," Halliday said. "We need a doctor right away. We're at the Stoneleigh Hotel, and could you send us a doctor?" Bessie Mae and Jac contacted their family physician, and he managed to get Mary well enough to perform on Monday. "I could tell by the look of Mary's face that she was ill," Bessie Mae said. "There was a puffiness, and I think it was a reaction to the medication she was taking." Also, Mary was depressed and crying a great deal, which was not like her at all.

The tour went on to Houston, Memphis, Cleveland, Charlotte, Greensboro, Richmond, Washington, D.C., Baltimore, and Detroit. On a Saturday in February 1969, Mary collapsed onstage just before the opening number, the victim of an intestinal infection, and was rushed to a local hospital. "She was obviously in pain during her Friday night's performance," Robert Preston said. "I could see it in her eyes." The Monday night and Tuesday shows were cancelled, and then the announcement was made that the rest of the tour would have to be scrapped. "Bob Preston was as sick as I was at the end," Mary said. "We both nearly died. I had this huge tumor in my stomach and I didn't know it."

Before she opened in *I Do! I Do!*, Mary and Richard had signed a pact with each other that they would spend two years at their ranch in Brazil without any trips back to the United States, no matter what the offers might be. Mary was so ill in Detroit that there seemed to be no other option for her but rest. She looked forward to a period of quiet, doing the things she'd never had time to do before. But Mary insisted that she had signed the pact with Richard for *his*

sake. "He and I had stresses and strains in our years together that we tried desperately to hide, not only from the world but also from ourselves," she said. "Now was our chance to be together with no outside interests." On Richard's birthday in April 1969, Mary gave him a card on which she had written: "This is for two years in Brazil. For you to be the greatest *fazendeiro* that ever was. No matter what comes up—shows, television, pictures—we will not come back." As it happened, they spent almost four years in Brazil, with only one trip back to New York, and Mary claimed those were the happiest years of their lives.

CHAPTER 12

Years of Adjustment

Although Mary would eventually return to the stage, she later
referred to *I Do! I Do!* as "the last show I did, I did." And it
was, in fact, her last musical. The years in Brazil that followed marked
a distinct transition in the star's life, personally and professionally.
After decades of single-minded effort, she became a lady of leisure,
living for four years on a sprawling farm deep within the Brazilian
interior, about two hundred miles southwest of the capital city of
Brasilia. "It's like leading a second exciting life," Mary said, "com-
pletely different from the first." In the pastoral stillness and quiet
of Brazil, the "first lady of the Broadway musical theater" was known
simply as Doña Maria, and Richard, her sometimes meddlesome
producer-husband, became a gentleman farmer. In contrast to their
years in the theater, they went to bed soon after nine in the evening
and got up at dawn. "Like the land," Mary said, "we have to lie fallow
from time to time."

Mary Martin was fifty-six years old when she "retired" to the
Halliday farm in Brazil. Deeply depressed after her hysterectomy,
she told a psychiatrist that she felt "caged," as indeed she was by
her regimen in the theater. She blamed herself for handing over
every practical detail of her life to Richard. With the last stops on
the tour of *I Do! I Do!* cancelled, Mary saw that her charmed life

244

had been a treadmill, and she was also feeling claustrophobic in her marriage to a man who was wrecking himself with liquor and pills. Mary, the very embodiment of enthusiasm, vitality, and joyous happiness, found herself swimming in pessimism, pouring out her frustrations to a psychoanalyst almost hysterically. "Never in my adult life have I been able to catch cold like other people and go to bed. I couldn't have a headache, or get tired, or feel out of sorts. I had to go out there and perform," she said. "I was raging at a life I had made, but in my heart I was blaming my husband." She knew it was time for a change. At the *fazenda* in Brazil the actress spent her days riding horseback through the lush valleys and over the mountains of a jungle paradise in a desperate effort to regain her lost exuberance.

The Broadway star learned to cook on a wood-burning stove, made friends with the workers on the farm and their children, began raising chickens, and did the ordinary things she'd never had time to do when she was appearing in a show. "I've been *on* all my life," Mary frequently said, but in Brazil she could relax, luxuriate in simplicity, and come to terms with herself. One of the things that haunted Mary was a belief that she had been a bad mother, particularly where her son was concerned. Larry and his family visited the Hallidays soon after they settled into their life in Brazil, and almost immediately there was a dreadful scene. "We have had an unbelievable year of emotions with our family," Mary wrote Bessie Mae Sue Ella in 1970. "I'm afraid Larry is going through all the Hollywood bit—pot, etc. I love him, but I don't like him anymore."

Heller and Tony Weir were having serious marital problems, and separated for a while. "So her 'boy friend' came to be with us!" Mary wrote Bessie Mae from Brazil, "and we don't even know him (or like him—he's *so* young and dull). Thank heaven she isn't marrying him. She and Tony are not together yet—legal papers must be signed—but apparently this is what she wants now (after one and a half years of lawyers getting her *out*). Oh dear—I think we're getting old. I don't understand *any* of them any more."

Yet, despite the family woes, Mary and Richard found contentment in South America. "We are just having a ball," Mary wrote

Bessie in February 1970. "We love our life here more than ever. Richard has accomplished more in seven months than most men do here in years! He has built dams, roads, lakes, bridges, and planted loads of flowers. I now have a rose garden with 300 roses!! We bought more property next to ours and will build another road." Eventually, the Halliday farm included some seven thousand chickens, which yielded an enormous egg production, ducks, a herd of cattle, and horses. The couple also raised wheat, rice, coffee, fruit, and vegetables and had their own brand—clasped hands—which greeted guests on a sign at the entrance to the property. Anapolis was the nearest town, and the farm's produce was sold there. Later the *fazenda* did get electricity but not a telephone. "Richard couldn't abide telephones in that lovely countryside," Mary remarked.

They decided to expand the house, adding a large office for Richard, a music room covered with white wicker, and a guesthouse with its own kitchen, bedroom, bath, and living room. In time they added a second guesthouse. "Our simple little country home kept growing and growing," Mary said. "We were never idle." By early 1970, the tired star felt her adrenaline flowing again. She let her hair go white and began making frequent trips into town, a seventeen-mile drive. Meanwhile, Richard supervised the building of seven waterfalls and the planting of 580 avocado trees.

After several months of quiet, Mary started getting restless. She decided to buy a little building with an extra lot in the center of Anapolis, population 100,000, and open a combination boutique and beauty shop that would sell her needlepoint and the dresses she'd design. "Aren't we mad?" Mary wrote Bessie Mae. "Well, after all I can just make so many kookie robes and dresses and saris for myself. If you have any crazy new ideas for my shop, send them down. (I'll sell anything!)"

Mary called the shop Nossa Loja (Our Boutique) and went into partnership with two local women. The boutique was located on a small curved street off the town's square and built like a Japanese pagoda, with columns of bright red, white, and black and doors a brilliant red. For the beauty shop—the only one in town—Mary got together with a Japanese ironmonger and a Brazilian sink maker

and had them build an armchair that tipped back so that customers could have a shampoo and rinse. Getting the shop ready took three months, but when it was finished, Mary said, "I felt like Edison." While she got busy designing the beginnings of a Mary Martin collection of dresses and accessories, Dema (the wife of the Hallidays' farm manager) converted the designs into clothes on an ancient pedal sewing machine that she operated barefoot. Within a few months, they had enough merchandise to hold a grand opening.

While a procession of family members and guests found their way to the Hallidays' tropical retreat, there was plenty of time in Brazil for relaxation and taking long coffee breaks and enjoying life with Richard. "The sun is out and the butterflies are doing their ballet," Mary said on a tape she made for Bessie Mae on Christmas Day, 1971. "Believe me, if I had to sing one note or dance or kick or do anything, I'd probably drop dead. I haven't done anything [like that] in two years." But she had learned some Portuguese, acquired a dog she named "Flaming Agnes," and doubled the previous year's business at Nossa Loja. "In all of my thirty-one years in the theater, I never sold so hard," Mary wrote Bessie.

Richard allowed a streak of gray to grow in his hair, gave up smoking, and gained twelve pounds. But later Mary found bags of speed stashed among her husband's possessions and learned then how serious his drug addiction was. Dozens of letters poured in with offers for Mary to return to Broadway, but the Hallidays said no to them all. They seemed to sense that their time together was running out, and they wanted to make the most of the few years they had left. For Richard the life of a country squire was salve to his tormented soul.

Mary and Larry continued to be estranged. Larry's wife, Maj, wrote occasionally, and out of the blue Mary received a letter from her son's eleven-year-old daughter, Heidi, saying that she would like to call Mary "grandma" and Richard "grandpapa," as she thought it odd that she never had since she loved them both. "Well, better late than never," Mary wrote Bessie Mae and Jac Austin, "and I am delighted."

Heller and Tony still hadn't gotten back together on a permanent basis; Heller seemed content with seeing her husband only

on weekends. "I don't know what my attitude toward Tony will be when we ever see them," Mary wrote Bessie Mae in 1971. "Heller's letters are all happiness. She is trying to right her 'wrong' and I guess Tony is." Mary thought perhaps Heller was spoiled. "If Heller had just once in any small way tried to do something except 'accept.' Just once made us feel that we were not the Bank of America, or that she didn't know how to cope with her responsibilities, I think we both would feel so much safer for her future. But then perhaps we have not been parents as you and Jac have been."

Mary often told Bessie Mae, "You're just the other half of me," and from Brazil she wrote that she wished they had corresponded more through the years. "I swear I would publish [your letters] or tour reading them in colleges to help young people," Mary said. "I, who have never envied anyone, envy your dear, dear tolerance." When Bessie sent the Hallidays a recording of *Jesus Christ, Superstar*, Mary found listening to the rock opera an experience. "I'm not sure I could take it every night and twice on Wednesdays and Saturdays," she wrote the Austins. "I told Richard the other night, 'I'm glad we had our period in the theater, as I'm not a part of this new constant, concentrated sound!' But it is all fascinating to hear. . . . Isn't it marvelous that this new generation has no inhibitions—no fears of expressing their thoughts. Maybe in all the mess that is going on, when the abscess finally breaks, something new and clean and beautiful will come about."

At the shop in Anapolis, Mary specialized in long, ethereal dresses and caftans, but she also sold Texas-style hats, bags, and jewelry. She had a fun sense of color and referred to herself as "the poor girl's Mainbocher." The first fifty dresses she designed, the most expensive of which was $100, sold within one week. She decorated the inside of the shop with masses of hanging ferns and wicker furniture. While the women sat under dryers in the beauty shop, Mary taught them how to do petit point and needlepoint. Within a year Nossa Loja was so successful that the Hallidays had ten seamstresses at work in homes all over Anapolis. For their second Christmas in Brazil, when the couple found out that Heller and her family were not coming down for the holidays, Mary and

Richard decided to open the shop during the evening and have a Christmas party there for their staff rather than spend Christmas Eve alone.

Richard understood that the energetic Mary needed to be busy and was delighted with the success of her shop. Before long, the pixie sparkle returned to Mary's eyes, along with her ability to laugh at herself. "I was driving Richard crazy," she said. "When I told him I'd like to expand the boutique, I think he cried for joy." Mary approached clothing design with the same zeal she had lavished on her shows, and she loved meeting and pleasing customers. She seemed to find supreme happiness in Brazil. "The climate is wonderful," the actress said, "never too hot or cold, and there's a breeze at night. When it rains it pours, but there's always a rainbow afterwards." Mary lived in South America for a year and a half before she visited Rio de Janeiro. "I have lost a sense of time," she said. "I've never had so much fun in my life."

During the Nossa Loja years, Janet Gaynor often visited the Hallidays. The film actress had left Brazil after Adrian died in 1959. But Gaynor returned several times with her third husband, Paul Gregory, whom the Hallidays had known for years. Gossip persisted that Mary was romantically involved with Janet, a rumor strengthened by the supposition that all three of Gaynor's husbands were either homosexual or bisexual. But the exact nature of Mary's relationship with either Janet Gaynor or Jean Arthur is unknown.

In March 1972, Mary and Richard returned to New York for a celebration of Richard Rodgers' seventieth birthday at the Imperial Theatre, sponsored by the Friends of Music and Theatre of the Museum of the City of New York. The benefit was an all-star gala at which Mary had agreed to reprise songs from *South Pacific* and *The Sound of Music*. Her appearance on the tribute was made tense by the fact that Richard Halliday had to testify at a court hearing in which the Rodgers and Hammerstein lawyers and the Hallidays' lawyers were in a dispute over royalties from the soundtrack album of the movie *The Sound of Music*. Halliday and Leland Hayward, co-producers of the Broadway show, had been excluded from profits accruing from the sale of the RCA Victor album when the

recording was released. "As they say," Mary wrote Bessie Mae Sue Ella, "'that's show-biz!'"

Mary was eager to see Heller and her grandchildren when the couple returned to the United States in 1972 and eagerly anticipated talking to Bessie Mae. "Ye gods," she wrote Bessie, "we can even sing 'Sam, the Old Accordion Man' and 'Sweet Sue.'" Mary claimed that the only singing she'd done in the past two and a half years was to the chickens on the farm. "My feet are killing me," she told reporters in Manhattan. "I haven't put on a pair of shoes since we retired to Brazil." The first difference she and Richard noticed in New York was that the air in the city had gotten more polluted. "When we go back to the farm, we'll have to get used to fresh, clean air again," Mary said. But there were other changes. "We couldn't believe what we saw on the streets," the star said. "We couldn't tell men from women. I really thought it was a costume party."

The lawsuit over the royalties from *The Sound of Music* album proved more complicated than Mary and Richard had expected. "You may or may not know that they—Rodgers and Hammerstein— were never the real producers [of the show], just Richard and Leland Hayward," Mary wrote Bessie Mae after the Hallidays returned to South America. "But way back there in rehearsals they [Rodgers and Hammerstein] asked to have their names first in the billing, in *name* only—not to receive additional money. Well, all went well until the picture came out and grossed more than any of all time! Everybody was happy until one day Richard Rodgers said to Leland (they were having lunch), 'What about that check we received for the first picture recordings?'" Neither Hayward nor Richard Halliday had gotten a check. "Oh! what a kettle of fish [Rodgers] opened," Mary said. Rodgers and Hammerstein's lawyers had put all rights to films and recordings in the Rodgers and Hammerstein name. By the time that was discovered, Mary told Bessie Mae, "darling Oscar (who we feel truly didn't ever know any of this) was in Heaven, and 'darlin' Dick R. was home studying those figures. You see, Bessie, he *really* does like money!" So Richard Halliday had to testify before several lawyers and a couple of judges, since by 1972 Leland Hayward was also deceased. "And there was nobody down

here but the lawyers and the two Richards left to 'tell it to the Judge,'" Mary said. The Hallidays and the Hayward estate ended up with a settlement of over $1 million.

Rodgers and his wife, Dorothy, sent Mary flowers upon her arrival in New York before the composer's birthday tribute and had a dinner party for the Hallidays the night before Richard's appearance in court. "I think we kissed in about 1,000 pictures," Mary wrote Bessie Mae. "In the middle of kiss 500, a man from the press asked who was writing my next show. I like an idiot replied, 'He is,' pointing at Richard Rodgers. After he got his eyebrow down, he said, 'Oh?' I said, 'Aren't you writing *Arsenic and Old Lace* as a musical for Ethel and me?' For that remark my Richard says I deserve to get back in that mad, mad world!!"

Heller had definitely decided to divorce Tony Weir, but she seemed happy, so Mary and Richard left New York feeling at peace with her decision. They flew to California for five days, where they visited Janet Gaynor and Paul Gregory at their home in Palm Springs. Richard had a lump removed from his mouth while they were in California, but a report showed that the growth was not malignant. Mary then visited her ailing sister, Jerry, for a few days in Fort Worth, and the Hallidays returned to Brazil by way of Mexico City. "What a lovely way to go on and on!" Mary wrote Bessie Mae from the farm in June 1972.

Shortly after the Hallidays returned to South America, Bessie got a call from Ralph Edwards, inviting her to participate in a *This Is Your Life* program honoring Mary to be taped in Brazil for broadcast. The Austins few from Dallas to Los Angeles, where they met Mary's sister, Heller, and Heller's two boys, Timmy and Matthew. (Because of "a prior commitment," Larry Hagman did not participate in the show.) When they all arrived in Brasilia, Edwards and Paul Gregory were on hand to greet them, and the guests were hidden in a hotel in the capital city until time for the program to be taped. "We went in cars to the farm," Bessie Mae recalled, "and Mary was really surprised when we showed up. Janet and Paul were visiting Mary and Richard at the time, and they had told Mary that some newspaper and television people wanted to do a

television special on two American actresses who made Brazil their home. So Mary was dressed and had her hair fixed. Richard had arranged everything without Mary's knowing." The show aired in the United States on November 13, 1972.

The Austins stayed in Brazil for about ten days, including a trip to Rio. "Mary's place was so isolated and beautiful," Bessie said. "One day Mary drove us up into the hills behind their house to show us what the property had looked like before they improved it. I've never seen such beautiful roses as those in the rose garden Richard made for Mary." On Sunday the Hallidays let their servants have the evening off, and Mary and her guests cooked dinner themselves. "Jerry was in charge of the salad," Bessie said, "and I made a rice and grit souffle. Since I wasn't accustomed to cooking at that altitude, it took forever for the water to boil, and my souffle was ready before we were prepared to eat our salad! But we all dined in the kitchen that night."

Having been professionally inactive for over two years, Mary was finally ready to get back to work. Richard called Joshua Logan from Brazil and said, "Josh, find something for Mary. . . . She's only happy when she's busy, and I'm sure you can find a story that she'll like." Logan and the Hallidays had made up by that time, and Logan's respect for Mary remained boundless. "To me," the director said, "artists are the aristocrats of today, and Mary is an aristocrat of aristocrats. A production is blessed to have her as the star." Thrilled that the Hallidays wanted to work with him again, Logan made several phone calls to friends in the theater, and one of them, actress Margalo Gillmore, suggested a musical version of *The Corn Is Green* for Mary. Miss Moffat, the Welsh schoolteacher in Emlyn Williams's play, was the right age for the star, and the story is filled with emotion that could lead easily to songs. Logan called Richard and told him the idea, and Richard assured the director that his wife loved *The Corn Is Green.*

Emlyn Williams insisted on changing the locale of the musical from a mining town in Wales to the cane fields of the American South and on transforming Miss Moffat's most promising pupil, Morgan Evans, into a black field hand. "I was enormously impressed

with Emlyn's ability to assume the American idiom," Logan said of the results. Albert Hague, who had composed scores for the Broadway musicals *Plain and Fancy* and *Redhead*, wrote songs for the show, by then called *Miss Moffat*, and Hague, Williams, and Logan flew to Brazil to discuss the production with Mary and Richard. Mary ran out to greet her guests, hugged and kissed Williams and Logan, and was gracious to Hague, but it was obvious that she was nervous when talk turned to her doing another Broadway show. When Hague sat down at the wicker piano in Mary's music room to play the songs he'd written, it was discovered that mice had eaten the felt off the hammers.

Logan later learned that Mary had no idea that Richard had called him. "She must have thought we were just being pushy," Logan said. "It was a mixed-up time." Mary listened politely to the songs Hague had written. Yet at the airport she told her visitors, "We would like you to go on working on it, but we can't say yes or no in the present condition of the score. There's just not enough of it yet to hold onto." Logan, Williams, and Hague remained hopeful enough to say that they'd return to Brazil once the songs were completed. When they did, the composer played the entire score, and Mary sang several of the numbers. "We could tell how exciting she would be in the part," Logan said. But Richard was suffering terrible pain in his stomach, and Mary seemed distracted. When Logan got the actress alone, he urged her to make Richard go to a doctor. "Oh, God, if he only would," Mary said. "I'm sick with worry. But you know how strong-willed he is, and he can be very stubborn about anything concerning his health."

Two weeks later, March 3, 1973, at the age of sixty-seven, Richard was dead. He died in a hospital in Brasilia with an enormous blockage in his intestine. "I had to watch my love fill with poison," Mary said. "In the end it was pneumonia that took him away. Everything stopped functioning—his lungs, kidneys, his brilliant brain." She tried to carry out her husband's wish to be cremated, but that was not possible in a Catholic country. So Mary flew Richard's body to Miami, and his ashes were taken from there to Texas for burial in the family plot in Weatherford, the hometown that Richard had

consistently refused to visit. From Florida, the star called Josh Logan to say that she would not be able to do *Miss Moffat*. She was too grief-stricken. The show opened at the Shubert Theatre in Philadelphia on October 7, 1974, with Bette Davis recreating the role she had performed in the Warner Bros. movie, but it closed after only fifteen performances.

The next four years were the darkest of Mary's life. The woman with the boundless energy and zest for work found her ambition gone. She had no desire to return to the stage, had no impulse to sing, and felt she couldn't go back to Brazil except just long enough to close up the house with Janet and Heller as steadying companions. Mary knew that she couldn't live in Brazil again without Richard. She seemed lost, unable to make decisions. "I didn't know how it would be possible to continue," she said. "Richard had edited me and planned everything three to five years in advance." She was disappointed in her attitude but found she was relying on old friends for direction. "I'm afraid my performance is not a good one this time," Mary wrote Cheryl Crawford a few weeks after Richard's death. "Even though I am desperately trying, my heart isn't in it. It is just almost impossible for me to imagine life without Richard—because he is half of me. The half that is left is not the vital, 'radiant,' fun loving person he knew. But I know I *must* come back to life someday. Otherwise all the years his love, devotion, and sacrifice of the things he didn't do would be in vain. I can only thank God that he had at least three-and-a-half years of joy in the land, the earth, that meant so much to him."

The one positive thing to come out of her losing Richard was that Larry called while his mother was closing up the house in Brazil, and they reconciled. In later years Mary and Larry would become great friends, although he refused to discuss their earlier strained relationship and the intense dislike he still harbored for Richard. "Now finally we have found each other and love each other," Mary said, and she doted on her four, and ultimately six, grandchildren.

In July 1973, Heller married businessman Bromley DeMeritt, Jr., and Mary spent that summer on Martha's Vineyard, close to her friend Katharine Cornell. She would attend parties where people

asked her to sing. "I tried," Mary said, "but it wouldn't come out. The words, the notes, the sound simply wouldn't come out. I thought there was something wrong with my vocal cords." In the fall of 1973, she went to England to try to pull herself together and decide where she wanted to live. "First, I had to learn to grow up," Mary said. "I'd always had someone to take care of me—my parents, then Richard." She visited Paris, Munich, and Greece and began taking ballet and voice lessons in London—"just to have a normal routine," she wrote Cheryl Crawford. "Life is still difficult without Richard, so keeping busy is the only solution."

She returned to New York in November, then visited her sister in Texas, spent time with Larry and Maj in California, and decided to buy a house in Palm Springs to be near Janet Gaynor and Paul Gregory. For months Mary couldn't relax or read anything and felt guilty about not wanting to work. "I don't like indulgence in any form," she said. "You go on. You stay involved in life." With Janet's encouragement, she finally started painting and doing needle-point again. When asked when she'd do another show, Mary answered, "When I feel like singing again. . . . I know producers' problems, and I don't want to add my problems to theirs." Fearful of facing a future without Richard, she turned to her religious beliefs, which were not the formal, organized kind, but rather a belief that there was Someone within her waiting to give her guidance. "All I had to do was call on Him," Mary said. "I have never prayed for anything except the wisdom to solve my own problems."

By 1974, she had decided to resume work on her autobiography. "I'd been running long enough," she said. Mary devoted the next year and a half to writing her life story, which she found both fun and frustrating. "The early parts just rolled out," she said. "I have total recall, so that part was easy. But other parts were very, very, very difficult and painful. It was like analysis, like being on the couch." But she couldn't bear the thought of giving up and spent four or five hours a day taping her thoughts for a secretary to transcribe at night. "I loved your suggestion of *Enter on Cue* as a title," Mary wrote Cheryl Crawford from Palm Springs. "I have many titles in mind. Anyway, it really is going well. I guess it's therapeutic

but it sort of destroys me every now and then, and I do a lot of weeping at night." In April she signed a book contract with William Morrow and Company. "You know how I never liked to read contracts," Mary wrote Crawford, "never did. Richard read them."

Much to the star's surprise, she decided to buy a house in Palm Springs. "I've never wanted to live here, ever," she said. "Richard and I both just loathed Palm Springs, so it must be the age or something, because I love it. I love the kind of life that we lead. We bicycle to town and do our shopping, and it's really quite marvelous." Mary had Janet and Paul Gregory to dinner frequently, and Walter Annenberg, William Powell, Alice Faye, and former President and Mrs. Gerald Ford were neighbors. "Mary had to have a home somewhere," Bessie Mae Sue Ella said. "She couldn't just go from resort to resort according to the fashion of the season. She didn't live like that."

The house Mary bought was battleship gray, but she painted it pink and turned the back of the place into the front. It was a rambling house with a red tile roof. Mary planted a lovely garden around the pool, began having friends in for cocktails, and talked about making a comeback on the stage as her memoirs neared completion. "How this dear lady by the name of Dodie Hamblin (who is transcribing the book) can hear me by tape all day and by night . . . while she transcribes the same bloody voice by banging away at her typewriter is beyond my comprehension," the actress wrote Bessie Mae. "We do, at intervals, swim in the heated pool *while still taping*. My voice actually sounds better underwater!" Mary found writing about Richard's death the most difficult part. "I put it off and put it off and finally didn't come through with it until the last minute," she said. "It took something as dramatic as seeing a new tree in bloom before I could finally do it."

"I want to work, and I will," Mary said, but making a decision was not easy for her. "I'll do one thing or another because one has to." She was still not singing and realized she was reluctant to try. The despondent star consulted various doctors who could find nothing wrong with her vocal cords. Finally, she consulted a psychologist, who told her that she could sing if she wanted to. "You're afraid to sing," the therapist told her. "Why?" Mary was stunned at his analysis;

she'd never been afraid of anything! "Me, Mary Martin, afraid to *sing?*" she said incredulously. "I discovered that I had developed a guilt complex about not singing."

She sold the penthouse in New York and grew closer to Larry and Maj, visiting them often. Mary thought about opening a boutique in California with her daughter-in-law and took pride in her son's rapidly advancing career. She went to see Bessie Mae and Jac Austin in the spring of 1975, spoke at the Dallas Women's Club, her first public commitment aside from her book, and visited Weatherford, where she turned the first shovel of earth for a new $300,000 public library. In July she flew to Brazil, planning to spend the summer at the farm, but sold the Loja and left after three weeks, finding the loneliness at the home she'd shared with Richard excruciating. Mary spent Christmas that year with Heller and her family and was present at the christening of her granddaughter and partial namesake, Mary Devon DeMeritt.

Long-time friend and confirmed bachelor Ben Washer became Mary's full-time publicist and confidant, as well as the person who handled her business affairs. She learned to enjoy living in Palm Springs, particularly the cool evenings there. "Every morning and night, when Ben and I go in the pool, with the palm trees and the moon," she wrote Cheryl Crawford, "we feel we are Nelson Eddy and Jeanette MacDonald (very old ones!). I just had two speakers installed on the outside, so now we even have music everywhere. Ben has been sensational, and we have fun cooking outside, both trying to stay on diets." Broadway shows were offered to the star regularly, as were television appearances, Las Vegas engagements, and benefits, but Mary refused them all. Without Richard, her professional life didn't seem to mean much. "I don't care what anyone says," Mary wrote Bessie Mae a year after her husband's death, "it does *not* get easier."

She finished her autobiography and began taking daily voice lessons. "I never said that I was retiring," Mary told reporters, "just that I was tired." Sooner or later she knew show business would beckon. "I have to decide if I want to return to that kind of life again," she had said while shopping in Brazil in 1975. "You know,

when you're doing a show—and that's how I lived most of my life—
you're like a nun or a hermit." Yet it was a matter of time before
she was offered an appearance she couldn't refuse. "I've got too
much energy just to ride bicycles," Mary told a *New York Post* reporter.
"I'm having a lovely time being free to do something besides eight
shows a week. But I have to make up my mind just what I want to
do. . . . I am just now learning the millions and millions and
millions of things that my blessed Richard did."

Her autobiography, *My Heart Belongs*, was published in 1976,
and that entailed a lengthy book tour with lots of appearances on
talk shows. "When they sent out the itinerary, I'd never seen any-
thing like it," Mary said. "This is all new to me. I've never done any
talk shows before because I was always having to save my voice for
a show." She found the tour grueling, but enjoyed meeting her
public. She assured interviewers that she would definitely be back
on the stage at some point, but she couldn't say when.

A platinum blonde Mary celebrated the bicentennial Fourth
of July in Weatherford, unveiling a bronze statute of herself as
Peter Pan at her hometown's new library. On the pedestal was this
inscription: "Peter Pan: a tribute to the genius of Weatherford's
Mary Martin who brought a myth to life for millions." Mary quipped
that the statue would be "nice for the pigeons," but added that she'd
discovered that "Never-Land was right there in Mary Martin's backyard."

In August the star rented a cruiser and spent a month sitting
on its deck and trying to make decisions about what to do next.
"Right now I'm just relaxing and doing all the things I've never
done," she said. "I'm learning to walk by myself. . . . There's no
way of anticipating what it is to lose a loved one. You hear a car
and think it's him—or see someone, or hear a voice." The only
thing she was sure of was that she didn't want to redo a show she'd
already done.

Mary told friends that she was in the "Me" phase of her life.
"One of the joys is being able to be with people I love," she said,
"to be able to talk at length and not be facing a nightly show. And
to have time to spend with my son Larry and his family and Heller
and her family, and be able to sing at the top of my lungs putting

my granddaughter to sleep." Mary was delighted when one of her grandsons introduced her to a playmate saying, "I want you to meet my grandmother—Peter Pan!"

After thirty-seven years in the public eye, Mary thought she was finally learning about herself and finding personal fulfillment. "How wonderful it is to be the age I am!" she said. "What a lovely time of life! I gave to audiences what belonged to my children, got back from audiences the love my children longed to give to me." She felt she was living her life at full capacity, simply being successful in another realm. But from time to time she thought she saw Richard standing before her saying, "Don't indulge your sadness." Finally, she knew it was time to sing again. "I thought, 'This is not right.' Richard did too much to make the career not to do something more with it. I knew it wouldn't be easy getting back. But I knew I didn't want to stop performing, even though I knew nothing about business."

Mary's reentry as a Broadway star occurred on Sunday, May 15, 1977, at a sold-out, one-night benefit for the Friends of Theatre and Music of the Museum of the City of New York. Called *Together with Music*, the gala was a joint concert with Ethel Merman. The two superstars—Mary in her sailor suit from *South Pacific* and Merman in Mama Rose's ratty old bed-blanket coat—made their entrances by jumping through two huge paper hoops to the strains of "Send in the Clowns." They were greeted with a roar of applause from an audience that had paid upward to $125 for seats. In the celebrity-filled house were Lillian Gish, Ginger Rogers, Claudette Colbert, Lauren Bacall, Jack Paar, Margaret Truman, and a smiling Larry Hagman. A single ad in the *New York Times* had brought such an avalanche of ticket orders that $40,000 in checks had to be returned because the Broadway Theatre, where the gala took place, was already filled to capacity. "They work together most remarkably," Walter Kerr said of the legendary stars in his *Times* review. "Ethel Merman is the bonfire and Mary Martin is the smoke. Smoke is always changing shape, so that you can't be sure from moment to moment just what it most resembles; heaven knows you can't catch it."

Through the years, Mary's voice had gotten lower, but she sang well and held her own with Merman. "Deciding to do that show took a lot of will power," Mary said, "because I hadn't sung for four years. Coming back was traumatic. But Richard was always there in spirit." The gala proved a love-in, with repeated ovations from a zealous audience. Toward the end of the show, two identical crimson Dollys descended two mauve staircases while singing "Hello, Dolly!" with a chorus line that included Yul Brynner, Joel Grey, and Burgess Meredith. "Both Mary Martin and Ethel Merman were past sixty years of age by then," lighting designer Ken Billington said. "My job was to chat with them, make them feel secure that they were going to be displayed to their best advantage, and see to it that those two superstars looked fabulous onstage."

Feeling that she had gone too long without definite goals, Mary signed a five-year agreement with Fieldcrest to design and promote a collection of sheets, pillowcases, and towels for the company. "They thought of me, I guess, because of my needlepoint book, which had come out in 1969," Mary said in the paperback edition of her autobiography, "and because I had designed dresses and hats, handbags, needlepoint rugs and pillows, all sorts of things for my shop in Brazil." The jungles of Brazil continued to inspire most of her designs. Mary introduced the Fieldcrest line to the press at a cocktail reception in the Rainbow Room in New York and traveled extensively for the company over the years ahead. On tour she did presentations, spent at least two hours a day signing autographs for customers in department stores (sometimes writing "J. R.'s mom" for those who requested it), and enjoyed making new friends wherever she went. "I can't imagine Mary *not* having a career," Bessie Mae Sue Ella said. "She would never have been content to stay at home and play bridge."

In 1977, Mary agreed to perform in a play, hoping to take it to Broadway. The two-character nonmusical was a translation of a comedy by Russian playwright Aleksei Arbuzov, and Mary's costar was Anthony Quayle. The show in its American version was called *Do You Turn Somersaults?* and depicted the developing romance between two older people. Mary played Lidya Vasilyevna, a former

actress who had become a cashier in a circus, whereas Quayle was a physician who directed a sanitarium at Riga on the Baltic Sea. The two meet when Lidya comes to the sanitarium for a rest cure. She is a vivacious eccentric who jumps out of her window after curfew, breaks into song at odd times, and gradually wins over the stuffy, reproving doctor with her free spirit. Quayle had done the play in London with Dame Peggy Ashcroft for the Royal Shakespeare Company under the title *Old World*, and he and Mary gave splendid, adorable performances. In the course of falling in love, the play's characters danced the Charleston onstage, and Mary did the shimmy. Until she fell from a revolving platform and was grounded by her physician, she also did backward somersaults. The actress was eager to get back to work and thought this comedy had the zing necessary to succeed in New York.

"Well, here we go! With courage and joyous abandon," Mary wrote the show's producer, Cheryl Crawford, in August 1977. "Let us pray that Lidya Vasilyevna does right by us." The play, directed by Edwin Sherin, opened in Knoxville at the University of Tennessee's Clarence Brown Theater on August 6. Two nights later Mary tore a ligament during rehearsal and had to wear an ankle-to-thigh leg cast during performances. Nonetheless, the effervescent star said, "I am alive and it feels good to be involved in the theater again." Ken Billington, who had worked on the Martin-Merman concert, again designed the lighting for the show, aware that it was to Mary's advantage to have footlights when she was onstage. Billington said, "I remember at the first tech rehearsal of *Do You Turn Somersaults?*, Mary walked out from the wings and the footlights came up, and she stopped and looked out front and said, 'Thank you, Ken.' Later I heard her talking to Anthony Quayle and she said, 'My Richard told me that I always have to have footlights to make me look good. I didn't tell Ken that, he just knows it.'"

From Knoxville the show went to the Kennedy Center in Washington, D.C., for a five-week run. "A confection that could easily have dissolved into a soup of mawkish sentiment gets souffleed into an amusing and often touching entertainment," *Time* magazine reported. Few doubted that any actress could convey the winsome joy of

living quite so well as Mary Martin did. The star told the press that she had no desire to get back on the stage until this play came along. The story of two older people beginning to fill the gaps in their lives after spouses and children had gone appealed to her, and she could relate to its message. But when David Richards of the *Washington Star* called the comedy "rather insipid entertainment," and similar reviews said much the same, Mary began to have doubts about the show's potential in New York.

Do You Turn Somersaults? continued on to Fort Lauderdale, Florida, and opened at the 46th Street Theatre in New York on January 15, 1978, during a major snowstorm. On Broadway the comedy lasted a bare three weeks. "*Somersaults* is not a play," Mort Young said in the *Los Angeles Herald-Examiner*. "It is a series of slow skits lightly connected by a dreary thread of story. . . . Miss Martin plays a Russian circus performer in a sanitarium as if she were Doris Day cajoling Rock Hudson for falling asleep at a beach blanket party." The critic thought the actors' biggest mistake was in accepting roles in this play, which in his opinion "floundered almost from its opening lines." Mary, who had rented Dorothy Hammerstein's apartment in Manhattan through March, admitted that *Somersaults* should never have come into New York and expected that ticket-holders would be disappointed when she didn't sing in the show. Still, she enjoyed her six months of performing in the play and was happiest when she was on the stage. Between shows in New York, the star had a chance to dine at Sardi's with such old friends as Richard Rodgers, Josh Logan, Ethel Merman, Yul Brynner, Dolly Haas, and Al Hirschfeld. But tastes in theater had changed. Rock, operas, concept musicals, and British imports currently dominated. "I think what's happened to Broadway is devastating," Mary said. "The only interesting musicals are revivals."

Although Mary loved to work and thought of work simply as a creative aspect of living, most of the scripts that producers sent her in her later years were unappealing. "I've turned down things left and right," she said. Finally another love story of two older people came along that Mary thought was warm, touching, and hopeful. It was a television movie called simply *Valentine*, to be

aired in December 1979 on ABC. Jack Albertson was her costar, and Mary played a seventy-one-year-old widow living in a California retirement center. "When this offer came, they needed an answer overnight," she said. "I flew out from New York, stayed up all night reading the script, and said yes."

Most of *Valentine* was shot outdoors at the beach in Venice, California, and around Lake Tahoe. The cast rehearsed the script for two weeks before filming began, and the show turned out to be one of the most agreeable experiences of Mary's later career. "We were a marvelously close family for twenty-three days," the actress said. "I felt . . . it would be exciting to do a story for people in the lovely September years." But while critics found the honey blonde Mary delightful in the older role, most thought the script was cloying and overromanticized. A reviewer for *Variety* called the writing "pedestrian" and said that the telefilm droned on "in desperate attempts at being jolly," but proved "a bust" since the actors failed to make the love affair convincing.

After *Valentine*, every script Mary received seemed to cast her as a seventy-year-old. "I'm not ready for the geriatric set yet!" she said. "I try to learn something new every day." But age was catching up with the perky performer. Mary's sister, Geraldine, died in May 1979 at the age of seventy-six and her death brought mortality home to Mary. Although the star was still interested in working, her priorities had changed. She wanted to spend more time with her family. Heller had her fourth baby in 1979, and Mary continued to grow closer to Larry and Maj and her grandchildren. "It's like having a rebirth and starting over," she said. "Larry has changed completely. He's so dear and so good at home. And he's very bright about his career." Mary loved watching her son as J. R. Ewing on *Dallas*, a character who stopped at nothing to attain his devious goals. "Larry is marvelous," his mother said, "he is so *awful!* How could I have raised such a rotten kid?"

In the last original episode of *Dallas* for the 1979–80 season, an unknown assailant shot J. R. Ewing. All summer long the question raged around the globe, "Who shot J. R.?" Mary was asked to divulge the secret dozens of times but swore she didn't know. Betting

parlors took in millions of dollars in wagers on who of the many
with reason to hate J. R. actually pulled the trigger. Mary was elated
to bask in her son's eminence and told him so when they were
together at a Hollywood party celebrating Ben Washer's seventy-
second birthday. To Bessie Mae Sue Ella, Larry's godmother, Mary
wrote, "It warms my heart that you love your godson. He *is* a dear,
dear man!! Isn't it marvelous that it just takes the right time for us
all to know each other!"

Producer Martin Jurow had in mind casting Mary and Larry in
a film version of *A Trip to Bountiful,* but Mary thought the mother's
part in the Horton Foote play was too old and frumpy for her. She
doubted that she'd ever do another musical, although she said she
might do something with songs. "A big musical now costs over a
million dollars," Mary said, "and I would never leave any show
until it had paid off its investors and made a lot of money. I don't
want to be tied up that long. I want to spend more time with my
family now that I've discovered them again."

The star returned to Brazil with Ben in 1978 long enough to
sell the farm, continued to tour for Fieldcrest, spent time with friends
during trips to New York, and was in the audience the night Janet
Gaynor made her Broadway debut in *Harold and Maude.* The years
of adjustment and reflection had given Mary an inner peace that
she had never known before. "I think God is within all of us," she
said. "I don't have a new romance . . . but my life is filled now with
other kinds of love. Love for my children and my grandchildren—
the kind of love I missed so much in my career. I am so happy that
finally we are as close as we all are now. . . . I do feel that I've
caught up."

Final Decade

Mary Martin, the symbol of perpetual youth for hundreds of thousands of fans, was approaching her sixty-seventh birthday in 1980. Still vibrant, with a mischievous smile, Mary believed in living life, even as a senior citizen, to the hilt. Grateful for a charmed career, she wished to continue being part of the world and use her talent to make others happy. "Life is really like a tapestry," she said. "There's a thread here, another there, and then it picks up over here." Delighted that she and her family had at last grown close, she resolved to spend the rest of her days putting them first. To Larry, Heller, and her grandchildren, she gave affection and friendship that was constant and reveled in the happiness their love brought her. "I thank God for this second chance to have this joy, to be with my children on birthdays, at Thanksgiving and Christmas," she said. "I don't think I deserve it, but I certainly enjoy it."

Thrilled that Larry had come into prominence as an actor, she established a playful relationship of equals with her son. When asked what it was like being the mother of the *Dallas* icon J. R. Ewing, Mary replied, "My son is a star. I am an icon." When Larry gave his mother a pair of jeans with the label "J. R.'s Private Stock" sewn on the back pocket, she wore them proudly. At the height of the J. R. Ewing craze, the two of them were waiting outside a hotel

in Las Vegas for a cab en route to a nightclub. A cab driver pulled up, slammed on the brakes, and shouted, "Hey, J. R., get in! I just got room for you!" Hagman hopped in, and as the cab spun off, he rolled down a window and shouted to his bewildered mother, "That's show business, Mom!" Later at the nightclub, Hagman was introduced by performer Joel Grey and received an enthusiastic round of applause. Then Mary was introduced as Peter Pan, and the audience gave her a five-minute standing ovation. As she sat down, Mary tapped Larry on the knee and declared, "And that's show business, too, baby!" They both loved to tell the story.

When the big mystery of who shot J. R. was revealed, the culprit turned out to be J. R.'s mistress, Kristin, played on the television series by Bing Crosby's daughter, Mary. "Who would have thought when I was making all those movies with Bing that his daughter would shoot my son and have an illegitimate baby with him?" Mary said in jest.

The Broadway star still dressed to perfection and carried herself regally. "One of the things I learned from all those hours of fittings with Mainbocher was what looks good on me and how clothes should fit," Mary said. She never lost her basic simplicity and candor and claimed that she still felt Richard's presence in her dreams. One particular dream haunted her. "There was a big rolling cloud coming toward me," she recalled. "It looked like curtains, and by the time it got to me the curtains parted. And there was Richard on a stage, wearing a dinner jacket. He called to me to come see the stage. 'It's unbelievable,' he said, 'the biggest stage you've ever played on.' And behind him I saw Oscar Hammerstein moving forward. Then he faded, and all I saw was Richard beckoning me to join him on that great stage. As I started toward him, the curtains closed, and I awakened screaming, 'I can't!'" Mary reasoned that she wasn't ready to die yet. "It wasn't my time," she said.

In Palm Springs she liked to get up around 6 AM to see the rising sun reflected against the mountains. She had overcome her fear of singing, performed at the farewell gala for opera star Beverly Sills at Lincoln Center, and made a surprise appearance with Larry at London's Palladium, singing "Honey Bun" in her floppy

sailor outfit at a tribute commemorating the eightieth birthday of England's Queen Mother. Mary continued to be a spokeswoman for Fieldcrest and in May 1980 played hostess to the fashion press at a cocktail party in the lobby of Radio City Music Hall. She spent that summer at Larry's house in Malibu while her son was on location in Texas shooting *Dallas.*

Mary was begged to come out of retirement and return to the Broadway stage, but she refused to be tied down to a long-term commitment. Producer Harry Rigby desperately sought her for a production of *Colette* in New York, but Mary said she wanted to be free to travel and move between Palm Springs, Houston (where Heller lived), and Malibu. There was talk of her doing another one-woman concert show, although that never materialized. The still bouncy star let her short hair go natural and assured reporters that she was enjoying the happiest years of her life. "I feel no one should ever really grow up or old," she said. "I'm aging, but I don't pay any attention to that. I absolutely refuse to admit that my joints ache a bit occasionally. . . . Growing old is a state of mind. I have no intention of letting it become part of me."

When Larry celebrated his fiftieth birthday in 1981, Mary was present for the occasion and danced disco with her son. "We didn't talk for three years, when I was away living in Brazil," she said. "I'm with my grandchildren now more than I was ever with my own children, and it is heaven." When Larry's daughter, Heidi, gave an exhibition of her oil and watercolor paintings in Palm Springs, Mary hosted a Mexican buffet at her house on opening night.

The singing star made an appearance with the Boston Pops Orchestra in May 1981, visited London and Dublin briefly during the summer with Ben Washer to publicize her Fieldcrest line, then took off for Australia to christen a new Fieldcrest mill. "There will never be enough time in the day for me," she said. "There never has been. There never will be." Although she suffered from a mild case of arthritis, Mary refused to consider the possibility of slowing down. "I really love living," she said. "I love every second of it."

When television talk show anchors Hugh Downs and Frank Blair left *Over Easy,* a thirty-minute series aimed at older people originating

from San Francisco, the producers felt the talk show needed a woman's touch. They asked Mary to host the program with former newscaster Jim Hartz. The idea appealed to Mary. "I can talk forever on any subject, whether I know anything about it or not," she said. "I thought I could be helpful. I know so many older people who just sit back and say, 'Oh, my life is over.' Then they start getting afraid to do things, to try things, which is a tragedy. I've watched it with people I love. They're afraid of breaking a hip or something."

Over Easy aired nationally on 235 stations and focused on issues facing Americans past the age of forty. "The series is a tremendous way to show people how to prepare themselves for their later years," Mary said. She made her debut on September 29, 1981, with Pearl Bailey as her first guest. Mary said her forty-one-year-old co-anchor, Jim Hartz, had to cue her during the first tapings. "He would press one finger into my back to remind me to ask another question," she said. "Two fingers meant 'shut up.'" Gradually, the star got used to reading a teleprompter and learned to find the camera for close-ups. "Jim's like another son," Mary said of her *Over Easy* co-host. "We're a perfect match. I'm over and he's easy."

The star gave the show a sense of personal involvement through anecdotes, personal observations, and her off-the-cuff feelings about matters of concern to senior citizens. "Keep busy, keep your mind active," was her advice. "Don't become a sitter or a recluse. Do something. There is so much to do, so much older people can do to help others." Over the next year James Stewart, Lillian Gish, Bob Hope, Maureen Stapleton, Joel Grey, Josh Logan, Eva Le Gallienne, Hume Cronyn, Ethel Merman, and Milton Berle were guests on the show. "I got more 'Texas' as we went along," Mary said. Her constant theme to viewers was "even if you have to retire from your job, you should never retire from life." Seniors found her upbeat message inspiring. "After forty it's patch, patch, patch all the time," Mary liked to say, "but so what?" The important thing was to try new experiences. "There is so much new to learn and so little time in the world." For Mary, *Over Easy* proved another challenge and a venue that allowed her to stay active and have stimulating conversations.

On Sunday, September 5, 1982, Mary, Ben Washer, Janet Gaynor, and Paul Gregory were riding in a taxicab on their way to dinner in Chinatown, after the two actresses had taped a segment for *Over Easy*. Mary remembered that the cab driver had the longest hair she'd ever seen on a man, and she thought, "If I had scissors, I'd snip it right off." That was the last conscious thought she had until she woke up in a San Francisco hospital with Larry and Heller standing over her. As the cab in which the actress and her party were riding approached the intersection of Franklin and California streets, a bare two and a half minutes from where Mary was staying, the driver of a speeding van failed to stop for a red light and slammed into the taxi. The impact sent the mangled cab skidding for more than eighty feet before it smashed into a tree on the opposite side of California Street.

Seventy-six-year-old Ben Washer was killed instantly. Janet Gaynor hovered between life and death in the intensive care unit at San Francisco General Hospital after four hours of emergency surgery to repair a torn bladder and remained in critical condition for weeks with internal bleeding. Mary's pelvis was broken in three places, and she suffered two broken ribs and a punctured lung. Doctors feared she would never walk again. Paul Gregory escaped with only three broken ribs and a bruised right kidney.

Robert Cato, the driver of the van that hit the cab and a former security guard, suffered only minor injuries but was charged with driving while intoxicated and vehicular manslaughter. In February 1983, Mary, Gaynor, and Gregory were served with subpoenas to report to the District Attorney in San Francisco to testify in a trial against the driver. Later, Mary accepted a $100,000 insurance settlement for damages incurred in the collision.

For several days after the accident, Mary's condition remained serious, while Gaynor's was so critical that the actress had to be connected to a ventilator to aid her breathing. For weeks Mary's closest friend continued to risk infection because her body was so injured. "By the grace of God, Paul Gregory, Janet Gaynor, and I are here," Mary told the press a week after the crash. "No one can take the place in our hearts of 'Uncle Ben.'" She attributed her

own quick recovery to luck, good genes, and her faith in God. When doctors told Mary that she would be able to walk, she was given a walker and told to stroll through the hospital's corridors. The star took off down a hall but soon noticed that everyone was staring at her. The battered patient glanced down and saw that she was carrying the walker!

Mary remained in the San Francisco General Hospital for nine days, released on September 14. A nurse took her to the basement of the hospital in a wheelchair, where the star demanded a walker, saying that she would walk to her waiting car to prove to herself that she could do it. The actress made her way slowly, while doctors and nurses hung out of windows on the upper flour clapping and crowing and yelling, "We believe, Mary! We believe!" It was just like the children in her audiences had done when she was playing Peter Pan. "That really got to me," Mary said. "I burst into tears." She blew them a kiss, but was too emotional to say anything.

Three weeks later Mary was back on *Over Easy*, still limping and using a walker. She wanted her message to be "it could happen to you, so whatever you do, keep moving." Her guests on that show, about how traumatic events affect lives, were Larry Hagman and Heller DeMeritt, who told how they had rushed to their mother's side when they heard of her injuries. "Welcome Back, Mary" buttons and signs greeted the star as she entered the television studio, and she was showered with confetti as she came through the door.

By then Janet Gaynor's condition had been upgraded from serious to fair. The celebrated movie star died two years later, having never fully recovered from the accident. Mary suffered prolonged remorse over the loss of Ben Washer and spent the winter in her home in Palm Springs meditating and recuperating. "I tend to think I'm nineteen," she told a reporter in January 1983. "I'm sort of retarded that way." By February, she was back in New York, peddling Velvaderm, a skin renewal product, at Bloomingdale's.

The accident made Mary a deeper person philosophically. "I don't remember having a thought till I was thirty," she said. "Now I'm sixty-nine and I've thought a lot." She appeared in an episode of *The Love Boat* on television, still stiff from her injuries. She accepted

the Weatherford Chamber of Commerce award for outstanding citizen of 1983 and performed at the White House in a nationally televised show before an audience that included President and Mrs. Reagan. For her final number she sang "My Heart Belongs to Daddy," wearing a copy of her original costume. "There was my daughter and my son-in-law and my granddaughter, who was having her thirteenth birthday, sitting with Nancy and Ronnie," Mary recalled. "I don't like to get mixed up in politics, but I'm so fond of the Reagans . . . , so I said yes."

In 1984, the star headed a benefit at Davies Symphony Hall in San Francisco for the trauma center at the city's General Hospital, where she'd been treated after the accident. In spite of the objections of her friends and family, Mary decided to fly again during the performance. So she contacted the fellow who had rigged the wires in Las Vegas and got her Peter Pan costume from the Museum of the City of New York and—at the age of seventy—flew up to the third balcony, crowing wildly and sprinkling the astonished audience with fairy dust. "I proved that you can overcome anything if you try," she told the press. Also performing at the benefit were Robert Preston, Florence Henderson, John Raitt, Van Johnson, Billy Daniels, Sammy Cahn, and Larry Hagman, and the show was staged by Miriam Nelson, dancer Gene Nelson's former wife. Toward the end of the show, Mary dedicated "The Way You Look Tonight" to Janet Gaynor, who had died several weeks earlier of complications stemming from the auto accident. The benefit was a triumph, and the hospital's trauma center was subsequently renamed in Mary's honor.

"I am still crowing about life," the aging star said. "I think it's a privilege to be alive. I have a joy of life, and the greatest thing right now is to get on in years, as I am doing, with my health and with fun." Then she smiled and added, "Here's to us never growing up— never, never, never." But Larry thought it was time for his mother to get back to steady work and urged her to return to her first love, the stage. Mary was frightened by the prospect and doubted that she was ready, particularly without the support system she had depended on for so many years. Underneath her happy exterior was a bittersweet mood, as she thought of the people she'd lost—

Richard, Oscar Hammerstein, her sister, Janet Gaynor, Ben Washer, Yul Brynner, Ethel Merman, the roll seemed endless.

When a preliminary script of *Legends* was sent to her in Palm Springs in April 1985, it had been eight years since Mary had done a play on the stage. The comedy, written by James Kirkwood, the Pulitzer Prize–winning author of *A Chorus Line*, was about two former screen idols, bitter enemies, who are given the chance for a comeback if they can overcome their differences and work together in the same show. Mary didn't like the script, largely because it was liberally laced with four-letter words, and turned the offer down four times before finally agreeing to do the play. The script went through several revisions, and finally Kirkwood flew to Los Angeles to read his latest draft to Larry Hagman, who urged his mother to do the show, convinced that she needed the activity. Mary insisted that she had to think it over, feeling neither confident nor secure. "Jimmy [Kirkwood] said he wanted me for this role because I'm a survivor," she said, "but I've never thought of myself that way. With all the knocks I've taken, and the pits I've been in, I never expected to make it this far." It was a negative stance for the fearless tomboy who had never ducked a challenge. Yet without the support she had depended on for so long and with old age racing toward her, Mary—despite a brave front—was terrified. She tried to remind herself of the lines from William Blake that Josh Logan had recited to her in London—that if the sun and moon should doubt, they would go out—but her fear was too great to heed the message. She remembered the failure of *Do You Turn Somersaults?* and felt vulnerable and alone.

With *Legends* she was not in the hands of masters the size of Joshua Logan, Oscar Hammerstein, and Richard Rodgers, and the script she reluctantly agreed to perform was nowhere near ready for audiences, much less the New York critics. Mary would be playing Leatrice, a prim, proper Hollywood has-been, outwardly sweet but capable of being as catty as her rival, Sylvia, the tougher, more openly ruthless and bitchy of the two former stars. The two actresses in the play had always loathed each other, and Sylvia had even stolen Leatrice's husband. Both were living in New York and approaching

seventy when a brash young producer got the idea of starring them in a new play. Alone, neither would have much public appeal, but together, because of their tempestuous past, they might be big box office.

Kirkwood wanted Mary in the show because he knew she wore clothes well and that audiences had always adored her. For Sylvia, the author and producer considered casting Eve Arden or Irene Worth. "If only Ethel Merman were still alive," Mary said. Eventually, Carol Channing was given the role, even though some thought the blonde star, most closely identified with *Gentlemen Prefer Blondes* and *Hello, Dolly!* would make Sylvia too much of a caricature. Channing liked the concept of *Legends* because she said, "We play the two meanest women that ever happened in show business." Mary still had reservations about the script, dreaded playing eight shows a week if the show made it to New York, and said she accepted the part in *Legends* when Kirkwood "just wore me down."

The reluctant star rented a house in England during the summer of 1985, where she rested and tried to make up her mind about whether or not she should do the play. In September she agreed but insisted on numerous script changes. That fall Carol Channing took a house near Mary's in Palm Springs and bicycled over every morning so that they could learn their lines together. Mary still wasn't convinced that she liked the play, had trouble remembering dialogue, and told James Kirkwood early, "You know, there are some words in the script that I could never say." Later she claimed that she gave all the four-letter words to Channing.

When rehearsals began in Los Angeles, Mary struck the play-wright as being "down to earth, eminently likeable and fun." She still had a touch of Texas accent, which the author found appealing and disarming. No grandiose star, Mary was warm and affectionate, free with her hugs and kisses, flattering about everybody's work, and did her best to make everyone involved feel important. From time to time she voiced concern that audiences wouldn't accept her as Leatrice, telling Kirkwood, "I just don't want to harm your wonderful play." Although Mary persistently refused to say the F-word, off-stage she had a slightly bawdy streak combined with a little girl

quality. Sometimes she had difficulty making up her mind, but on most issues she was reluctant to say no.

Mary stuck with *Legends* primarily because her son thought it was a funny play and urged her to do it. "Larry said if he wasn't so busy right now, he'd buy the play and produce it as a film," she said. "He even kidded me and said, 'Mother, I don't see why you can't say every word in that script.'" The show's costume designer gave Channing a dark wig, so that she'd look like Joan Crawford or Rosalind Russell or one of the other vintage movie queens, but Mary's look was harder to establish. She was still trying to decide on her appearance when the show opened in Dallas. Everybody agreed that her look should be distinctly different from Channing's, since she was playing a genteel moralist somewhat in the Loretta Young vein. Yet finding the right costume for Mary proved a problem. Bessie Mae Sue Ella went with her friend to a costume fitting in Dallas, during which Mary dismissed the design suggested as too matronly. "I love Helen Hayes," she said, "but I don't want to look like her!"

The nervous star often came to rehearsals whistling, yet became far more reserved when business matters were brought up, often resorting to her little girl stance, which others found frustrating. "How dispiriting to pull this delaying tactic," James Kirkwood wrote, "to let Carol sit there with egg on her face, to play the little girl who just didn't want to get involved in nasty business details." Yet when pushed, Mary could be obstinate. Although the show was not a musical and required no singing, she insisted that she could only do seven performances a week, not the usual eight, even though an eighth performance could mean the difference between a profit and a loss. "Darling, I wasn't trying to be difficult at all," Mary told the playwright. "It's just that I've never missed performances. I'm older, but even so I don't want to start missing them now. I love you and the play. And won't Carol be absolutely wonderful? I adore her." That was Mary's gracious way of holding firm.

Even before rehearsals began, she had demanded repeated cuts and made constant suggestions for changes in the script. Kirkwood

responded that he hoped there would be a minimum of these requests. His experience was that when stars kept coming to the author for changes, the authority of the director was undermined. Then Channing called the playwright, very upset. "Darling," she said, "those cuts! Now that I look over them, they totally diminish my character. My whole reason for being an actress. You can't do that."

As rehearsals progressed, Mary seemed lost and confused and had difficulty remembering her lines. "Mary would finally get it," Kirkwood said. "Then, after a five or ten-minute break, work would resume, and it was as if it had never been rehearsed." Frustrated, Mary would say to the author, "Jimmy, I'm just so upset about all this. Maybe you'd give Larry a call and see what he might suggest." Larry came to a rehearsal and told his mother, "Stop worrying. You're going to be all right. It will come through."

Mary admitted to the press that it was hard to get back into harness. "You know, if you don't play tennis for a long time, you don't keep your tennis arm," she said. "And if you don't do anything, your brain goes. When I think back, I've always known every single word of the script before we even started rehearsals for a musical. And I knew every song. Also, there's a certain rhythm in musicals. There isn't that much dialogue. You go from rhythm in a song to rhythm in dialogue. So this is a whole new thing for me to take on—and at a very *late* age." Yet the realization that she couldn't remember lines came as a blow to the star, who prided herself on perfection.

Kirkwood felt that the cuts and changes the two women wanted gradually whittled his play away. Neither Channing nor Mary thought much of the show's British director. "We would have understood each other better if he were Chinese," Channing said. But Mary claimed that her costar made her nervous, and she didn't want anyone in the rehearsal hall except the person who was playing the scene with her. Gradually, the thought struck Kirkwood and the producer that Mary was not going to be able to give a cogent performance. When the star realized they were losing faith in her, she

began to cry. "She seemed so very tiny with all of us surrounding her," Kirkwood remembered. "It had to be so humiliating for her. Here was Nellie Forbush and Peter Pan and Maria von Trapp falling apart, all of them collapsing in on Mary Martin—in public."

Legends opened at the Majestic Theater in Dallas on January 9, 1986, still nowhere near ready for public scrutiny. Mary had so much trouble remembering her lines that she was finally given an earplug through which she could be prompted. At one rehearsal the stage director suggested they run through the end of both acts, during which Mary got flustered and wasn't sure which act she was in. Larry Hagman came in to lend support to his mother and eventually took over the direction of the show. "He had a fine divining rod as a director," Carol Channing remembered.

Mary kept up a happy façade in the face of disaster, but even her fans found the show weak and parts of it in extremely bad taste. Jac Austin left the theater on opening night in Dallas muttering, "If Richard Halliday were still alive, Mary Martin would not be doing this show!" Suddenly, the vivacious star of *South Pacific* and *Peter Pan* seemed to be an old lady dolled up to appear youthful. She still needed the battery-operated earphone to remember dialogue, and the audience could sometimes hear the prompter feeding her lines. "It was incredible to us that an actress, any actress, could get through an entire play having to listen to someone offstage and pay attention to actors speaking to her onstage," Kirkwood said. To make matters worse, busloads of Mary's Texas friends arrived to see the girl from Weatherford, who had become a national treasure, perform one last time. "It was so confusing," the star said of the Dallas performances. "We weren't ready for anybody to see the show. It was murder, absolute murder."

From Dallas the show went back to Los Angeles, where it opened at the Ahmanson Theater on January 25. The rewrites continued, and nerves within the company were frayed. Mary showed amazing resilience despite her problems. "No matter what was going on inside," Kirkwood wrote, "she presented a bounce-back picture on the outside." Most members of the audience applauded the two stars for what they had done in the past, and for some it was

painful to watch these two legends soiling their reputations with such inferior material as Kirkwood's play. Mary decided that the show should end with her and Channing singing a song. "It was difficult to imagine how they'd burst into song in that apartment [set] after fighting all night," the playwright said, "but it was, as Mary said, probably right that the audience would like to hear them warble, and certainly the present ending was a copout." So they put in "Accentuate the Positive," a cheery number from an old Bing Crosby movie, but Mary had trouble learning Peter Gennaro's choreography for the end of the song.

In New Orleans there was talk about building up Mary's character, since the audience knew so much more about Sylvia. In part, that was true because so much of Mary's dialogue had been cut. In June the hesitant star was still using an earplug when the show opened in Phoenix, but had to take it out at intermission because she was picking up taxi calls on it. Mary was so ecstatic when she discovered that she could do without the crutch that she swore she'd never put it in again. That gave her a new freedom, and she actually began responding to the other actors. "Mary was high as a kite without the ear bug," Kirkwood said. "She seemed to have dropped ten years, maybe fifteen. She was all sunshine and smiles."

There had been talk of taking the play to London, but by the time it reached Philadelphia, Mary was unhappy with Channing and growing short-tempered. When the producers wanted to cut her mastectomy scene, which was the heart of her character, the irate star slapped her script shut and gave a final edict in an emotional but cool voice. "I don't need to work," she said. "I don't ever have to work again. I wanted to quit in Dallas, but I stuck with it and I worked on and on and now I know [the lines] and I like doing that speech. It means a lot to me." She paused, took a deep breath, and added, "This is a very rare moment in my professional career. Not only is the speech ruined for me, but also the play is ruined for me. I will go on, but I will not play London, and I will not come to New York. I'll fulfill my contract, and then you can get someone else and cut anything you want. . . . I don't think I've ever had a moment like this before in my entire career. It's very

sad, and I don't think I will ever forget it." With that she walked off the stage, carrying her script and her dignity with her.

Altogether Mary and Carol Channing played *Legends* to sold-out houses for slightly over a year, with Mary never missing a performance. "It took its toll," the star said, "but Carol and I ended up friends." Channing maintained that the two stars were never competitive. "Mary and I held hands all the way through this one year and one month tour," said Channing, "and we sustained each other."

After *Legends*, Mary had little desire to do another show. She continued to take voice lessons and vocalized at home every day. She said she'd like to end her career the way she'd begun it—singing in a bar. She was still a clotheshorse, spent a couple of hours each day fixing her hair and doing her makeup, and in her seventies continued to exude a spirit of eternal youth. She tended to talk nonstop, was an inveterate shopper, and had the ability to make fans she met casually seem important to her, chatting with them in a natural, folksy way. "I guess once you're corny, you're always going to be corny," she said. "It's just a state of being."

Mary halfheartedly believed in reincarnation and said, "If I do get to come back, I want to be a carpenter, an electrician, or a plumber. I want to do all the *practical* things I didn't get to do in this life." She insisted that she still felt Richard's presence in dreams and requested that she be cremated and buried in the same plot with her beloved husband in Weatherford. Then with a mischievous grin, she added, "But I'll have top billing!"

In old age, Mary reflected a lot on the circles in her life, events that happened and people she'd met that recurred. "Age is a state of mind," she said. "There are days when it's easy and days and nights when it's not. I find the only solution is to keep as busy as possible." The important thing, she felt, is not to give in to tragedies. "If some crazy problem is bothering me, I can work it out if I just listen to my inner voice." She continued to look upon her talent as a gift. "Talent is given to everyone," she said, "and it comes in all forms. Seek and you'll find it. But if you don't take care of that talent, it's easily taken away."

Mary celebrated her fiftieth year in show business in 1988 by again singing at the Rainbow Room. "It was joyous," she said, "just like opening night fifty years before." She and Susan Grushkin, her secretary-companion after Ben Washer's death, spent two months that summer in San Miguel de Allende, Mexico, happily visiting with Bessie Mae and Jac Austin, and left in time for Mary to appear with Placido Domingo doing excerpts from *South Pacific* at the Hollywood Bowl. Considerate person that Mary was, she spent days browsing through Mexican shops looking for just the right outfit to wear when she sang opposite the Spanish tenor who had been raised in Mexico.

"The trick is to do something every single day and do it to the top of your ability," Mary said. "I mean never let down—go to the hilt." She claimed that she'd love to do a Western—"on television, not in movies" and toyed with the idea of doing another musical. The show under consideration was *Grover's Corners*, a musical version of Thornton Wilder's *Our Town*, written by Tom Jones with songs composed by Harvey Schmidt, the team responsible for *I Do! I Do!* Mary would have played the Stage Manager in the musical. "She said yes, she said no, she said yes, she said no," book writer Tom Jones said in March 1989. "She hasn't signed a contract, and we're doing some rewrites for her right now. She wants to do the show, but part of her doesn't want to do it. This is very different from anything she's ever done, because she's not the active verb in the piece. That's troubling her. She likes the piece, finds herself very moved by it, and connects with it. I think it would be a wonderful finale to her career."

But by early June any thought of Mary's doing *Grover's Corners* ended when the star underwent surgery for colon cancer at Cedars-Sinai Hospital in Los Angeles. She had suffered from back pain, but the ailment proved far more serious. The actress spent the summer recuperating from the operation on Martha's Vineyard, walking on the beach and meditating. In December 1989, Mary, Harry Belafonte, Claudette Colbert, Alexandra Danilova, and William Schuman were honored with life achievement awards at the Kennedy Center. Still

battling cancer, Mary said she'd like to do one more flight as Peter Pan—in a big arena like Madison Square Garden, then fly out an open window at the top and never come back. "Don't give in to anything until you have to," she said.

In October 1990, Mary was hospitalized at the Eisenhower Medical Center in Rancho Mirage for tests but was released a few days later. She knew the end was near and considered death just another opening night. "She'd never liked Bach," Larry Hagman said of his last visit with his mother, "yet she knew I enjoyed whistling Bach inventions. So she started whistling one of my favorites. I did counterpoint. We whistled while holding hands until she grew too tired. I sat for a while longer, then kissed her goodbye."

Mary died in a coma in her home late on Saturday, November 3, at the age of seventy-six. Her ashes were taken to the family plot in Weatherford, with her children, grandchildren, Bessie Mae Sue Ella and Jac Austin, and Weatherford friends at the graveside to bid a tearful farewell. Larry put pictures of the family in with her ashes, and Heller added a miniature bottle of Kahlúa, Mary's favorite drink. "I'll keep living until it's time," the bubbly performer had said. "Then I'll just go on to another stage. That doesn't bother me. That's the way life is. The secret is to accept it and enjoy it."

A memorial celebration of the star's life was held on January 28, 1991, at the Majestic Theater in New York, the same theater where *South Pacific* had played. Invited guests were admitted first, then as many of the fans waiting in a line that stretched for blocks as the fire marshal would permit. "Mother always liked a full house," Larry said from the stage. The tribute was upbeat, classy, and affectionate. Helen Hayes, Jerome Robbins, and Van Johnson spoke, and Carol Channing, Florence Henderson, John Raitt, and Carol Lawrence entertained. In the audience were Glenn Close, Peter Fonda, Jane Powell, Dickie Moore, Margaret Whiting, Delores Gray, Benay Venuta, and Mary Rodgers. The consensus was that Mary Martin was indeed one of the brightest stars ever to grace the Broadway stage, a true legend of the American theater.

Notes on Sources

The beginning point for any study of Mary Martin is the star's autobiography, *My Heart Belongs* (New York: Morrow, 1976; New York: Quill, 1984). I was fortunate in being able to tape a three-part oral history with the Broadway performer in Dallas and San Miguel de Allende, Mexico, on June 11, 1986, and July 18 and 19, 1988. A transcript of that interview, as well as many others relevant to the actress, may be found in the DeGolyer Library at Southern Methodist University. The ten days I spent in Mexico with Mary and her friend Bessie Mae Sue Ella Yeager Austin during the summer of 1988 gave me insight into their relationship and the personalities of the two women. The oral history I taped with Bessie Mae Sue Ella Yeager Austin on May 4, 1976, marked the start of a fifteen-year friendship that included countless conversations about Mary Martin, past and current. Eventually, Bessie Mae deposited her papers relating to the star in the DeGolyer Library at SMU. Those include correspondence and a program and a review of Bessie Mae Sue Ella's recital with her friend in Mineral Wells, Texas, in March 1929.

Larry Hagman's autobiography, *Hello Darlin'* (New York: Simon and Schuster, 2001), proved helpful in writing this book, since it details his side of his relationship with his famous mother and her husband-manager, Richard Halliday. Extensive clipping files in the

Margaret Herrick Library of the Academy of Motion Picture Arts and Sciences in Los Angeles, the Billy Rose Theatre Collection at the New York Public Library, and the Fine Arts section of the Dallas Public Library contain a wealth of information on the musical comedy star, mostly newspaper items. At present the Mary Martin Collection in the Weatherford Public Library is small, but a new wing is anticipated to house additional memorabilia. The Harry Ransom Humanities Research Center at the University of Texas in Austin houses the Ogden Nash, Ray Walston, Alfred A. Knopf, and Gloria Swanson papers, each of which includes manuscript material on Mary Martin. The Cheryl Crawford papers, offering significant data on Martin's career, are at the University of Houston, and the Oral History Collection at Columbia University is a major source on this as well as many other Broadway subjects.

Additional interviews that proved helpful in writing about Mary's early life included sessions with her cousin, Don Martin, and a childhood neighbor and friend, Virginia May Milmo, both taped in Weatherford. The transcripts of these oral histories are in the DeGolyer Library at SMU. Copies of the Weatherford High School *Melon-Vine* for 1928 and 1929 are available in the Weatherford Public Library.

Among the articles containing insight into the star's growing up years in Texas are Hope Hammond (the performer's second mother-in-law), "Uncontrary Mary Martin," *House and Garden* 98 (July 1950); Pete Martin, "I Call on Mary Martin," *Saturday Evening Post* 221 (March 28, 1959); Mary Martin, as told to Charles D. Rice, "Everybody Sing!" *Reader's Digest* 74 (Apr. 1959); Charlotte and Denis Plimmer, "Her Heart Belongs to Broadway," *Coronet* 35 (Mar. 1954); Fred Robbins, "The Unsinkable Mary Martin," *50 Plus* (Jan. 1988); and Mary Martin, "The Best Advice I Ever Had," *Reader's Digest* 76 (June 1960).

Valuable on the star's months of auditioning in Hollywood are Lupton A. Wilkinson, "The Mistakes of Mary," *Los Angeles Times*, Jan. 18, 1942; Mary Martin, "Fame Is a Song," *Liberty*, Feb. 24, 1940; Kyle Crichton, "Mary Had a Little Talent," *Collier's* (Mar. 2, 1946); and Heller Halliday Weir, "My Mother, Mary Martin," *Good Housekeeping* (Jan. 1963). The quotes from Lillian Burns on Martin's audition

for Republic Pictures came from my interview with the drama coach in the SMU Oral History Collection, taped in Los Angeles on Aug. 17, 1986.

Sophie Tucker's recollections of Mary Martin during rehearsals for *Leave It to Me* may be found in *Some of These Days* (Garden City, N.Y.: Garden City Publishing, 1946). Gene Kelly's response to the future star's impact in the Cole Porter show and his encounter with the composer are from the dancer's interview in the SMU Oral History Collection, taped in Dallas on June 20, 21, and 25, 1974. Reviews of *Leave It to Me* include Rosamond Gilder's in *Theatre Arts Monthly* 23 (Jan. 1939) and Brooks Atkinson's in the *New York Times*, Nov. 10, 1938, and Nov. 20, 1939.

For more information on Mary's midnight appearances at the Rainbow Room during her first Broadway show, see Ronald L. Davis, *Van Johnson: MGM's Golden Boy* (Jackson: University Press of Mississippi, 2001).

Oral histories with director Andrew Stone and singer Allan Jones, both in the SMU collection, hold data pertaining to the making of *The Great Victor Herbert*, the former taped in Los Angeles on July 15, 1985, and the latter recorded in New York City on Jan. 9, 1985. Hedda Hopper's comment on early Mary Martin came from the columnist's book with James Brough, *The Whole Truth and Nothing But* (Garden City, N.Y.: Doubleday, 1963). Slim (Hawks) Keith discusses Mary in her book with Annette Tappert, *Slim: Memories of a Rich and Imperfect Life* (New York: Simon and Schuster, 1990). Jean Arthur's friendship with Mary is briefly chronicled in John Oller, *Jean Arthur: The Actress Nobody Knew* (New York: Limelight, 1997), whereas Jean Porter's remarks about her fellow Texan came from Porter's oral history for SMU, taped in Dallas and Austin on Apr. 18, 1980, and Apr. 4. 1981.

Conversations in Los Angeles with musical comedy performer Carol Bruce rendered the most complete information on the show *Nice Goin'*, although Tom Ewell referred to the musical in his oral history for SMU, taped in Dallas on Jan. 24, 1974.

Mary's article, "My Mother-in-Law and Me," *Good Housekeeping* 144 (June 1959), details early problems in the star's second marriage.

Also revealing is Irving Stone's "The Happy Hallidays," *Los Angeles Examiner*, Jan. 15, 1956.

Cheryl Crawford's *One Naked Individual: My Fifty Years in the Theatre* (Indianapolis: Bobbs-Merrill, 1977) and Elia Kazan's *A Life* (New York: Knopf, 1988) are essential to understanding the preparation and production of *One Touch of Venus*. Also invaluable are letters from John Wildberg in the Crawford papers. Worth consulting on the show's composer is Ronald Sanders, *The Days Grow Short: The Life and Music of Kurt Weill* (New York: Holt, Rinehart and Winston, 1980). On the star's glamorous image after her marriage to Halliday, see "Mary Martin's Dress," *Life* 15 (Nov. 22, 1943).

Reviews of *One Touch of Venus* include Mary Morris, "The Name Mary Martin Is Familiar, " *P.M.*, Dec. 12, 1943, those in the *New York Times* and the *New York Post* on October 17, 1943, and the one in the *New York Herald Tribune* on Oct. 31, 1943. Notices also appeared in *Life* 15 (Oct. 25, 1943) and *Time* 42 (Oct. 18, 1943).

Mary Martin's letter of thanks to Cheryl Crawford from Philadelphia, written on Feb. 14, 1945, is in the Crawford papers. Her letter to Ogden Nash regarding the continued success of *One Touch of Venus* on the road, written on May 11, 1945, is in the Humanities Research Center at UT.

Richard Halliday's statement that theater people learn to live with emotional stress was taken from an item in the *New York Times*, Mar. 4, 1973.

The turmoil behind putting the production of *Lute Song* together is told in detail by John Houseman in *Front and Center* (New York: Simon and Schuster, 1979). Also informative are the interviews with Yul Brynner and Dolly Haas in the SMU oral history collection, the former taped in Los Angeles on Aug. 1, 1975, and the latter in New York City on Oct. 6, 1986. Reviews of *Lute Song* may be found in the *New York Times* and the *New York Post* on Feb. 7, 1946, as well as in Steven Suskin, *Opening Night on Broadway* (New York: Schirmer, 1990).

The best source on *Pacific 1860* is Graham Payn and Sheridan Morley (eds.), *The Noel Coward Diaries* (Boston: Little, Brown, 1982). Mary's letter to Ogden Nash, dated Dec. 28, 1946, describing the

opening of the Coward operetta is in the Humanities Research Center at UT. Critic Mollie Panter-Downes's reaction to the show appeared in *The New Yorker* 22 (January 4, 1947). Heller Halliday's reaction to her mother in the London musical was recalled in Nelson Lansdale, "Her Heart Belongs to the Road," *Theatre Arts* 42 (Sept. 1958).

Mary's contention that she and Noel Coward didn't speak for two years after their fight during the staging of *Pacific 1860* is related in *Women's Wear Daily*, Dec. 11, 1970. Lucinda Ballard recalled hearing about the Martin-Coward squabble in her oral history for SMU, taped in New York City in five sessions between Jan. 12, 1985 and Mar. 19, 1987. Joshua Logan wrote abut overhearing Coward say that Mary was "not very good" in the London show in *Josh: My Up and Down, In and Out Life* (New York: Delacorte, 1976).

Elia Kazan mentions that he tentatively suggested Mary for the role of Blanche in *A Streetcar Named Desire* in his autobiography, *A Life.*

Important to understanding the staging of the national company of *Annie Get Your Gun* is Joshua Logan's autobiography, *Josh*, although the director's oral history in the SMU collection, recorded in New York City on Jan. 3. 1979, is an illuminating supplement. Dorothy Fields's interview in the Columbia University Oral History collection is worth consulting on the show, and Lucinda Ballard's candid comments in her several sessions for SMU are matchless. Tom Ewell recalled for an SMU interviewer seeing Mary Martin and the national company of *Annie* perform; his oral history session was held in Dallas on Jan. 24, 1974. Bob Thomas describes Merman's sitting in the front row and applauding with white gloves on in *I Got Rhythm! The Ethel Merman Story* (New York: Putnam, 1985). For more on Mary Martin's success during *Annie*'s run in Dallas, see Ronald L. Davis, *John Rosenfield's Dallas* (Dallas: Three Forks Press, 2002). A later review of the show appeared in the *Pittsburgh Post Gazette* on June 12, 1948, and film director George Sidney told of seeing Mary in the musical in his interview for the SMU collection, recorded in Los Angeles on Aug. 22, 1980. The star is quoted in the *Los Angeles Examiner* on Sept. 5, 1954, as saying that she felt like crying when her company of *Annie Get Your Gun* closed.

Richard Halliday's letter to Cheryl Crawford regarding *Love Life*, dated Oct. 16, 1947, is in the Crawford papers at the University of Houston, as is Kurt Weill and Alan Lerner's response to Crawford, dated Oct. 21, 1947. Nanette Fabray's feeling that the part in *Love Life* was a little beyond her talent was expressed in her oral history for SMU, taped in Los Angeles on Aug. 5 and 12, 1975.

Gretchen Wyler's contention that to be a star of the first magnitude a performer must be a killer was expressed in her oral history for SMU, recorded in Los Angeles on May 23, 1985.

Richard Rodgers discusses the problems with the book of *South Pacific* in *Musical Stages: An Autobiography* (New York: Random House, 1975) and also talks about the show in his lengthy oral history for Columbia University. His daughter, Mary Rodgers, analyses the composer's music and talks about the subtle difficulties of being Jewish in her interview for the SMU oral history collection, taped in New York City on Mar. 15, 1990.

Joshua Logan's autobiography and his oral history for SMU contain essential data on both the original production of *South Pacific* and the first staging of the show in London. Ezio Pinza reveals his problems with the musical in "Enchanted Evenings," *Theatre Arts* 34 (June 1950), and Slim Keith gives some insight in *Slim*. Reid Shelton describes the cinematic nature of the Logan staging of *South Pacific* in his SMU interview, taped in New York City on Oct. 19, 1979.

The Billy Rose Theater Collection in the New York Public Library has an entire scrapbook devoted to *South Pacific* and is also rich in newspaper clippings on the show.

Reviews for the Rodgers and Hammerstein musical may be found in *Variety*, Mar. 8, 1949; *New York Times, New York Post*, and *New York Herald Tribune* (all Apr. 8, 1949); *Time* 53 (Apr. 18, 1949); *Nation* 168 (Apr. 23, 1949), *New Republic* 120 (Apr. 25, 1949); *Saturday Review of Literature* 32 (May 28, 1949), and *Theatre Arts* 33 (June 1949). Ethel Merman's comment that Mary was okay in *South Pacific* "if you like talent" is quoted in Thomas's *I Got Rhythm!*, and Noel Coward's various assessments of Mary in the show and the act they performed together at the Café de Paris were taken from Payn and Morley, *Coward Diaries*.

Lewis Funke in the *New York Times Magazine*, Nov. 27, 1949, and Bennett Cerf in the *Saturday Review of Literature* 33 (Jan. 14, 1950) wrote about how difficult it was to come by tickets for *South Pacific* during the early years of the show's New York run. Letters regarding Bessie Mae Sue Ella and Jac Austin's visit to New York in 1949 are in the Austin papers at SMU.

Mary wrote about creating the role of Nellie Forbush in "My Year of *South Pacific*," *Reader's Digest* 56 (June 1950). Reviews of the London opening of the show appeared in *The Spectator*, Nov. 9, 1951, and *Punch*, Nov. 14, 1951. Ray Walston's remark that no one could compare with Mary as Nellie was made during the actor's interview for SMU, taped in Los Angeles on Aug. 11, 1988. The letter Walston received from the *South Pacific* star after he left the cast, dated Sept. 26, 1952, is in the Humanities Research Center at UT.

Hedda Hopper describes the Broadway star at a bullfight in Spain in "My Mary Martin," Sept. 9, 1955, a manuscript in the Herrick Library in Los Angeles. Mary wrote about her troubled relationship with her son in "The Lights in the Halliday Home," *Coronet* 39 (Nov. 1955).

Greg Lawrence, *Dance with Demons: The Life of Jerome Robbins* (New York: Putnam's, 2001) is an excellent source on Mary's work with Jerome Robbins, both on the Ford anniversary show for television and the staging of *Peter Pan*.

Yul Brynner credited Mary with getting him the role in *The King and I* in his oral history for SMU, and Felix Jackson remembered the actor's enthusiasm for the part of the King in his interview in the SMU collection, taped in Los Angeles on July 16, 1984.

Mary told of recording two songs with Larry Hagman in "'That's My Boy,'" *Time* 56 (Dec. 18, 1950), whereas Mitch Miller acknowledged her as a real pro in his oral history for SMU, taped in New York on Mar. 25, 1986.

Cheryl Crawford's attempt to find another show to produce for Mary is mentioned in a letter to Richard Halliday, dated Feb. 26, 1952, in the Crawford papers. Also included in the Crawford correspondence at the University of Houston are letters to Halliday regarding Mary's work in *Peter Pan*.

Dorothy Stickney talked about Joshua Logan's difficulties during the rehearsals of *Kind Sir* in her interview for SMU, taped in New York City on Jan. 9, 1979, and in *Openings and Closings: Memoir of a Lady of the Theatre* (Garden City, N. Y.: Doubleday, 1979).

Hedda Hopper's comments about the Norman Krasna comedy appeared in *The Whole Truth and Nothing But.* Reviews of *Kind Sir* may be found in the *Dallas Morning News*, Sept. 28, 1953; *New York Times*, Nov. 15, 1953; *Time* 62 (Nov. 16, 1953), and *Nation* 177. (Nov. 21,1953).

Edwin Lester recalled Mary Martin's loving nature in his oral history for SMU, taped in Los Angeles on July 15, 1985. Stacy Wolf makes the observation that, although Mary kept her mass audience, the star became an icon of lesbians in her book *A Problem Like Maria: Gender and Sexuality in the American Musical* (Ann Arbor: University of Michigan Press, 2002).

Reviews of Martin in *Peter Pan* are to be found in the *New York Times, New York World-Telegram and Sun,* and *New York Herald Tribune,* all on Oct. 21, 1954, as well as in *New Republic* 131 (Nov. 1, 1954) and *Nation* 179 (Nov. 13, 1954). Mary told of going out front and personally thanking the children in her *Peter Pan* audiences in *American Home* (Aug. 1961). Harry Sosnik discussed the television adaptation of the Barrie show during his oral history for Columbia University.

Mary expressed gratitude for the exceptional career she had had in Seymour Peck, "She's Worked that Gal Right Outa Her Hair," *New York Times Magazine*, Sept. 20, 1953, whereas Mary Rodgers' assessment of the star's intellectual capacity came during Rodgers' interview for SMU.

Jay Lerner remembered Mary's reaction to the first songs she heard from *My Fair Lady* in his autobiography, *The Street Where I Live* (New York: Norton, 1978). Hedda Hopper's contention to Joshua Logan that there were makeup men in Hollywood who could make the Broadway actress look like a young girl appears in *The Whole Truth and Nothing But.*

Alan Schneider talked about directing Mary in *The Skin of Our Teeth* in Joseph F. McCrindle, *Behind the Scenes* (New York: Holt,

Rinehart and Winston, 1971) and *Entrances: An American Director's Journey* (New York: Viking, 1986). Don Murray discussed his fondness for the star in his oral history for SMU, taped in Montecito, California, on July 20, 1989. George Abbott gave his evaluation of Mary as Sabina in his interview for SMU, taped in Miami Beach, Florida, on Nov. 16, 1979.

Reviews of Martin in *The Skin of Our Teeth* may be found in the *New York Times*, Aug. 18 and 28, 1955, and in *Saturday Review* 38 (Aug. 27, 1955).

Heller Halliday's comment that her mother hadn't grown up yet was reported in the *Los Angeles Times*, Apr. 12, 1979.

Noel Coward's recollections of the television special he did with Mary came from Payn and Morley, *Coward Diaries*, whereas *Variety*, Oct. 24, 1955, contains a review of the show.

Duane Bogie mentioned the disapproval he faced over Mary's being cast in *Born Yesterday* in his oral history for SMU, taped in Dallas on Nov. 4, 1985. Arthur Hill recalled the television production of the Kanin play in his interview for SMU, taped in Los Angeles on Jan. 5, 1977.

John Raitt talked about working with Mary in the revival of *Annie Get Your Gun* in his SMU oral history, taped in Dallas on Oct. 22, 1976.

Cheryl Crawford wrote her observation that Mary seemed more relaxed than ever in a letter to Mary and Richard, dated Dec. 5, 1957, in the Crawford papers. Richard's remark about his wife's perpetual joy was quoted in "How Mary Martin Stays Young," *Hollywood Citizen*, Jan. 18, 1959.

Mary Rodgers compared Mary and Richard during the preparation of the children's show Rodgers and her sister composed for the star in an oral history for SMU. The star's double television appearances on Easter, 1959, were covered in *Newsweek* 68 (Mar. 30, 1959), and critic John Rosenfield reviewed *Music with Mary Martin* for the *Dallas Morning News* on Jan. 31, 1959.

Maria von Trapp's statement that Mary was the ideal person to play her in *The Sound of Music* was reported in *Newsweek* 54 (Nov. 30, 1959). Lucinda Ballard and Theodore Bikel's recollections of the show are from their oral histories for SMU, the latter taped in

Los Angeles on May 4, 1990. Richard Rodgers wrote about the musical in *Musical Stages* and talked about the production in his oral history for Columbia. Also worth consulting is Meryle Secrest, *Somewhere for Me: A Biography of Richard Rodgers* (New York: Knopf, 2001).

Agent Lucy Kroll made interesting observations about Vincent Donehue and putting *The Sound of Music* together in her interview for SMU, taped in Dallas on Feb. 15 and Mar. 1, 1990. Fred Robbins told of Oscar Hammerstein's writing special lyrics for Mary in "The Unsinkable Mary Martin," *50 Plus*. The *Dallas Morning News* reported that Margaret Truman had been offered a part in the upcoming Rodgers and Hammerstein musical on July 13, 1959.

The *New York Times* reviewed *The Sound of Music* on Nov. 17, 1959, and *New Republic* 141, on Dec. 28, 1959. Mary was quoted as saying the show was the hardest she had ever done in "Rx for Hit: Mary, Music, Kids," *Coronet* 47 (March 1960). Merman's comment about losing the Tony Award to Mary came from Ethel Merman, with George Eells, *Merman—An Autobiography* (New York: Simon and Schuster, 1978). Andrea Marcovici recalled going backstage after a performance to meet Mary in her oral history for SMU, taped in New York City during a spring vacation.

The letter to Bessie Mae Sue Ella Austin from Mary's friend in Bermuda, signed simply Puss, is in the Austin Collection at SMU, as are Mary's letters to Bessie Mae after their vacation together, the closing of *Daughter of Silence*, and Heller's first wedding.

Florence Henderson told of Mary Martin's coming to see her perform *The Sound of Music* in her oral history for SMU, taped in Los Angeles on Aug. 18, 1983.

Mary's initial enthusiasm for the show that became *Jennie* was expressed in a letter, dated Feb. 5, 1962, in the Austin collection. Howard Dietz remembered the musical in *Dancing in the Dark* (New York: Quadrangle, 1974), and Lucinda Ballard offered some biting comments in her oral history for SMU. Cheryl Crawford talked about the problems with the production in *One Naked Individual.* Mary recalled how she needed a doctor daily during rehearsals for *Jennie* and her distress after the show's failure in "The Healing in Solitude," *Guideposts* (June 1969).

Reviews of *Jennie* may by found in the *New York Times* and the *New York Herald Tribune* on Oct. 18, 1963. Noel Coward's appraisal of the show came from the *Coward Diaries*.

Mary wrote a letter to Blanche Knopf, dated July 1, 1963, telling how deeply she and Richard loved their place in Brazil, part of the correspondence in the Humanities Research Center at UT.

Richard Halliday wrote the Austins on Feb. 15, 1965, stating how peaceful Mary seemed to be while rehearsing *Hello, Dolly!* The star's contention to Hedda Hopper during the tour of the Herman musical that she'd "never felt so much love from audiences" was quoted in the *Kansas City Times*, May 14, 1965. The *New Orleans Times-Picayune*, May 12, 1965, contains a review of Mary in *Hello, Dolly!* Some of the star's experiences on the Vietnam tour were recounted in *Variety*, Nov. 3, 1965, and in the *Los Angeles Times*, Feb. 4, 1966. The *New York Times*, Dec. 3, 1965, described Mary's success as Dolly Levi in London. Noel Coward stated his opinion of the musical in *Coward Diaries*.

Harvey Schmidt and Tom Jones recounted their memories of the preparation and tryouts for *I Do! I Do!* in their respective oral histories for SMU, recorded in New York City on Mar. 15, 1988, and Mar. 22, 1989. Tharon Musser explained the importance of Jean Rosenthal's lighting design in her interview for SMU, taped in New York on March 25, 1986.

Reviews of *I Do! I Do!* appeared in the *New York Times* on December 6, 1966, and *The New Yorker* 42 (Dec. 17, 1966). Mary described her daily life during the run of the two-person show in *Newsweek* 80 (Sept. 4, 1972). The star's exhaustion toward the end of the national tour was reported in the *Dallas Times Herald*, Feb. 27, 1969.

Mary wrote Bessie Mae Sue Ella frequently from Brazil, telling her friend of family problems, legal hassles over the *Sound of Music* album, and describing the Halliday's life on their remote ranch. All of these letters, as well as the tape Mary made on Dec. 25, 1971, are in the Austin collection at SMU.

Joshua Logan wrote about trying to entice Mary into doing a musical version of *The Corn Is Green* in *Movie Stars, Real People, and Me.* The star wrote several letters to Cheryl Crawford confessing

the problems she was having adjusting to Richard's death. Those are in the Crawford papers at the University of Houston. Mary's reunion with Larry Hagman was reported in the *Christian Science Monitor*, Oct. 19, 1981. Mary insisted that she was happy not working in *Woman's Wear Daily*, Mar. 14 and Aug. 25, 1975.

Ken Billington recalled designing the lighting for the concert Mary did with Ethel Merman and for *Do You Turn Somersaults?* in his oral history for SMU, taped in New York City on Mar. 17, 1990. Reviews of the Arbuzov play may be found in *Time*, Sept. 5, 1977, and the *Los Angeles Herald-Examiner*, Jan 16, 1978.

The most complete source on *Legends* is James Kirkwood, *Diary of a Mad Playwright* (New York: Dutton, 1989), although Carol Channing, *Just Lucky I Guess* (New York: Simon and Schuster, 2002) also provides information.

Tom Jones talked about Mary Martin's reluctance to do *Grover's Corners* in his oral history for SMU.

Career Appearances

Broadway Shows

Leave It to Me (1938), songs by Cole Porter, book by Bella and Samuel Spewack, produced by Vinton Freedley, directed by Samuel Spewack, choreography by Robert Alton, and starring William Gaxton, Victor Moore, Sophie Tucker, and Tamara.

One Touch of Venus (1943), music by Kurt Weill, lyrics by Ogden Nash, book by S. J. Perelman and Ogden Nash, produced by Cheryl Crawford in conjunction with John Wildberg, directed by Elia Kazan, choreography by Agnes de Mille, and also starring Kenny Baker and John Boles.

Lute Song (1946), music by Raymond Scott, lyrics by Bernard Hanighen, book by Sidney Howard and Will Irwin, produced by Michael Meyerberg, directed by John Houseman, choreography by Yeichi Nimura, designed by Robert Edmond Jones, and also starring Yul Brynner.

South Pacific (1949), music by Richard Rodgers, lyrics by Oscar Hammerstein II, book by Oscar Hammerstein II and Joshua Logan, produced by Richard Rodgers and Oscar Hammerstein II in association

with Leland Hayward and Joshua Logan, directed by Joshua Logan, and also starring Ezio Pinza, Myron McCormick, Juanita Hall, and William Tabbert.

Kind Sir (1953), play by Norman Krasna, produced and directed by Joshua Logan, and also starring Charles Boyer, with Dorothy Stickney, Frank Conroy, Margalo Gillmore, and Robert Ross in the cast.

Peter Pan (1954), a musical version of Sir James M. Barrie's play, music by Mark Charlap and Jule Styne, lyrics by Carolyn Leigh, Betty Comden, and Adolph Green, produced by Edwin Lester and Richard Halliday, directed by Jerome Robbins, and also starring Cyril Ritchard, with Kathy Nolan, Margalo Gillmore, Sondra Lee, and Heller Halliday in the cast.

The Skin of Our Teeth (1955), play by Thornton Wilder, directed by Alan Schneider, produced under the auspices of the American National Theatre and Academy, and also starring Helen Hayes, George Abbott, and Don Murray.

The Sound of Music (1959), music by Richard Rodgers, lyrics by Oscar Hammerstein II, book by Howard Lindsay and Russel Crouse, produced by Leland Hayward, Richard Halliday, Richard Rodgers, and Oscar Hammerstein II, directed by Vincent Donehue, choreographed by Joe Layton, and also featuring Theodore Bikel, Patricia Neway, Kurt Kasznar, Marion Marlowe, and Lauri Peters.

Jennie (1963), music by Arthur Schwartz, lyrics by Howard Dietz, book by Arnold Schulman, produced by Cheryl Crawford and Richard Halliday, directed by Vincent Donehue, choreography by Matt Mattox, and also featuring George Wallace, Robin Bailey, and Ethel Shutta.

I Do! I Do! (1966), music by Harvey Schmidt, lyrics by Tom Jones, book by Tom Jones, based on *The Fourposter* by Jan de Hartog, produced by David Merrick, directed by Gower Champion, and also starring Robert Preston.

Do You Turn Somersaults? (1978), an Americanized version of a play by Aleksei Arbuzov, directed by Edwin Sherin, costarring Anthony Quayle.

Other Stage Shows

Nice Goin' (1939), closed during tryouts in Boston.

Dancing in the Streets (1943), closed during tryouts.

Pacific 1860 (1946), book and songs by Noel Coward, played four months at the Drury Lane Theatre in London.

Annie Get Your Gun (1947), songs by Irving Berlin, book by Herbert and Dorothy Fields, produced by Richard Rodgers and Oscar Hammerstein II, directed by Joshua Logan, choreography by Helen Tamiris, performed on a national tour.

South Pacific (1951), original London production of the Rodgers and Hammerstein show, directed by Joshua Logan, with Wilbur Evans as Emile.

South Pacific (1957), revival of the Rodgers and Hammerstein musical, produced by the Los Angeles Civic Light Opera Association, staged by Albert Marre, and also starring Giorgio Tozzi and Myron McCormick.

Annie Get Your Gun (1957), revival of the Irving Berlin musical, produced by the Los Angeles Civic Light Opera Association, directed by Vincent Donehue, and also starring John Raitt.

Music with Mary Martin (1958), a concert with costumes, performed on a national tour.

Three to Make Music (1958), a matinee show for children with music by Richard Rodgers and his two daughters, performed on a national tour.

Hello, Dolly! (1965), music and lyrics by Jerry Herman, book by Michael Stewart, based on *The Matchmaker* by Thornton Wilder,

produced by David Merrick, directed and choreographed by Gower Champion, performed on a national tour and in Asia and London.

Together with Music (1977), a concert in New York with Ethel Merman.

Legends (1986), a comedy by James Kirkwood that costarred Carol Channing, performed on a national tour for over a year.

Films

The Great Victor Herbert (1939), Paramount, directed by Andrew L. Stone, and also featuring Allan Jones, Walter Connolly, Lee Bowman, Susanna Foster, and Jerome Cowan.

Rhythm on the River (1940), Paramount, directed by Victor Schertzinger, and also featuring Bing Crosby, Basil Rathbone, Oscar Levant, Charley Grapewin, and William Frawley.

Love Thy Neighbor (1940), Paramount, directed by Mark Sandrich, and also featuring Jack Benny, Fred Allen, Eddie (Rochester) Anderson, and Virginia Dale.

Kiss the Boys Goodbye (1941), Paramount, directed by Victor Schertzinger, and also featuring Don Ameche, Oscar Levant, Virginia Dale, Vera Vague, Elizabeth Patterson, and Connee Boswell.

New York Town (1941), Paramount, directed by Charles Vidor, and also featuring Fred MacMurray, Robert Preston, Akim Tamiroff, Lynne Overman, Eric Blore, and Fuzzy Knight.

Birth of the Blues (1941), Paramount, directed by Victor Schertzinger, and also featuring Bing Crosby, Brian Donlevy, Carolyn Lee, and Eddie (Rochester) Anderson.

Star Spangled Rhythm (1942), Paramount, directed by George Marshall, and also featuring Betty Hutton, Eddie Bracken, Bing Crosby, Ray Milland, Bob Hope, Veronica Lake, Dorothy Lamour, Susan Hayward, Dick Powell, Alan Ladd, Paulette Goddard, Cecil B. DeMille, Arthur Treacher, and William Bendix.

Happy-Go-Lucky (1943), Paramount, directed by Curtis Bernhardt, and also featuring Dick Powell, Eddie Bracken, Betty Hutton, Rudy Vallee, and Mabel Paige.

True to Life (1943), Paramount, directed by George Marshall, and also featuring Franchot Tone, Dick Powell, Victor Moore, Mabel Paige, and William Demarest.

Night and Day (1946), Warner Bros., directed by Michael Curtiz, and also featuring Cary Grant, Alexis Smith, Monty Woolley, Ginny Simms, Jane Wyman, Eve Arden, Alan Hale, and Dorothy Malone.

Main Street to Broadway (1953), directed by Tay Garnett and Tom Morton, and also featuring Ethel Barrymore, Lionel Barrymore, Shirley Booth, Rex Harrison, Lilli Palmer, Helen Hayes, Henry Fonda, Tallulah Bankhead, Mary Murphy, and Rosemary DeCamp.

Major Television Performances

Ford's Fiftieth Anniversary Show (1953), produced by Leland Hayward and Lawrence White, directed by Jerome Robbins, and costarring Ethel Merman.

Peter Pan (1955, 1956, and 1960), recreations live and on tape of the Broadway production.

The Skin of Our Teeth (1955), an abridgment of the production that had opened in Paris and played in Washington, D.C., Chicago, and New York, directed by Vincent Donehue.

Together with Music (1955), a television special that costarred Noel Coward.

Born Yesterday (1956), play by Garson Kanin, presented on the Hallmark Hall of Fame, directed by Garson Kanin, and also starring Paul Douglas and Arthur Hill.

Annie Get Your Gun (1957), a recreation of the Los Angeles Civic Light Opera Association production.

Music with Mary Martin (1959), a recreation of the concert performed nationally.

Three to Make Music (1959), a shortened version of the children's show performed on a national tour.

Valentine (1979), a made-for-television movie that costarred Jack Albertson.

Over Easy (1981), talk show for senior citizens originating in San Francisco, co-hosted by Jim Hartz.

Index

Mary Martin, *continued*
100, 110, 116, 122, 171, 172, 181–82,
185, 188–89, 196–97, 207, 218, 223,
224, 245, 247–48, 251, 254, 257,
258–59, 263, 264, 265, 267, 269, 270,
271, 280; relationship with Hender-
son, 222–23; relationship with House-
man, 93, 96, 97–99; relationship with
Van Johnson, 46; relationship with
Billie Jones, 5; relationship with
Juanita (mother), 4, 5, 6, 7, 8, 9, 10,
11, 12, 15, 16, 17, 18–19, 20–21, 22,
23, 26, 27–28, 29, 33, 35, 45, 51, 52,
53, 60, 61, 83, 144, 201, 255; relation-
ship with Kazan, 76–77; relationship
with Kirkwood, 272–78; relationship
with Larry, 18, 19, 24, 26, 33, 34–35,
45, 51, 52, 53, 60, 83, 84–85, 89, 110,
115–16, 146–48, 152, 154, 172, 173,
183, 190, 207, 220, 245, 247, 251, 254,
255, 257, 258, 259, 263–64, 265–67,
269, 270, 271, 272, 274, 275, 276, 280;
relationship with Logan, 107, 109,
112, 134, 135, 148–51, 152–53, 154,
176, 177, 180, 195, 252–53, 254, 262,
268, 272; relationship with Maj, 172,
193, 220, 247, 255, 257, 263; relation-
ship with Marcus, 43; relationship with
Merman, 115, 140, 174–75, 259–60,
262, 268, 272, 273, 281; relationship
with Milmo, 7–8, 25, 32, 34; relation-
ship with Jean Porter, 65–66; relation-
ship with Preston (father), 4, 5–6, 7, 8,
9, 11, 12, 14, 17, 19, 20, 21–22, 23, 26,
27, 28, 31, 35, 43, 44–45, 64–65, 255;
relationship with Robbins, 181, 183;
relationship with Rodgers, 85, 109,
111, 123–24, 125, 149, 180, 192,
203–204, 210, 211, 212, 249, 250–51,
262, 272; relationship with Rose,
25–26, 27; relationship with Rosen-
field, 22–23, 206; relationship with
Schneider, 193, 194–95; relationship
with Schwab, 34, 36, 51, 54, 56, 61;
relationship with Laurette Taylor, 226;
relationship with Washer, 218, 257,
264, 267, 269, 270, 272; relationship
with Ford White, 8; relationship with
Wilder, 97; relationship with Woods,
26, 27–29, 31, 32, 33, 35–36, 38, 43,

44, 48, 51; relations with newspaper
reporters, 42; residence in Palm
Springs, 255, 256, 257, 266, 267, 270,
272, 273; sexuality of, 20–21, 65, 70,
249; voice of, 27, 28, 30, 31–32, 33–34,
38, 43–44, 46, 49, 82, 92–93, 113, 122,
125–26, 142, 148, 184, 206, 212, 213,
216, 241, 256–57, 260, 278; at
Ward–Belmont, 15–17, 31. *See also*
Martin, Mary, comments by; Martin,
Mary, relationship with Richard
Martin, Mary, comments by: on age, 267,
268, 271, 275, 278; on *Annie Get Your
Gun,* 108, 113, 114, 115, 122, 202; on
auditions in Hollywood, 28, 29, 35; on
auditions in New York City, 36–38; on
Blood and Thunder, 223; on *Born
Yesterday,* 200; on Brazil, 244, 246, 247,
249, 250, 267; on Gower Champion,
237; on curtain in mother's bedroom,
3; on *Do You Do Somersaults?,* 261, 262;
on Fanchon and Marco, 21; on *Fanny,*
180; on God, 255, 264, 269–70; on
Hello Dolly!, 232–33, 234–35, 236; on
her appearance, 49, 73, 74, 75; on
herself, 69–70, 73, 270, 271, 278; on *I
Do! I Do!,* 237, 238, 241, 242, 244; on
Jennie, 225–26, 227, 229–30, 231; on
Jesus Christ, Superstar, 248; on *Kind Sir,*
176, 177; on Larry, 19, 26, 45, 83, 89,
263, 264, 265–66, 267; on *Leave It To
Me,* 37–38, 39, 40–41; on *Legends,* 272,
274, 275–76, 277–78; on Lerner and
Lowe, 191; on life, 265, 267, 271, 279,
280; on Logan, 134, 135, 154, 176,
177, 180, 195; on *Lute Song,* 91, 93, 95,
97, 99, 100; on motion pictures, 11,
49–50, 57, 59, 62, 66, 67, 68, 266; on
music, 5, 6, 9, 10, 22, 25, 28, 37–38,
48, 57, 241, 248; on *Music with Mary
Martin,* 205, 206; on New York City,
36; on *One Touch of Venus,* 73, 74, 75,
76–79, 82–83, 85, 86, 87–88; on *Over
Easy,* 268; on *Pacific 1860,* 101, 102,
103, 105; on performing, 6, 7, 10, 11,
22, 23, 31, 33, 34, 40, 48, 68, 83, 86,
87–88, 91, 222, 241, 244–45, 247, 254,
255, 256–58, 264, 275; on *Peter Pan,*
180, 183, 184, 186, 188, 218, 219, 258,
270, 280; on Pinza, 130, 133, 138, 140,

Wilson, Earl, 42
Winchell, Walter, 42
Wolff, Nat, 200
Wood, Audrey, 72
Woodruff, Charles, 215
Woods, Mildred: relationship with Mary,
 26, 27–29, 31, 32, 33, 35–36, 38, 43,
 44, 48, 51
Worth, Irene, 273
Wright, Jim, 178–79

Wright, Martha, 147, 219
Wyler, Gretchen, 120–21
Wyman, Jane, 91

Yeager, Ben, 21
Young, Mort, 262

Zolotow, Sam, 139
Zorina, Vera, 45, 72, 215